LEADERSHIP IN MINISTRY

Bowen Theory in the Congregational Context

Edited by

ISRAEL GALINDO

Leadership in Ministry:
Bowen Theory in the Congregational Context
Edited by Israel Galindo
Copyright © 2017, Israel Galindo
All rights reserved.

Cover design by Israel Galindo

Published by Didache Press

CONTENTS

Acknowledgements

Introduction 1

1. The Pedagogy of Leadership in Ministry 2
   Israel Galindo

2. Leadership Through a Bowen Systems Lens 9
   Lawrence E. Matthews

3. Navigating the Triangles in Interim Ministry............... 16
   William T. Pyle

4. On Sibling Position 18
   Margaret Marcuson

5. Common Misunderstandings of
   Systems Theory 20
   Israel Galindo

6. Bowen Family Systems Theory and
   Congregational Life 25
   Ronald W. Richardson

7. Systems Theory and Congregational Leadership 55
   James E. Lamkin

8. Long-tenured Ministry and
   Bowen Systems Theory 91
   Israel Galindo and Betty Pugh Mills

9. Pastoral Care Triage: BFST and Leading With
    Heart and Mind 127
        Jim Boyer

10. Leadership is Easy – Or Is It? 139
        Elaine Boomer

11. Self-Differentiated Pastoral Leaders 143
        Michael Lee Cook

12. Reciprocity in the Emotional Field 149
        Israel Galindo

13. Theology and Family Systems
    Theory in Dialogue 163
        Lawrence Matthews

14. The Possibility of Change 185
        Carla Toenniessen

15. How to Let Go of the Outcome 190
        Margaret Marcuson

16. Five Necessary Shifts in Thinking 193
        Israel Galindo

17. Herding in the Bovine and the Human 202
        William T. Pyle

18. Exploring the Ninth Concept 216
        Israel Galindo

19. Understanding and Being Understood.......................240
    Rebecca Werner Maccini

20. Anxiety Makes the World Go Round.........................243
    Margaret B. Hess

21. Leadership, Self-Differentiation, and
    Team Empowerment.......................................252
    Brian Virtue

Appendix: An Interview with Lawrence E. Matthews
on the LIM Experience

Bibliography

Acknowledgements

We thank the following persons who have granted permission to use the following works: Richardson, Ronald, "Bowen Family Systems Theory and Congregational Life," is reprinted with permission from *Review & Expositor* summer 2004. Matthews, Lawrence, "Leadership Through a Bowen Systems Lens" is reprinted with permission from *Review & Expositor* summer 2004. Lamkin, James, "Systems Theory and Congregational Leadership: Leaves from an Alchemist's Journal," is reprinted with permission from *Review & Expositor* summer 2004. Galindo, Israel and Betty Pugh Mills, "Long-tenured Ministry and Systems Theory," is reprinted with permission from *Review & Expositor* Vol. 113 Issue 3, August 2016. Marcuson, Margaret, "On Sibling Position" is reprinted from the Leadership in Ministry Newsletter, Summer 2010. Galindo, Israel, "Misunderstandings," reprinted from *Perspectives on Congregational Leadership* (Educational Consultants, 2009). Brian Virtue, "Leadership, Self-Differentiation, and Team Empowerment," used by permission.

Introduction

Founded in 1992 by Dr. Lawrence Matthews, Leadership in Ministry (LIM) has been helping pastors, congregational leaders, and organizational leaders grow in competence through a theory-based, peer learning model. Matthews served as coordinator through 2010. Dr. Robert Dibble served as the coordinator since then, retiring in 2016. Subsequently, LIM has found a home at the Center for Lifelong Learning of the Columbia Theological Seminary, with Dr. Israel Galindo as director.

The goal of the Leadership in Ministry workshops is to help clergy and organizational leaders acquire ways of conceptualizing emotional phenomena and its influence in their contexts, rather than merely teaching techniques for handling ministry challenges. The program is designed to assure that long-term, in-depth training in family systems theory be available to congregations and clergy leaders.

The workshops draw clergy from a variety of denominations, including Presbyterian, Episcopal, Lutheran, Baptist, Methodist, Orthodox, Jewish, Unitarian Universalist, Pentecostal, and United Church of Christ among others.

This book collects articles from faculty members of the LIM workshops, and from some of its participants and presenters from over the years.

1

The Pedagogy of Leadership in Ministry

Israel Galindo

Israel Galindo is Associate Dean for Lifelong Learning and Director of Online Education at the Columbia Theological Seminary. He directs the LIM workshops. This chapter presents the pedagogy used in the LIM workshops.

The Rationale for the LIM Workshops Model

The Leadership in Ministry workshop model follows the format used by Edwin Friedman, with some modifications developed over years of practice in the workshops. The format provides for the exploration and exposition of BFST as a "theory of practice" for leadership in the congregational and other contexts. Through reflection on practice and peer groups, the workshop experience encourages participants to focus the three primary relationship systems in which the theory is applied: one's family of origin, one's work context, and one's immediate family and extended relationships. While the didactic theory presentation component is an important part of the pedagogy of the workshop, the transformative learning tends to take place in the peer group genogram and case study presentations through reflection-on-experience.

Family of Origin Work Through Genograms

Providing opportunity for participants to create and present their genograms is a key component of the LIM learning model. One entire small group session is devoted to presenting the genogram and family of origin dynamics. Reviewing the genogram in the first small group session facilitates referencing emotional process issues in subsequent small group presentations. Below are some pedagogical benefits of using the genogram in small groups:

- Through looking at the facts of one's family genogram one can identify common and persistent patterns of behavior in family members across generations, and, the ways those patterns influence relationship in the ministry context and the nuclear family.
- Identifying patterns of behavior across the generations allows one to see these patterns as being facts about the family that have histories and influence that precede and transcend the history and influence of any one family member.
- Understanding emotional process in one's family of origin allows one to develop a more objective understanding of behavior patterns, family members, and the parts that self and other family members play in creating and perpetuating these behavioral and relationship patterns.
- Through family of origin work one can become more neutral and less reactive toward those family patterns, family members, and oneself.
- Progress in family of origin work can lead to less blaming and more acceptance of self and other family members for

the patterns in the family while simultaneously encouraging one to assume responsibility for the part that self plays in creating and maintaining these patterns.

- Family of origin work can result in a shift in perspective and in goals and pursuits to change that were impulsive, willful, and driven by emotions. One can pursue new life changes, goals, and aspirations in a more thoughtful and less reactive manner.
- Clarity of emotional processes (like reactivity and homeostasis) in one's family of origin can help one have greater success at being able to sustain changes, recognize reactivity, and function in differentiated ways when the family puts pressure on one to "change back."

Plenary Presentations

The purpose of the LIM plenary presentations, typically delivered by faculty members, is to:

- Help the framework of the workshops remain grounded in the theory
- Challenge participants to acquire accurate understanding of the concepts of the theory
- Demonstrate how "thinking about the theory" influences aspects of the presenter's life and self through work and professional case studies, family of origin case studies, or study
- Provide opportunity for peer learning through dialogue and reflection
- To continue to advance the theory through imaginative thinking and interpretation.

The plenary presentations provide an opportunity to practice differentiation of self on the part of the presenter and participants. Differentiation of self in the instructional context involves thinking through pedagogical principles of teaching and learning, the content, methods, and relationships in ways that are consistent with BFST. For example: calmly stating one's convictions without debate or explanation; acting on one's principles; observing the reactivity in response to challenge; managing one's own reactivity in a responsible fashion.

In the instructional context there are two aspects of differentiation of self: the differentiation of thinking and feeling within the presenter, and the differentiation of self and other.[1] Pedagogical goals when presenting, then, include (1) fostering reflection to the extent to which thinking can be distinguished from feeling, and (2) fostering conversation to the extent to which dialoguing with others leads to the expression of ideas that allows interaction in which each person can state what he or she thinks and be heard (vs. uncritical reception of information, fusion, or reactivity).

Peer Learning Groups

The peer learning groups component of the LIM workshop experience facilitates the pedagogy of reflection-on-experience through the lens of BFST as a theory of practice in a peer-learning context. The following axioms highlight the distinctiveness of the small group experience from a BFST perspective:

- To the extent appropriate for the group, the faculty-coach should encourage confidentiality, mutual respectfulness, neutrality, and attentiveness (being emotionally and mindfully present).

- To the extent possible the faculty-coach should promote an environment of trust, challenge, and relatively low anxiety
- Participants should be encouraged to make connections with BFST in their small group presentations. Those listening to the presentation should avoid advice-giving.
- The purpose of the small group is not therapy nor "group building," rather, it is to help participants present thoughtful observations about their own families, relationships, or work situations to gain insight through reflection-on-experience and to allow other group members to listen and learn.
- When responding to or questioning a small group presenter, participants should be encouraged to focus on observable facts rather than interpretations. Asking who, what, where, when, how, and "why now?" but avoiding "why" questions of the type that solicit mind-reading and interpretation of others' motivations or of causality.
- When presenting their genograms in small groups participants should be encouraged to start with a focus on themselves, their spouses or partners, and their children and then move toward observations about their families of origin and multigenerational families.
- Participants should be encouraged to focus on facts of chronology and nodal events and then identify patterns and themes in family relationships across generations. Greatest value is gained on focusing on emotional process dynamics across generations and among and between individuals than on over-focusing on individuals and their

personalities.

The Case Study Method

The case study method is used to facilitate reflection on experience and practice in the participant's life and work contexts. Participants write 300-500 word case studies prior to the workshop and present them in peer small groups. Two case studies are presented: (1) a case study related to leadership in their ministry setting (congregation or work); (2) a case study involving a family or individual in their ministry or work context. It is important for participants to prepare a written case and share copies with participants as this is part of the pedagogy of reflection on experience. The act of writing is the vehicle for a first pass at reflecting on experience and provides a focus for the small group work. A short outline for preparing a case study is available to participants. Most faculty coaches will ask the presenting participant to diagram the case while the rest of the small group members read the case prior to the small group work.

The Process

The diagram below illustrates the pedagogy of the Leadership in Ministry workshops. Three major components help participants arrive at meaningful learning: (1) Bowen Systems Theory as a theory of practice for ministry—a lens through which to interpret experience, apply a framework for thinking, observe emotional process in contexts; (2) the participant's own experience in relationship contexts (family of origin, nuclear family, work/ministry setting); and (3) the act of reflection on experience and practice. This third component is facilitated by the use of three methods: case study, genogram, and peer group dialogue.[2]

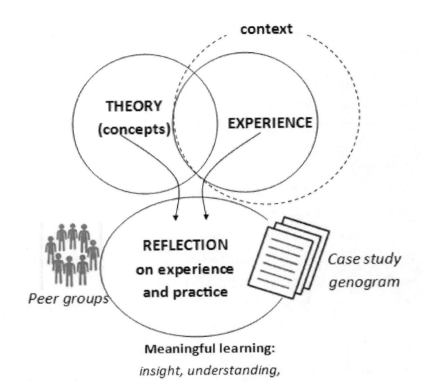

Meaningful learning:

insight, understanding,

change, growth, maturation

---

[1]Murray Bowen, *Family Therapy in Clinical Practice,* (NY and London, Jason Aronson, 1978), pp. 362-366.

[2]Some content adapted from Cheryl B. Lester, "Integrating Bowen Theory with Academic Research, Teaching, and Service,"; "Thomas J. Shur, A Supervision Model Based in Bowen Theory and Language," and Katherine G. Baker & Peter Titleman, "Bowen Theory in Russia: A Training Program for Russian Psychologists," in *Bringing Systems Thinking to Life: Expanding the Horizons for Bowen Family Systems Theory,* ed. Ona C. Bregman and Charles White (New York: Routledge, 2011).

2

Leadership Through a Bowen Systems Lens

Lawrence E. Matthews

Lawrence Matthews served on the faculty of Edwin Friedman's program. He founded the Leadership in Ministry workshops while pastor of the Vienna Baptist Church, Vienna VA where he retired in 1998. Matthews continued to serve as coordinator of the workshops until 2010.

There are multiple perspectives from which one can try to understand the concept of "leadership." When viewed through a Bowen family systems (BFST) lens, I understand leadership as a functioning position that is present in all relational systems. From this perspective, how that position is filled—how the "leader" is present in the system—is the crucial issue. A system will either benefit or suffer from the way the leader is present because the functioning of the leader (or leaders) affects the emotional processes themselves.

As author Edwin Friedman applied Bowen Family Systems Theory to leadership, he focused upon Bowen's core concept of self-differentiation. As he spoke and wrote about leadership through self-differentiation, "through" was always the determinative word. His emphasis was upon the direct relationship between the leadership function of a person and her or his self-differentiation. He maintained that when the "L" position is occupied by a leader who is moving forward in his/her own process of self-differentiation, any system stands the best chance of dealing creatively with, rather than simply reacting to, change and challenge.

When leadership is understood in this way, the crucial question becomes: how does one do it, be it? To phrase the question differently, if leadership is about "being," what are the qualities of leaders engaged in the process of self-differentiation?

Friedman taught that there are at least four dimensions to leadership understood in this way: self-regulation, self-definition, connectedness and response to resistance. I label them "dimensions" because it seems to me that they are inextricably bound to one another. To examine them individually may be practically helpful, but in doing so we should not forget that each one is simply one dimension of a unified process being lived out by unique human beings. These are not "three tips for would-be leaders" or "three simple steps to more effective parenting or pastoring." Rather they are some of the more visible signs of the presence of the life-long process of growing "self" from the inside.

Self- Regulation

Anxiety encompasses the total human response to the perception of threat, real or imagined. Basic to the process of self-differentiation is the task of consciously working at regulating one's anxiety. This includes acknowledging the anxiety and intentionally regulating one's reactivity to it. It is hard, daily work, but the leader engaged in self-differentiation accepts the challenge. Leaders know that change in the emotional process is facilitated by focusing upon the modification of one's own behavior rather than the functioning of others.

One of the most significant contributions of family systems theory is its awareness of the multi-generational nature of much of our anxiety. Not only does our anxiety come with the territory of being human, it comes in unique ways as part of the territory of being human in our particular family systems. This can be a source of despair as we find ourselves living out the reactive patterns of past generations, but it can also be a source of growth and change as we consciously face and rework those patterns. Therapy and healing in a family systems model involves such reworking, and the freedom discovered through this process enables one to better regulate reactivity in the present.

I have learned from personal experience, my experience with parents I have coached, and pastors and other leaders who participate in our workshops, that the people who are able to become less anxious and less reactive are the ones who are involved in learning more about their own family of origin.

Michael Kerr wrote, "Learning enough about the multi-generational emotional history of one's family to change the way one thinks about the family and about oneself probably contributes more to the effort to 'grow up' than anything else a person can do." [1]

The concept of the emotional triangle enables one to actually observe the emotional process which—although always present and ultimately determinative—is in most situations outside of conscious awareness. It allows one to "see" the impact of others upon oneself, the impact one has on others and the impact others have on each other equips leaders with a valuable resource for self-regulation. This is why understanding the theory is so essential, and why the ongoing Leadership in Ministry Workshops were the main focus of my ministry prior to my retirement. A person does not learn to think this way by reading a book or attending a seminar. Learning to "think process" and not focus only upon content is a multi-year process itself.

Self-definition

Self-regulation is the internal dimension of this process; self-definition is the external dimension. Here the focus shifts to the communication of self to other selves, and I include all the various forms communication can and will take. To define self is to give expression to the thoughts, values and goals one holds dear. It includes taking stands. To use biblical language, it is self-revelation. I have come to understand this as one of my major tasks as a pastor. My responsibility is to get clear about what I think and believe and communicate those thoughts and beliefs in words and actions, not to get others straight about what they should think and believe.

To focus on clarifying and communicating one's own ideas and goals is an invitation for others to do the same. When a parent takes a stand that clearly expresses his or her true thoughts and values, other family members are challenged to function differently. When a pastor is able to preach the sermon that clearly and non-reactively expresses what the pastor believes about the emotionally loaded issue facing the congregation, the people are invited and challenged to clarify and express their beliefs, and some will. And when the resistance of those who are most reactive surfaces, as it most probably will, if the pastor and other leaders are able to maintain that clarity of definition, the congregation stands its best chance of actually responding to the situation in faithfulness and obedience. It might even act redemptively.

It is my experience that leaders who are working at their own self-definition are better able to resist the temptation to will others into compliance with their ideas and goals. Whatever is meant by the phrase "the will of God," it does not mean that God violates the freedom and responsibility that is part and parcel of our God-created humanity. When willing others to "be" or "do" is the posture of a leader, trust in self-definition has been abandoned and a path of coercion that can only lead to a conflict of wills has been chosen.

Connectedness

Self-differentiating leaders work at self-regulation and self-definition while maintaining connection to their relational systems. They realize that they cannot affect an emotional system of which they are not a part. It is important for newly arrived leaders to take the time to become connected to their new system. It is especially important to maintain this connectedness when resistance is encountered because of the leader's self-differentiating behavior.

At such times a leader is tempted to either give up or cut off. If the leader persists, does not withdraw or quit, but rather remains connected and on course, a system stands the best chance of dealing creatively with challenge.

Response to Resistance

Friedman referred to a leader's ability to maintain a posture of non-reactive persistence, staying on course in the face of resistance, as "the key to the kingdom." Although leaders may seem surprised and disappointed by the reactivity of others to what they consider their creative self-differentiated leadership efforts, resistance is actually systemic in nature. It comes with the territory. Self-differentiated leadership disturbs the homeostasis, the "balance", of an emotional system. The resistance is the "kickback" of the systemic forces themselves to this "loss of balance"—even if the original condition was one of "stuckness." In contrast to the "rearrangement of symptoms" that often passes for change, systemic change includes resistance to the unfamiliar and therefore uncomfortable readjustment that is necessary to move to a new state of balance.

The resistance will most probably be experienced by leaders in one or both of its two major expressions: sabotage and/or seduction. Resistance as sabotage is perhaps most easily recognizable. Although the sabotage can take many forms, it is usually expressed through acts of either active or passive attempts to block the change or attack the perceived would be "changers," usually the leadership. Resistance as seduction, although less easily recognized as resistance, may be the more subversive and effective form.

It may even be experienced as support for the leader, when in reality it is an invitation for the leader not to stay the course. After I went public with my decision to retire from pastoral ministry, I encountered both forms of resistance from the same couple.

On one occasion the husband angrily attacked me for thoughtlessly "forsaking the congregation," while at another time the wife tearfully told me that the congregation just could not get along without my wonderful leadership.

A Concluding Word of Caution

Experience has not changed my belief that when the leadership ("L") position is filled by a leader (or leaders) who is moving forward in his/her own process of self-differentiation, any system stands the best chance of dealing creatively with, rather than simply reacting to, change and challenge. However, because I am increasingly aware that such creative responses do not come easily or quickly, I am learning to add a word of caution. They may not even come at all. The presence of self-differentiated leadership offers "the best chance" of such a possibility happening, but it is not a guarantee that the system will respond instead of react.

The payoff of leadership through self-differentiation may not be what we think such a supposedly more insightful understanding of leadership ought to deliver success of the endeavor and approval for the leader. This understanding of leadership focuses upon the leader and not upon the outcome of the leader's efforts. Viewed through the emotional process lens of family systems theory, "leadership" is not about "them" or "success" but about self, self-regulation, self-definition, self-differentiation. The payoff is self.

---

[1]Kerr, Michael E. & Bowen, Murray, *Family Evaluation* (W. W. Norton & Co., 1988), p. 309.

❖

3

Navigating the Triangles in Interim Ministry

William T. Pyle

Dr. William T. Pyle is a long time participant in the LIM workshops and has served as intentional interim at numerous congregations. He has taught previously at Campbell University Divinity School, NC, Wesleyan College, and Southeastern Baptist Theological Seminary.
He joined the faculty of LIM in 2007.

I have been serving congregations as an interim pastor since 1990. I have been observing the ways that triangles develop as I enter and become a part of the emotional process of the congregation. In this essay, I will explore some of the triangles that I have encountered, the way that the triangles reveal the emotional process of the congregation, and ways that I choose to function as a part of the triangles.

The development of triangles begins to emerge with my first contact from a congregation. Often the chair of a search committee makes the first contact with me. That person will provide an overview of the church's recent history and describe what they need in an interim. While they are providing historical context, I am listening for emotional process. They are moving toward me and are often identifying the person(s) that will occupy the other point in the triangle. This is just the opening round of positioning. As soon as I am introduced to the search committee, or the Deacons, or the Church Council, other people begin offering their perspectives on the recent history of the church. By virtue of my position as an interim leader, it becomes important to them that I hear their perspectives. And while I want to be attentive to the content, I also need to keep making process notes. What are the emerging triangles revealing about the emotional process of the congregation and the ways they deal with anxiety?

I recognize that when I sit in the former Pastor's chair, I have also reactivated the triangle with her detractors and her supporters. It's not personal and I don't need to make it personal. While it isn't fair, it is an opportunity to model a different way of functioning in this triangle. I work to maintain significant contact with the people involved and remain an observer of the emotional process as it unfolds. Of course, this also gives me a great opportunity to work on my own issues surrounding closeness and individuality. My personal challenge is to avoid moving into the close position with one of the sides and putting the other point of the triangle in the outside position. The inside close position is the coveted, comfortable position in my family of origin. As a leader, I compromise my ability to lead the system when I move to the comfortable inside position in the triangle.

The time between installed Pastors is an opportune time for a congregation to explore its heritage and to think about necessary changes that are appropriate for their changing context. Conversations about "how did we get here?" and "where are we going?" are necessary, important, and natural anxiety-binders. My responsibility as an interim minister is to facilitate these kinds of conversations without being responsible for the outcomes or the decisions the congregation makes. One triangle that I have consistently encountered is minister, congregation, and the future. In this triangle, I am in the outside position and the church is in the inside position with its future. And that is appropriate. It is their future. My responsibility is to be a good dialogue partner who can tease out mature, reality-based thinking. My personal challenge is to avoid the willfulness that would move toward trying to control their side of the triangle. Again, my issues around boundaries provide an opportunity for personal growth. The clearer I can be about the congregation's responsibility for its future, the clearer I can be about my role as coach and facilitator.

While I wanted to write an essay about churches and their triangles, this is turning into a confessional about how working with churches and managing their triangles has been a great opportunity for me to grow as a person and as a leader. I have learned that I cannot be responsible for the relationship between the other two points of the triangle; that is their business. I can be responsible in maintaining healthy one-on-one relationships with each individual point of the triangle. If I can maintain healthy one-on-one relationships without intruding into their responsibility, I encourage the kind of environment where others can step up in their functioning, or not. That is their responsibility and choice.

4

On Sibling Position

Margaret Marcuson

Marcuson is founder of the Marcuson Leadership Circle and lives in Portland, Oregon. She works with clergy and other leaders who want to practice an easier, more effective way to lead. Margaret was pastor of the First Baptist Church of Gardner, Massachusetts, for thirteen years. She began her studies with Ed

Friedman in 1995 and continued to study at the Center for Family Process in Bethesda for six years. She joined the LIM faculty in 1999.

My younger brother told me recently that one of his most enduring childhood memories is chasing after me on his tricycle while I and my friends shot away from him on our bikes. What memories do you have of your siblings, if you had them?

"Sibling position" is one of the eight foundational concepts of Bowen Family Systems Theory. Michael Kerr suggests that, for example, "a first born, all things being equal (as Dr. Bowen liked to say) is born into a different sets of needs and expectations of the system than a second born."[1]

Over time, as we work on our own differentiation we can better manage the automatic responses we learn from our functioning position in the family. Kerr himself says, "I'm less of a youngest than I used to be."[2] For me, this has to do with managing my overfunctioning and being less bossy. I recognize that when my anxiety goes up, my irritability with the perceived underfunctioning ("irresponsibility!") of others increases. I can now see it more clearly, and regulate it better, on a good day.

Many in ministry are oldest or only children. This can work well, to a degree. They know instinctively how to take charge and articulate a vision. Still, when the pattern becomes compulsive, it can be a problem. People at higher levels of differentiation will have a wider repertoire than those who are less mature.

Beth Norton, director of music at First Parish Church, Concord, MA and long-time LIM workshop participant, notes that in a high-functioning staff like theirs, the sibling dynamics are a bit less important on an ongoing basis. But, she says, at times of higher anxiety the patterns emerge more strongly: "It's predictable who is going to be the caretaker, who are going to be the ones who underfunction when it gets really stressful, who are going to be the ones who try to take care of them and restore harmony, and who are going to go into a room and close the door."

Here are some questions to consider:

- What is your sibling position in your family, and that of your parents?
- How have your own siblings fared in life? Your aunts and uncles?
- What do you notice about how you function in your ministry role based on your sibling position?
- Can you try it another way, lightening up if you're an oldest, or getting more serious if you're a youngest, just for a day?

---

[1]Michael Kerr, telephone interview, June 5, 2008.
[2]Ibid.

5

Common Misunderstandings of Systems Theory

Israel Galindo

Few things escape the consequences of their own success. This axiom seems true even of Bowen Family Systems Theory. It seems that systems theory is now the "in" thing—never have there been as many courses on it, or more "experts" on the matter. And a sure sign of its popularity is the rate of books being turned out that claim to have a "systems approach to" something or other (this book being one of them!). This is, overall, a good thing. The more the theory is propagated, the better, I say. But one consequence of the theory's fast dissemination is the risk of misunderstandings—like in that old parlor game, "telegraph." What goes in one ear at one end may come out as something completely different at the other—the message gets lost in translation as it is passed from one person to another.

I continue to hear many "misunderstandings" related to Bowen Family Systems Theory (BFST) and its application to leadership. And while I'm no self-appointed guardian of orthodoxy, I am enough of an advocate for critical thinking—and admittedly have little patience for "fuzzy thinking"—that I often find myself offering correctives when I hear a misapplication or misunderstanding of the theory. After all, both, I think, can have dire consequences. Below, then, are correctives to some of the more common "systems misunderstandings."

Systems theory is about leadership. The fact is that BFST is primarily about therapy. But the theory identifies principles about relationships and relationship systems that are universally applicable to any context in which people form attachments or live and work together. The application of this theory to the concerns of leadership is appropriate. But to believe that systems theory is a "style of leadership" is a fundamental misunderstanding.

Systems theory is about managing conflict. For those unfortunate enough to occupy a leadership position, this is the cold hard truth: conflict exists and it cannot be managed. To assume that systems theory provides a way to manage other people's behaviors, emotions, beliefs, or anxiety is a fundamental error. What system theory offers the leader is a way to manage him or herself amid the conflict that arises as a natural course of events in any relationship system.

Systems theory is about managing change. Sorry, it's not about this either. How do you "manage" the nature of the cosmos? Change, in both evolution and entropy, is the nature of the world we live in. The typical misunderstanding here is that systems theory is a tool to use in managing other people, relationships, organizations, and circumstance. Holding on to that misunderstanding will do a leader in every time. If systems theory is about anything, it is about managing self in the midst of the constant changes around us.

Busyness is the same as overfunctioning. The complexity of congregational ministry means that pastoral leaders will always be busy. In fact, the longer one stays in one context, assuming the leader is working at organizational development and institutional evolution, the more complex the ministry becomes, and, the busier the job. Overfunctioning involves taking responsibility for things that are not yours to take on: other people's jobs, anxieties, or responsibilities. Effective leaders are busy about the things for which they are responsible—and they will always be busy. The point is to avoid overfunctioning—being busy because you are doing other people's jobs, or worse, perpetuating patterns of overfunctioning-underfunctioning reciprocity.

Self-definition is the same as Self-differentiation. Self-definition is merely the act of stating what you believe about yourself or about an issue. While that is important, it is not equivalent to self-differentiation, which is qualitatively different.

A bigot can self-define his position about a class of people — but self-differentiation allows the freedom and dignity of the other without feeling threatened or denying the other the right to define self also. The differentiated person is able to balance difference while staying connected, rather than cutting off.

Talking to another person is equivalent to "staying connected." BFST is about emotional process. Merely talking to another person is not equivalent to *functioning* at an emotional systemic level. Staying connected with another person in the system means making an *emotional* connection. That requires a form of communication that is deeper, reciprocal, and affective; not merely giving orders, stating an opinion, stating what we think, or airing our feelings.

Systems theory helps us get out of triangles. Whether we like it or not, we are always in triangles. And if you are in a leadership position, you likely are in some monster triangles that span a couple of generations — they come with the job. BFST is about being able to choose how we will *function* in the triangles we are in.

In Systems theory we never ask "Why?" We often hear that BFST strives to be scientific and so we should stick with observable facts rather than asking why questions (which go to motives). Asking who, what, where, how, and when are helpful to uncovering facts about functioning, and for avoiding over-interpretation. But that does not negate the importance of why. The notion that cautions against asking why question merely means we should not *start* with the why questions. Asking who, what, where, how, and when *first*, will help answer the why question ultimately.

There is no such thing as a non-anxious presence. It's curious to hear this oft-repeated sentiment given that the literature of BFST specifically refers to persons and leaders who are a non-anxious presence in anxious systems. Arguably, there may not be such a creature as a non-anxious *person*, but the concept here refers to the relative *functioning* of an individual in the midst of a context where high anxiety and reactivity, if not chaos, is rife. Many seem reluctant to own the term, perhaps due to their own challenge in "being non-anxious." But the fact is that persons can, and are, trained to be non-anxious in even the most chaotic and threatening of circumstances. Think of EMT personnel, police and rescue personnel, soldiers on the field of battle, trauma surgeons and nurses, etc. Being a non-anxious presence is merely the epitome of differentiation: separating one's functioning from the experience of feelings.

The leader should avoid or give up expectations of outcomes. This is sound advice, but it's a good example of how misunderstanding leads to misapplication. The error here is emphasizing the wrong part of this axiom. More often than not, leaders hear this as giving up on outcomes, and not taking responsibility for bringing about those outcomes. But that's not in keeping with the nature of leadership. If you're the leader, your job is to bring about appropriate and necessary outcomes—and a healthy system will hold the leader responsible for that. What is not helpful is holding on to our *expectations* related to outcomes, that's the trap: expectations about people's willingness to embrace or accept change; expecting that the first response to a call to vision or action will be an enthusiastic and sincere "yes!"; expectations about timetables for accomplishing goals; about how many will be supportive of a vision; about who accepts challenges and who will cut off, etc. Effective leaders are clear about the outcomes necessary for the system and organizations they lead, and their take appropriate responsibility for it.

The leader's job is to lower systemic anxiety. Yeah, good luck with that. An effective leader primarily takes responsibility for managing his or her own anxiety, rather than rescuing the system from the discomfort of anxiety. In fact, a savvy and playful leader understands that pain is an effective motivator for change. He or she knows when to allow the anxiety in the system to climb in order to facilitate emotional process or functioning on the part of those who need to own the anxiety that belongs to them. A helpful reminder: leave the pain where it belongs.

6

Bowen Family Systems Theory and Congregational Life

Ronald W. Richardson

Ronald Richardson is the author of several standard texts on BFST and clergy and congregations. He has presented numerous times at LIM workshops. Richardson observes that pastors and church leaders are increasingly using family systems theory as a way to understand normal relationship processes in their churches and to learn how to function within them. In this article he shows some of the relevance to church ministry of the eight primary concepts in Bowen family systems theory.

Introduction

Pastor Ralph came in for a consultation. He had been the head minister at the 700-member First Baptist church for just over three years. He had been doing family systems theory work for about the same amount of time. A situation was now emerging that he was both excited by and worried about. His excitement was over a shift in the church leadership system that he saw as beneficial; yet he feared that he could be somehow trapped in it. He was experiencing conflicting loyalties.

The Smith family was one of the pillars of First church. Jim and Jane Smith were now each 72 years old but still vital and active both at their work and in the church. Two of their three children were also active in the church along with their families. They were all major contributors and had served as valuable leaders for many years. As Ralph said, "The tradition of this church is to have on its board 50% men, 50% women and one member of the Smith family."

Jim and Jane had been the primary supporters of bringing Ralph to First church and they considered themselves the major interpreters to him of "what this church is about and what we need from our pastor." They often took Ralph and his wife out to their Golf Club for meals and Jim and Ralph had occasional golf games together. On nearly every such occasion some bit of guidance would be offered to Ralph about issues in the church. Ralph had, up to this point, mostly followed this advice.

Jane Smith (the current Smith family representative on the board) was absent at a recent board meeting where replacing the church computer system was being discussed. The old computers were frequently crashing. Pastor Ralph told them that the Smith's eldest son Jeff planned to give the church the computers from his law office, since he was replacing them with new ones. All previous gifts to the church from the Smith family came with strings of indebtedness, made known to the board members as well as the pastor. At the meeting, another member of the board, Harry, said he would buy the church "four new computers. They would not have to be 'hand-me-downs' from the Smiths." Ralph opined that the Smiths might be unhappy about having their gift refused and Harry said, "We don't have to do everything the Smiths want." At this many others board members jumped in with enthusiastic agreement.

Ralph kept quiet during the rest of this discussion but inwardly he was torn. He was happy to have the possibility of new computers and glad that some new leaders were challenging the hegemony of the Smiths. But he felt a loyalty to the Smiths and feared how they might react to this possible "mutiny" by the board. Pastor Ralph knew he was in what systems theory calls "a triangle" and he was wondering what to do now.

Bowen Family Systems Theory

Triangles are just one of the eight concepts that are a part of Bowen family systems theory. Dr. Murray Bowen was a Professor of Psychiatry at Georgetown University in Washington, D.C. He began developing his family systems theory in the 1950s and died in 1990. The late Rabbi Edwin Friedman, a student of Bowen's, was the first person to make a broad application of the theory to pastoral functioning in his book, *Generation to Generation*. Many other authors are now adding to the growing body of literature on systems thinking and the church as the theory becomes a primary framework for understanding pastoral functioning.

Family systems theory has some similarities to biblical anthropology. In both cases, the individual self is always a part of several larger wholes. The self does not exist alone. In the biblical world, individual identity is nearly always derived in part from what he or she belongs to, whether it is occupations, places, families, or tribes. The larger context helps to define the individual. The individual is often a particular expression of the larger corporate group. Paul's first Corinthian letter evokes the same idea where he describes how we are a part of the body of Christ. This idea is pervasive in both Testaments.

From the time of the enlightenment, we have been breaking reality down into discreet, constituent parts, losing the connection things have with each other, studying them separately, as if they existed on their own. In modern times, we have attempted to understand individuals apart from their communities of identity. Freud continued this process in his psychological language and worldview, separating the individual into discreet parts. Bowen has shifted the focus back to a more biblical view of the individual as a part of one or more larger wholes. For him, as well as for the ancient Hebrew authors, the family is the primary unit of interest.

Bowen theory is a source of hope for pastors and church leaders. It not only describes how we normally operate in relationships, it also offers directions for how growth can happen. The systemic approach includes the belief that when we change our part in a relationship process, others will then have to change their part. This approach is not about doing "tricky" things to others to get them to change. It is about a caring way to be closely connected with others that also allows us, at the same time, to be true to our own beliefs and values.

Bowen considered his theory incomplete because we do not yet know enough about human beings and how they function in relationships. Toward the end of his life he was considering a possible ninth concept that he tentatively called "spirituality." This had to do with the function of beliefs in human life and relationships. He was never able to develop this idea into a full concept. In the rest of this article I will describe the eight basic concepts in the theory and show some of their relevance to congregational life.

1. Triangles

Triangles are the basic molecules of emotional systems. They are the primary way we manage the inevitable anxiety that will occur in two-person relationships when they are stressed. When one member of the dyad begins to feel anxious, often around feeling either "too close" or "too distant," a third person (or group) will be brought in. Ralph had begun to develop some anxiety early in the relationship with the Smiths about being "in their pocket" and "controlled" by their wishes. He felt "too close" to them and was happy now to have the board members challenge the Smiths.

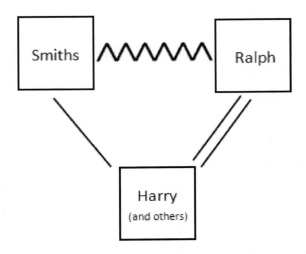

Fig. 1: A Church Triangle

However, Ralph knew once the Smiths heard about the board's decision about the computers they would focus their feelings of rejection and lack of appreciation on him. They would think he was drifting too far away from them and would put the pressure on him, through the expression of these feelings, to "reign him back in" and bring him back close to them. He feared their anger in particular. He knew he didn't want to have a confrontation, nor did he want to lose their otherwise valuable input to church life.

Triangles are a central feature of church life and every pastor is a part of numerous significant triangles every day. Once we learn to see them we realize they are everywhere; there is no escaping them. Each triangle has three corners. In this example, the Smith family is in one corner, Ralph in another, and the "rebel" board members in the third corner of a congregational triangle.

Generally two of the corners in a triangle represent the "close insider" position and the third corner is the "outside" position. Who is "in" or "out" is fluid and can shift about.

Understanding how triangles function and how we can manage ourselves within them can help us in most of our pastoral relationships. Conflicts between two people will often resolve themselves if a third person, who is important to them emotionally, can maintain contact with them both and remain neutral about their conflict. The principle involves learning how to manage our own anxiety and be a calmer presence with the conflicted parties. This is what family and couples therapy is based on and it is a useful principle for most pastoral functioning.

Triangles can be a place where we play a game of "let's you and them fight." Ralph could tell the Smiths that he wasn't able to dissuade the board and they need to take their concerns to the board. Therefore he could transfer his tension and anxiety to the two other parties and feel calmer and safer himself. However, if Jim Smith went to Harry and confronted him, Harry might say he was "sure that Pastor Ralph wanted those new computers I offered to buy," thus shifting the anxiety back to the other two corners. Or any of the three corners could bring in a fourth party, like a computer systems consultant, and create an interlocking second triangle. This process could continue with anxiety being passed around the congregational emotional system, through interlocking triangles, building as it goes while other parties add in their unresolved concerns, until it becomes an even bigger deal in the church. If there was enough anxiety about other unresolved issues, a major church fight could develop.

Triangles exist in our nuclear family, in our family of origin, in our friendships, and in our workplace. They also play out in social, cultural, economic, and political issues in the local community and in national and international arenas.

2. Nuclear family emotional system

The nuclear family emotional system concept describes the patterns of emotional functioning in a one-generation family, or, from the point of view of the church, within a primary administrative unit. This concept includes a number of sub-concepts.

Bowen defined "family" in the broadest terms possible in order to be inclusive of all the types of families that exist. He said, "A family is any number of people gathered around an emotional nucleus." The emotional nucleus is usually one or both parents or, in the church, it could be the pastor and one other staff person like the church secretary. While I don't believe that "the church family" is an accurate or useful term (and in some cases can include dangerous assumptions for both pastors and members), and I discourage the use of the term, it does recognize that a congregation can function like a family in many ways.

A major difference between systems thinking and the individual model of human functioning is the answer to the question "where does the problem lie?" The individual model suggests that the problem is within particular people like Ralph, or one of the Smiths, or the "rebel" board member Harry. This belief is bolstered by the many psychological approaches to human motivation and their diagnoses of individual problems. Bowen theory enlarges the field of vision. It recognizes the interconnectedness of people in emotional systems and how each person affects the others. Every involved person is included as a part of the problem and of the potential solution.

The concept of the nuclear family emotional system recognizes that members of a family or a church have a deep, interconnected way of being with each other in which each one affects the other. No one exists as a purely autonomous being and most of us are emotionally connected with a large number of people. How we think and feel about them and our relationship with them, and how they think and feel about us and relate to us is an ongoing, dynamic interactive process that deeply affects us all.

The functioning of the emotional system depends just as much on emotional process as on rational process. Emotional process is about how relationships develop as a result of the basic biological, automatic reactivity we have to each other. This process is often beyond awareness. It is deeper than our "feelings." We have little conscious control over it until we make a concerted effort to modify our part in it. Work systems are rarely governed simply by rationality, and the organizational chart rarely reflects the way things really work. This partly explains why our best-laid plans often go astray.

Theologically, this means our "care for souls" can be subsumed under the heading of the care for the community. Being aware of the emotional process in the community, and relating to it as a more emotionally mature person, is one of the best things we can do for individual members of the church in our pastoral care for them. A powerful emotionality was stimulated in the triangle of Ralph, the Smiths, and the board. A pastor who can get outside of this emotional process and stay emotionally connected to both other parties is doing pastoral care in an important way.

A variety of emotional systems can influence specific triangles and be interconnected with them. They can each affect process in the other systems. For example, there is Ralph's own family emotional system. Ralph's wife June has some strong feelings about Ralph as a husband and as a father and sometimes sees the church as a competitive third corner in a triangle. For her, the church is almost like Ralph's mistress. His preoccupation with church issues takes up emotional energy she wishes he would invest in her and their family.

Also, June has particularly resented the Smith's influence on Ralph and feels protective of his reputation in the church, wanting him to look less like he is in the Smith's corner. Her beliefs and feelings were in Ralph's head at that board meeting. He thought, "This will be a chance to show her I am not always on the Smiths' side." Colleagues in his Baptist conference, another emotional system, had also heard something about the influence of the Smiths at First church and Ralph felt their opinions affecting him as well. However, Ralph's parents, another emotional system, had aspirations for him to "make it big" as a pastor and encouraged him to pay special attention to "the really important members" of the church.

Ralph had always wanted to "just preach the gospel and encourage people to live a more Christian life." He once believed that church politics kept getting in the way of this goal and he wanted to get away from this or ignore it. But now he understood that these emotional system processes could be a major arena for him both to demonstrate a Christian life in action and to be a pastor to his people in the midst of their relationships.

Anxiety is pervasive in emotional systems. It has a major impact on emotional process. Anxiety results from the perception of threat, whether real or imagined. For example, the leaving of a former pastor (whether the departure is welcome or not) and the arrival of a new pastor is a time of anxiety for nearly everyone involved. There is a real threat related to whether this pastor and this church have a "fit" in terms of the skills needed for this particular church, at this point in time. There could be imagined threats for someone like the Smiths wondering if they would be able to influence the new pastor the way they did the old one.

People join the church with their own level of chronic anxiety already in place, just as we pastors come with ours. Our chronic anxiety is perpetually sensitive to certain imagined threats being activated. This will cause us, at some point, to be reactive. We all have our anxiety around different things so we can count on the fact that just about any topic or issue will raise somebody's level of anxiety.

Within emotional systems, different people can take on different functional positions. For example, pastors are often anxiety sponges for their congregations. In their desire to keep the peace, they become either the chief worrier or the focus of worry. This puts the pressure on them to solve something that may not be their responsibility. Usually this inclination to absorb anxiety comes first out of their way of functioning in their family of origin. They can easily get caught up in the problems of their parishioners and the church just as they did with their family. The pastor's implicit agreement to do the worrying helps the congregation stay calmer and more relaxed. Relieving people of their anxiety by taking it on one's self is not good pastoral care.

Over-responsible people usually fail to see how their over-functioning promotes under-responsibility in others. This is the traditional parent trap when dealing with less responsible children. Ideally, parenting is a process of taking less and less responsibility for the child and challenging the child to be more responsible for self. It is best to be ahead of children in this process rather than being reluctant to give up responsibility for them. If parents are more anxious about a child's life and future than the child is, then those parents are going to be over-responsible. Ed Friedman is famous for telling us we need to learn how to delegate anxiety rather than responsibility.

As anxiety builds in an emotional system and things begin to feel significantly unbalanced, someone or some relationship in the system may become problematic or symptomatic. Symptoms are an indication that anxiety has built to a fairly high level in the system. They are generally expressed in one or more of four types of relationship patterns: 1) significant emotional distance between people; 2) significant conflict between leaders in the church; 3) the physical, emotional, or social dysfunction of one of the leaders; or 4) the projection of anxiety to a lower level person or group who appears to be "dysfunctional."

3. Differentiation of Self

Differentiation of self is the primary focus for growth within the emotional system. Differentiation is the ability to be in significant emotional contact with others and still be able to function as a more autonomous self, without having the automatic emotional system processes determine our own thinking and behavior. This is emotional maturity.

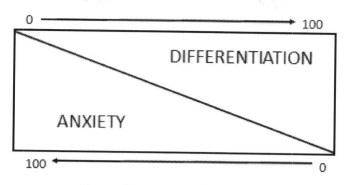

Fig. 2: The Inverse Relationship of
Anxiety and Differentiation

Anxiety and differentiation are two key variables in family systems thinking. Generally, the more imagined threats we experience in life, primarily in relation to others, the less differentiation we will have. The two are inversely related. As anxiety grows during stressful times we are less able to think with a broader perspective. We narrow in on the perceived threat, often represented by a particular person, and the larger systemic issues get lost. The impact of the anger or of the imagined potential abandonment by the Smiths was a perceived threat for Ralph.

During times of upset, if just one key leader can be less anxious, relate well to others in the group, and simply define self, this will have a beneficial impact on the life of the group as a whole. The more important this person is to the life of the group, the greater the impact. If this one person is more solid and less anxious, he or she can be an anchor for the whole system.

The average level of differentiation of a congregation is the critical element in determining whether a church is able to accomplish its stated mission. It decides to what extent a church is influenced by exterior social, cultural, political, or economic pressures and influences or, from the interior of the church, how much it is affected by the reactions and complaints of key people in the church. How much does the focus of church life and mission get blurred by anxiety and its related emotional patterns?

Differentiation is what allows us individually to fulfill our Christian calling more closely, to choose our principled ethical and moral stances with clarity, and to act with courage in fulfilling them. It allows us to relate to others in the loving way we would like without participating in the "party spirit" that destroys church life and ministry. It allows us the emotional flexibility to stay in contact with all important constituencies in the church, hear all points of view and understand them without being aggressive or defensive, or retaliating when hurt, or accommodating in response to emotional pressure from key others in the system. In addition, it allows us to know which battles to fight, when, how, and what the potential outcomes and costs may be.

Better-differentiated people are willing to be responsible for their part in the emotional process, and no more than that. They do not easily catch or become infected with more anxious peoples' anxiety. They are much less reactive to other peoples' way of expressing their anxiety, and can stay focused on their own goals for how they want to be and what they want to do in a cooperative and flexible way with others. They have relatively few relationship difficulties and those that do exist are normally resolved relatively quickly, unless they have decided to provoke an issue intentionally related to a differentiating stance of their own. They are better able to keep a focus on fulfilling the mission of the church while also relating well to all members of the congregation.

Bowen described a theoretical scale of differentiation of self that went from 0 to 100. Those toward the lower end of the scale are more emotionally fused with others and those toward the upper end are more able to connect with others emotionally while also functioning in a more autonomous way. Just as a point of reference, I would put myself in the high thirties on the scale. Most people would probably fit towards this lower end of the scale. This leaves us lots of room for growth. The scale is primarily useful for thinking about our issues of growth and development.

At the lower end of the scale (say around 20 to 25) issues of acceptance and approval are primary. People may quickly adjust their attitudes and beliefs or actions to those of others in order to fit in or be part of the group. Or they are expected to do so by the authorities in the group. Leaders at the lower end may dogmatically attempt to actively control others and make them conform. This begins the automatic reactive processes that are common in lower level communities. The bullies, the compliant chameleons, the rebels, the combative fighters, and the emotional distancers are all operating out of their deep emotionally fused connection with each other. We all have some of these in us.

Persons are lower levels of differentiation require more emotional support to function well. They need to believe that others are in their corner. Their functioning fluctuates depending on how well they feel in relation to others and that others like them. Emotional fusion reveals itself in this anxious focus on others and our preoccupation with what they think, feel, and do. We lose a focus on our own thoughts, beliefs, perceptions, feelings, and intentions. This is the case even if we are making a point of doing the opposite of what "they" want, in order to show them they can't control us. The rebel is controlled by others just as much as is the compliant, agreeable person who goes along with them. The focus is still on what the others want.

At the higher end of the scale, people realistically recognize their interdependence and take into account how the functioning of others can affect them and *vice versa*. They recognize the power of the group but attempt to think with their own head while making good emotional contact with others in the group. In the midst of conflict they will normally remain focused, calm, cool, and collected. When criticized or threatened with rejection they attempt to remain focused on whatever is factual and not get caught up in the emotionality of the event.

Better-differentiated people are able to distinguish between thinking guided by a fact-based rationality and thinking that is based on an emotionally driven reactivity. During their life, they have worked at clarifying their own principles for interacting with others and their beliefs about what is important about how to live. They tend not to have gurus that they give up their self to. They are better able to do what they say they will do, and live according to the personally chosen values they profess. They can choose to give selflessly toward the needs of the group and can have compassion for others in difficulty or they can avoid feeling-based loyalty pulls and compassion traps that keep systems stuck. They are also clear about what they are responsible for and what they are not responsible for.

Church systems themselves are more or less differentiated. Those with a lower level of differentiation will have many debilitating symptoms. The level of differentiation of a church community is something like an average of all the people in it, particularly its leadership. When better-differentiated people are in positions of authority, they can challenge the community to function at a higher level than it might otherwise do. Less well-differentiated and more anxious leaders can bring down the functioning of the congregation, spreading anxiety through the membership. In the case of First Baptist Church it turned out that Harry and a couple of other board members had a slightly higher level of differentiation than the average of the church. They were able to do a good job of relating to the Smiths, working in an open, sensitive, straightforward way with them, appreciating all that they had done for the church, without feeling beholden to them.

The more mature board members made the job easier for Ralph whose own anxiety in relation to the Smiths was indicative of unresolved emotional attachments related to his own family of origin. He had not been more able to differentiate a self in relation to his primary parental triangle at the time that he left home. Both he and his father had played a submissive role in relation to his mother. He had rarely openly gone against his mother's wishes. The very idea of doing this made him anxious. Even today, at age 45, he would wonder about his mother's reaction when he considered options for major life decisions. He dealt with her primarily through emotional and physical distance. This helped him to feel safer and more like his own person. But then he found that if mother was not actually present in his daily life, others could fill in for her. Sometimes his wife functioned as "mother" for him, and he discovered that the Smiths could also; they "knew best" for him, just like his mother.

Differentiation is always a work in progress. No one ever gets there. One of the primary ways of working on it is doing family of origin work. One of the goals of this work is to better differentiate a self within our family, with the people who are the original players in the development of our own way of emotional functioning as adults. It doesn't take long for most of us, in a visit home, or even in a phone call with our parents, to begin to slip back into our adolescent way of being with them. It is as if we never left home emotionally. One result of my consultation with Ralph is that he set a clear objective of working on being a self in relation to his mother and repositioning himself within the parental triangle. In doing his family work, Ralph would be better prepared to deal with the powerful triangles of the emotional system of his church and function as a better leader within it.

4. Family Projection Process

Projection is taking unresolved anxiety from one relationship and focusing it on another. The projection process is the primary way anxiety can be transmitted from an upper level in the church hierarchy to a lower level. Leaders at the top, who have significant disagreements with each other that they are too anxious to look at directly, may join in apparent agreement around someone at a lower level who is seen as a problem. The anxious focus can be on a particular committee, or chairperson, or church member, or another church employee like a janitor. Parents, rather than deal with the anxiety and un-addressed conflicts in their relationship, may project their anxiety onto a problematic child.

In doing his family work, Ralph discovered that his mother, while growing up, had great anxiety about the functioning of her own father. He learned from her that, as the oldest child in her family, she did everything she could to support her mother and to prop up her father. She saw him as weak and dealt with this by becoming his supportive confidant and counselor. Her father began to rely on her overfunctioning more and more and she thus helped keep the family on an even keel. In doing this, by keeping the family less upset, she felt less anxious herself.

Ralph learned that early in his life, his mother thought she saw similar kinds of weaknesses in him. She became anxious that he not turn out like her father and was vigilant for any signs of this direction emerging. As a result she and Ralph replicated the relationship she had with her father. Her husband was relieved to have the focus be on Ralph even though he perceived his wife as acting inappropriately. But he never made an issue of this and went along with her take charge style with Ralph. Like her father, Ralph also developed a dependency on his mother's guidance. At first, as a young boy, he really thought she knew best, but later, as an emerging adult, he began to resent her efforts to steer him in particular directions. He saw her as controlling. However, by adulthood he didn't know how to take more charge of his own life in relation to her wishes. He felt free only by keeping his emotional distance from her.

Generally, unless it is interrupted, the projection process leads to an unhappy outcome and everyone involved will end up feeling inadequate and like a failure. The relationship between the parties involved only becomes more intense, complicated, confusing, and impossible. Differentiation helps us to begin to clarify who is responsible for what and where the limits of our responsibility lie. It helps us to step out of this "responsibility tangle" and to begin to be clear that more loving and caring behavior involves not doing for others what they can actually do for themselves. It helps us to see that we need not spend our time looking for problems in other people to fix. Usually we have enough problems of our own to deal with.

5. Multigenerational Transmission Process

This concept explains how problems can be projected or handed down through the generations. Ralph had begun to see some tendencies in his oldest daughter that made him think of his mother. He had diagnosed this as "her problem" and he had begun to treat her as if this was the case. This was leading to an intense relationship in which each was getting more involved in the other's life. As his daughter moved into puberty, it became a highly conflictual relationship. He was beginning to assume now that the only way to deal with this was emotional distance from his daughter, repeating the pattern with his mother in the next generation. This distance left his daughter even more confused, hurt, and upset even though consciously she thought she welcomed it.

The unresolved issues from Ralph's mother and her father, then transmitted to his mother and him, were now being played out between Ralph and his daughter. A similar process had been at work in the Smith family. Both Jim and Jane Smith were the oldest children in their families and both of their father's had been oldest children. Oldest children know how to be in charge, but they may not be clear about the limits of their responsibility. If they have a parent who was also an oldest, they often get an extra dose of how to be an oldest. They may well learn to be anxious about anything that they are not in charge of. Oldest children can learn to feel responsible for their siblings, and they may often get the message from their parents that they are supposed to keep their siblings in line. If a sibling messes up, they might be held responsible, so again they learn to take care of their own anxiety by making sure everybody does what they should.

As a result of doing his own family work, Ralph began a project of getting to know more about the families of his church. As he learned more about the Smiths and their own families of origin, he began to see this oldest child pattern more clearly as it repeated down their generations. However, Jeff Smith, the Smiths' oldest son was different. He had always struggled with meeting their high expectations of him, getting into lots of trouble as an adolescent. The more his parents overfunctioned for him, the more he underfunctioned.

Significant behavior problems in adolescence are often indicative of the projection process at work. Even though he made it through law school and developed his own law office, with a lot of help from his parents, he still was not measuring up to their expectations. He was now in his second marriage and that one was rocky. He had ongoing drinking and debt problems.

After listening to each of the Smiths tell their family stories, Ralph even commented at one point, "So you both have had a lot of training in being in charge of things. Right? It must be very difficult for you if you begin to think things are beyond your control." Because he had worked hard at getting to know them and being interested in their family life, a higher level of trust had developed between them and they took his comment as a friendly one and readily agreed. Eventually they were able to begin to be different kind of parents with their grown children, and they became less anxious church members.

Getting to know more about the family life of his church leaders and members, Ralph began to be a better pastor to them.

They saw him as a person who was interested in them and that they could seek counsel from. They increasingly began to turn to him during times of crisis in their own family. His systems theory training was a major resource. This also resulted in fewer issues being projected into the church multigenerational emotional process.

6. Sibling Position

I have already touched on the significance of sibling position in some of the previous examples. This concept is the only one in the theory that did not originate with Bowen. As he was developing his theory he happened on the work of Walter Toman who had done extensive research on the impact that a person's birth order and their sex had on their personality. Toman's work fit with Bowen's own perceptions and helped to explain the variety of ways of functioning within a family.

Toman identified ten basic sibling positions: oldest brother of brothers, oldest brother of sisters, oldest sister of sisters, oldest sister of brothers, youngest brother of brothers, youngest brother of sisters, youngest sister of brothers, youngest sister of sisters, only children, and twins. Middle children are some mixture of these depending on the sibling they were closest to growing up. It is possible for middle children to have characteristics of both a youngest (in relation to their older siblings) and an oldest (in relation to their younger siblings).

Certain personality characteristics and functional styles tend to go with each position. Those who have the same sibling position as people from other families may have more similarities to each other than they have with their own siblings. In my pastoral counseling practice I found Toman's descriptions to be highly accurate and useful in helping people understand how they functioned in their important relationships.

People who didn't fit Toman's descriptions either came from better differentiated families or, more often, they were the object of the projection process (Jeff Smith would not be a typical oldest son, for example), or some unique event had happened like the early death of an older sibling.

Toman's research has shown how, for example, sibling position can affect marital issues and the way they are dealt with. He even shows which sibling combinations in the marriage may have more possibility for divorce. He described complementary and non-complementary couples. A complementary couple would be an oldest brother of sisters married to a youngest sister of brothers. If their experience growing up with their siblings was relatively positive, then this is likely to be a highly cooperative relationship with each bringing complementary gifts. A non-complementary couple might be an older brother of brothers married to an oldest sister of sisters. Each is used to be in charge (called a "rank conflict") and has little day-to-day experience of living with the opposite sex as a peer (a sex conflict).

Toman's first large research project was published in Germany in 1971. The sample was 2300 couples. At the time, the divorce rate in Germany was just 5%. It was the same in his sample. However, just as his model predicted, there were no divorces in the couples that had the most complementary positions and a 16% divorce rate in those with the least complementary birth orders. He replicated this research later on in another large sample of 5000 couples in Massachusetts and got almost the same results.

Each sibling position brings with it certain advantages and certain liabilities. Each position also implies a particular leadership style and perhaps even particular ways of looking at life and the world. The process of differentiation can help us to grow beyond the liabilities and to capitalize on the advantages of our sibling position.

Clearly, this suggests that people's characteristics at work and behavior in communities like the church will be affected by the functional roles they learned as a result of their birth orders. Church staffs would be well advised to pay attention to these issues. The older sister of brothers may make an excellent secretary for a male pastor, but there will be more challenges between them if she is working for an oldest female pastor. The insights that birth order functioning can play out in the congregational ministry setting can be extremely helpful to pastoral leaders when navigating staff conflicts.

7. Emotional Cutoff

Bowen decided to make significant emotional distancing into a separate concept because it was so prevalent. Emotional cutoff is primarily about distancing between generations. When we cutoff from other family members, the emotional issues that led to the cutoff do not get resolved. The unresolved emotional attachment does not just go away but is transferred into new adult relationships. The loss of parts of their family may lead people to make these new relationships "too important" as they attempt to compensate for the loss. Parts of families may be split off from each other and eventually, over the generations, the reasons are lost, but the family members may still continue to be affected by the intense underground emotional process that has resulted.

When Jane Smith decided to marry Jim, her parents tried to argue her out of the marriage. They were very reluctant to give their blessing because they thought Jim's family were snobs. As a result, she distanced significantly from her family and had only the rare, ritualized contact with them around holidays. She also restricted their access to her children. She was partly ashamed of her less cultured parents and didn't want their qualities to rub off onto her children. This cutoff only served to intensify her focus on her husband and children and pressure them to be the family she wished she'd had.

Most of our church members (as well as staff) will have cutoff in their lives. This is a major source of chronic anxiety in the church. People with a significant amount of cutoff tend to create substitute families and to invest a great deal of emotional importance in them. The church is one primary object for a substitute family. The cutoff may happen also with former churches when people have left a church with unresolved conflicts. They will carry the sensitivity and uneasiness into their new church relationships. The intensity of their reactivity to a current issue in their new church may seem higher than necessary, but that intensity may be fed by the unresolved attachment with their old church, which was probably fed by unresolved attachment to their families of origin. Church splits are a part of the cutoff phenomenon. Those who "leave" usually have more unresolved issues to deal with than those who are left.

The higher the level of differentiation of people the less cutoff there will be in their lives. These people will be able to deal comfortably with a wider range of differences with others and be more adaptive to novel challenges they may face in the church. They will have greater emotional flexibility in relationships and around conflictual issues that allow them to clearly define themselves, to work cooperatively with others, not get bogged down in emotionality, and work towards certain goals without being rigid and stubborn about it.

8. Societal Emotional Process

Each of the concepts in Bowen theory can be applied to non-family groups like our workplace, our social relationships, or our church. Bowen saw the theory as also applicable to larger social processes and understood society as having periods of regression or of progression. Social regression is prevalent generally when people are more focused on "rights" than they are on being responsible, and authorities are more focused on being "accepting and understanding" rather than expecting that certain standards be maintained.

During periods of societal regression people may feel more entitled to even their bad behavior. They may feel they have legitimate "excuses" for behaving as they do and that this should be understood and accepted no matter what the negative effect is on society. During such times the court system is also likely to agree with this stance. The general levels of violence and crime may increase, the divorce rates will rise, greater polarization will be prevalent in society in a number of areas, civic and business leaders will be less principled, the drug culture will flourish, people will become more litigious, and everyone will do their own thing rather than work together to overcome challenges.

Conclusion

Ralph already knew much of the content described here and had begun to sort through the issues for himself. I told him about some of the work of Robert Sapolsky, a primatologist who has been studying baboon tribes in Kenya for many years. One of his books is *Why Zebras Don't Get Ulcers*. In part it focuses on the stress response in baboons whose endocrine system is very similar to humans. There are, in fact, many parallels between how he describes baboon life in their tribes and how humans function. By studying them, we can get a bit more perspective on our own lives.

Being the alpha male, the leader of the baboon pack has many rewards like getting the most food and having sexual access to the females of the tribe. It is a highly desired position and there is never any want of secondary males and older adolescents trying to usurp the alpha's position from time to time. Once some sign of weakness in the alpha has been observed, due to general aging or illness or injury, triangular groups of challengers will take him on. Sometimes the females will participate in the process. If they manage to depose the alpha, then a period of chaos ensues while there is a struggle between the various challengers for who will be the new alpha male and reap the rewards of the position. The formerly cooperative challengers become competitive with each other but eventually a new leader of the pack emerges.

After describing some of this process to Ralph, I asked him where he would like to be in the story in relation to him and the Smiths and the challenge from the board. Did he want to be the alpha male or one of the challengers who would eventually emerge as leader of the pack or who would he want to be? It was, of course, a bit of a trick question. I said that I would want to be Sapolsky rather than one of the baboons. I would like to be studying their life and making observations on how they ran their life and what happened during times of anxiety in the tribe.

I suggested that too many pastors want to be the alpha in their churches and that this is usually how they get themselves in trouble. They successfully win the position and the church becomes dependent on them and they have to overfunction while also dealing with rebellious challengers. If they attempt to institute programmatic or procedural changes in the church and make it into their own image of "what the church should be," they end up in conflict with the indigenous leadership of the church and get booted out.

Everybody's polity will vary on this issue, but I suggested that none of us can be just another member of the church. By virtue of our position as pastors, we come and go. The church is their church. It belongs to the members. They were there before we came and they will be there after we leave. Christ is the Head of the Church and we are no substitutes for Christ. Sometimes some of us think we are, but we know where that fantasy leads.

Good pastoral care and leadership means we must function, at times, as process observers and systems consultants around the anxiety in the church. Of course we have the pulpit where we can lay out our own vision for what the gospel requires for this specific church at this specific time. No one else in the church has quite this opportunity and that is definitely a primary aspect of our leadership. Otherwise, we need to recognize that the church belongs to its members. Whether they take on our vision is up to them.

This kind of position of neutrality with regard to church life does not mean not having a position of your own. It is not simple passivity and going along with whatever way the wind blows. There will be times when we have to clearly define ourselves with both words and actions. Someone once said, "Pastoring is like being a stray dog at a whistler's convention." We could go crazy responding to every whistle. We need to define our own goals and direction in ministry. But that does not mean we define the congregation or set their goals.

Rather than the question "How can I change the church?" the question we ask ourselves should be "What do I need to work on to improve my functioning within the emotional system of the church so that I can better represent the gospel?" If we successfully begin to address this question, it will be amazing what begins to happen in our church. Our focus on the church as an emotional system and defining ourselves within it is a form of pastoral care in which every member will profit and do better, and we will be better, wiser, and healthier pastors.

7

Systems Theory and Congregational Leadership:
Leaves from an Alchemist's Journal

James E. Lamkin

James Lamkin has served on the faculty of Leadership in Ministry for several years, most recently at the Atlanta workshop. He is pastor of Northside Drive Baptist Church having previously served a church in Virginia and as Director of Pastoral Care at a medical center in Louisiana.

Introduction

Medieval metallurgists believed lead could be turned into gold. Within the caldron of secrets, alchemists searched for the golden formula. One part chemistry, plus one part mystery, might equal wealth by magic.

Though the mysterious formula is sought no longer, the quest for secret knowledge still beckons. However, the search is not for gold, but for great leadership. "What is the secret recipe for leadership?"

A plentitude of alchemists have offered answers. Their showcases include bookstores, conferences, motivational rallies, CD sets, workshops, and seminars. The answers are available for purchase. (Buy now while supplies last!). A casual sampling of methods includes notions such as one minute managers, or seven habits, or keys to unlocking hidden power within.

I appreciate the attempts of these various methods. (There's no use beating your clothes on a rock when a washing machine is available). However, for me, in the long run, all of these technique-driven approaches run out. Either I am too fickle or I'm too easily swayed by moods, or too arrogant in believing I can change people, or too vulnerable with my "need to please," or I start well but get discouraged as I encounter resistance, or I just get worn down. The truth is: all the above and more.

This litany of traits has makes me susceptible to the latest leadership fad. Jesus' words about looking anxiously for the Messiah in all the wrong places (Luke 21:8) were for folk like me. I'm gullible enough and needy enough to say, "Well, maybe the young guru with the big teeth on the late night marketing channel really does have THE answer."

However, none of these approaches has ever worked for me, or at least, they haven't worked longer than my three easy payments on the CD set. Why is this so, and why haven't I been able to make them work (for more than a few weeks)? This article is a partial answer to that question.

You've heard it said, "When the student is ready, the teacher will come." That is my testimony. This axiom names the necessary intersection of motivation, insight, and stamina. That trinity is the alchemy of a student's "readiness." When that conflagration is in place, there's an adventure ahead.

"How Can I Understand Without An Interpreter?"

I should have kept the restaurant napkin on which Larry Matthews drew a triangle. Like Lewis Carroll's *Alice in Wonderland*, a pen moved me from one way of seeing, to another.

"Where you stand determines what you see," said Robert MacAfee Brown.[1] And I was about to begin standing in a very different place. I sought out Larry at the recommendation of colleagues. I wanted someone to help me understand what was happening in the church where I was a new pastor. Larry Matthews had pastored Vienna Baptist Church in Vienna, Virginia, for nearly 30 years. When I met him he had been on Ed Friedman's teaching staff.

Three years before, I had read some of *Generation to Generation*, Friedman's perspective on how BFST impacts congregations and clergy, but let's just say that I was not motivated to appreciate it at that time. For the previous eight years, I had been a hospital chaplain; but now, I was the new pastor of Ravensworth Baptist Church in Annandale, Virginia. It was quite a change of ministerial terrain.

Though a new leader's presence always generates some reactivity, there seemed to be more in the congregation than I could produce (or for which I could take credit). Gratefully, the reactivity was not high on the Richter (or rector) scale; but it was more than I expected. In retrospect, at least part of it was the congregation's natural vigor.

Thus, I sought out Larry. I spoke to him of "our" expectations—the church and mine—and "our" vision for ministry. I told of my efforts at attempting to move the congregation toward the vision we'd agreed upon, but of my frustration and fatigue with the resistance.

Larry pulled out a pen, picked up a napkin, and drew a triangle, the Holy Grail of BFST. "Let's call Point A, the pastor," said Larry. "And B is the congregation; and C is the vision." Larry went on to note, "Friedman was saying the other day, that often in the clergy selection process, a search committee speaks to a prospective minister about the congregation's vision (ministries, membership growth, etc.). When the potential minister's vision matches that of the congregation, the relationship is off and running. However, as the new minister begins trying to move the congregation toward the vision, he or she encounters a surprising amount of resistance."

That pretty much said it for me. I was the "point A" pastor, trying to push together "Point B and C" of congregation and vision. Larry was telling my story. I was the Woman at the Well in the fourth chapter of John's Gospel who met a man who "told me everything I'd ever done."

That moment was one of those moments in life. I had put on a new set of eyeglasses and knew that life would be different. The triangle helped me see where I was standing.

As the reader may know, there are certain "rules" by which emotional triangles function. One rule is: you cannot change a side of the triangle to which you are not connected. In other words, "A" cannot change the relationship between "B" and "C." And, when "A" attempts to do so, "A" will end up with the stress of the relationship.

Larry's triangle on the back of the napkin held the seminal paradigm—and for me the primary gift—of BFST. It helped me step outside my anxiety that felt so personal, so that I could stand in a more objective position. By standing in a different vantage point, as an observer of the process, I saw my role in it differently.

Following our meeting, I read *again Generation to Generation* and found the formerly foggy content to be much clearer. The "ah ha" was something like the discovery of the

Ethiopian Eunuch in Acts 8. Through St. Philip's interpretation the Ethiopian found his place in the story.

From Cut-Off to Connected

My place in my own story got even more interesting when I began pastoral supervision with Bob Whitten, pastor of Westwood Baptist Church in Springfield, VA. Having just left a hospital chaplaincy position, and having observed the "lone ranger syndrome" among parish clergy, I decided upon reentering the pastorate, I would seek out a pastoral supervisor and go for monthly consultation. This was a gift—both to the congregation and to me. After all, it is great thing to give a congregation: a minister who is working on her or his maturity.

Almost right off the bat, Bob challenged me to invite my sister who is four years younger than I, to come for a visit. In BFST language, my sister and I were in a cut-off (cut-off is what one does in order to cope with the intensity of anxiety in a system by installing emotional distance). She and I are the only two siblings; and yet, I was emotionally far-away from her. Years ago I fled my small town upbringing and what felt like enmeshment with my parents. When I left home for college, I emotionally didn't come back. Though I was not aware of it, this cut-off really hurt my sister.

To my surprise, my sister said, "yes," to my invitation. I still have the four page letter that came later saying, "I thought this day would never come."

When she arrived we immediately got into the pain that installed the cut-off in the first place. Through Bob Whitten's mid-wifery, we reconnected. Words cannot describe what that reunion has meant to me and to my ministry. To this day, I see the rediscovery of that relationship to be the most significant breakthrough I have made as an adult. We now phone each other weekly, seek each other's counsel, and keep each other informed as to the triangles (more about that later) in our family, with our parents, and extended family. She and I are cheerleaders for the other's growth.

The impact of this reconnection echoed beyond our family. There's a BFST saying that "self encourages self." That is, when one person or one part of a system matures and behaves more healthily, it may have a stimulating effect to other parts of the system.

A Congregational Cut-Of Healed

My reconnection with my sister paralleled Ravensworth Baptist Church reconnecting to its first pastor, Rev. Grady Hutchinson. Grady had left about twenty-five years before by a forced resignation. The ensuing years brought little interaction between the church and his family.

However, when I finally found Grady, he was suffering from a terminal pulmonary problem and living just a few miles away. I worked at staying connected with both Grady and the church—relaying my evolving relationship to each. During his dying, individuals in the church reconnected with him and his family. In spite of years of minimal contact, when Grady died the family held his funeral in Ravensworth Baptist Church.

I had noted that the church hallway contained pictures of former pastors. Yet, Grady's picture was not among them. Several weeks later, there was a ceremony—a "Hanging of the Grady." All of his family came for the presentation and were overwhelmed with gratitude.

Words fail to describe what I believe happened that day, but it seemed as if a rip in the space/time continuum was healed. The ceremony and ritual around this reconnection mattered more than I knew.

Though you'll never find "work at healing cut-offs" in a book on how-to-grow-a-church, I believe it made a difference. Visitors began to join and a sense of joy emerged in the church and in me. Energy was unleashed.

When it comes to BFST, there is little use for the language of cause and effect. Blame is not in the vocabulary. Since all actions and behaviors are part of a larger whole, one life always is influencing other lives and vice versa. For instance, in this story, was it my emotional growth that encouraged the church to do the same? Or, was the church getting healthier and their actions toward healing a cut-off challenged me to reconnect with my sister? Or, was it God who instigated the healing in all of us? Systemically speaking, the answer to all is yes.

The Method for This Article

Let me describe how I use BFST to reflect on my own life and how I use it in my ministry as a pastor. The opening story of healing of a cut-off in my family and its occurrence within a congregational context is an apt image for this article. It illustrates the interlocking layers of the minister's family, families within the congregation, and the congregation as a family.[2]

Autobiographical writing is tricky. Thus, I've tried to write with four intentions in mind. First, all personal stories must be pertinent beyond the personal. That is, there must be the possibility of impact outside of the writer with the hope that this montage of "ah ha's," representing twelve years of living with BFST, will be illuminating to the reader.

Second, parish examples are to be specific enough to be enlightening, yet discrete regarding appropriate confidentiality. I will forever be grateful to Ravensworth Baptist Church and Northside Drive Baptist Church. They have encouraged, witnessed, and put up with my unfolding. They've allowed me to accompany them and learn from our journeys.

Third, the material is conversational in tone for both laity and clergy. Fourth, "a sense of the spiritual" underlies every page. God is present within in the soul of every congregation and within the life of the world. All of life is a layered landscape with a spiritual dimension permeating all existence. The very notion of relationship points to a quality that transcends one life and connects it to another. Though BFST does not intend to "explain the spiritual," it does seek to observe the impact of the (spiritual) relationships that underlie behavior.

Following a general description of BFST, I will use four main components of the theory as a framework. These are: The Emotional Triangle, Self-Differentiation, The Emotional Field, and Multi-Generational Transmission. Under each concept will be: a definition, an interpretation, and stories.

Family Systems Theory—A Way of Seeing

Definition: *Family Systems Theory is a conceptualization of the behavioral processes at work in relationships which observes the components as not functioning according to the individual identity of each, but rather according to their position in the overall structure.* [3]

Each piece of a system is a part of the whole. The particular affects the whole, and vice versa. All life is connected in this way. As Ed Friedman would say, "This is true for all protoplasm on the planet." It is true of an amoeba. It is true of families. It is true of congregations.

In working with the theory, a student can start at any piece of a system and go from there—micro to macro, or macro to micro. All points are starting points.

Take the story of the cut-off told above. You could start with the church's behavior; then look at my (the pastor's) behavior. Or start with the pastor and then go to the church. Or start with my sister and Grady Hutchinson (the cut-offs), then go to the folk who cut them off. Regardless of the beginning point, "systems thinking" asks the observer to pay attention to the processes between the relationships and the sum total of those processes.

From this perspective, alchemy does happen. Lead does turn to gold. However, the gold is nothing external; it is internal. The gold is the "wealth of self," the personal adventure of maturity. That is where the pay-off comes. Maturity is taking responsibility for emotional and spiritual health of one's own self.

The tandem telling of these reunion stories contains the soul of this article: (1) the "self" of the minister and the "self" of the congregation are connected, yet differentiated; (2) the push-and-pull of this drama is the intriguing, grueling, and invigorating stage on which parish ministry occurs; (3) BFST is a lens through which to see this play, and it assists the minister in making his or her choices on where to stand on the stage.

As the reader may know, Murray Bowen of Georgetown University was one of the founding fathers of BFST. He observed that a "systems" way of thinking varied from models of psychotherapy that were based on individuals without primary consideration for the role played by the person in the family from which he/she comes.

An individualistic approach would not ask, "What part might this individual's (or committee's) behavior play in the extended family's emotional processes? For example, rather than just observing a wife as depressed, BFST would ask, "How might her depression serve the family?" Could it be that her depressive episodes are a counter-weight to her husband's workaholism? Or, are the long office hours spent by the husband an attempt to escape the gravity of his wife's melancholy? And beyond the two spouses—could their parents also be part of the story?

The very act of asking these questions invites the pastor to think through the actions he or she might take in this situation. In fact, just reflecting on these questions is an action taken by the pastor.

BFST challenges me to think through issues and be as clear as possible regarding what I believe—but it reminds me that I am only one part of the whole. Though I am important as a leader and pastoral caregiver, I cannot change other people. This echoes the wisdom of the Serenity Prayer: "God, grant me the serenity to accept the things I cannot change, the courage to change the things I can, and the wisdom to know the difference."

With this perspective of "keeping the whole in mind," I'll turn to the four primary components of the theory.

The Emotional Triangle

Definition: *An emotional triangle is any three members of a relationship system or any two members plus an issue or symptom.*[4]

Congregational examples of triangles may include: (A) a pastor offering counseling to (B) a husband and (C) wife; (A) a minister working with (B) the Youth Committee on (C) its vision; (A) a committee, (B) the chair, and (C) the pastor; and (A) the Finance Committee, (B) the congregation, and (C) the budget pledging process.

Emotional triangles exist because life seeks balance and stability. Life wants homeostasis. A tripod is more stable than a dyad. Thus, two human beings will often manage their anxiety by "triangling in" a third. Imagine a husband and wife in an intense discussion of "their relationship." How long will the conversation go before one says, "You are acting just like your mother!" Consequently, the reference to father, mother, or whomever is the making of the triangle.

I've heard Larry Matthews say it a thousand times. "BFST is about anxiety. BFST is about anxiety. BFST is about anxiety." It is a way of paying attention to what anxiety is doing to the system. I've also heard Larry quote Mike Kerr, the former director of the Family Center at Georgetown University: "If you are not thinking triangles, you are not thinking systems."

The Emotional Triangle is what humans do attempting to manage anxiety. It is a huge piece of BFST. In my opinion, it is the window into other components of the theory. It is also the easiest to communicate. Thus, I will spend an extended time pointing at and looking through this window.

Emotional Triangle Systems Snapshot No. 1: The New Minister's Visits

Remember the A=pastor, B=congregation, C=vision, triangle Larry Matthews drew on the napkin? Let's change vision to expectations. One of the expectations of any church is the pastoral care of its membership. At Northside Drive Baptist Church in Atlanta, GA, the congregation within which I am presently serving, there was some anxiety within the Pastor Search Committee, about the new pastor's attending to older persons in the congregation. This is natural, and I was glad they voiced their concern.

Since every Pastor Search Committee is invested in the success of their recommended candidate, they needed reassurance that this expectation regarding pastoral care to older congregants would be addressed. So, I included the committee in the process.

To handle my anxiety—and to practice my theology of pastoral care as a congregational responsibility—I asked the chair of the Pastor Search Committee to accompany me during my first six months while I made introductory pastoral visits.

I said, "I value connecting with parishioners, but I don't know who to see first. Would you help me by: (1) making calls with me every Tuesday afternoon, and (2) booking the appointments with whomever you think I should meet?"

See the triangle? A=pastor. B=church's and search committee's expectations regarding pastoral care. C=the responsible action of pastoral visitation. This was win/win all around. Since the chair and the committee were connected with the needs of the congregation, they provided the list of whom to see and when. Thus, to each person we visited, I said something like, "You are important to this congregation. Jim (the committee chair) wanted me to meet you and I am grateful that he did."

It was an immediate connection between the expectations of pastoral care, the actions of pastoral care, and the systemic communication between the two. The search committee members got to participate in the success; plus, the bond between the pastor and these leading lay persons was strengthened.

One more peripheral story. I'd have folk say on the church steps, "I heard you came to visit my neighbor, and I need a visit too!" So—and watch the triangle—I'd say, "I'd love to visit you! Jim is scheduling my 'get to know you' visits these first few months. Please tell him I want you put on the visitation schedule!"

If you haven't guessed, I believe (and BFST supports) that playfulness is vital to handling one's own anxiety. Sometimes there is a thin line between being playful and being a smart-aleck. The difference is the amount of anxiety. When I am grounded in my own skin—and not taking myself too seriously—a playful word can keep me connected but not responsible for the emotional freight of the relationship. However, when I'm anxious, an intended playful word can come across biting—and bite me, too.

Emotional Triangle Systems Snapshot No. 2: Preachin' But Not Meddlin'

Preaching is a triangle. A=preacher. B=congregation. C=God. Also, C could be "text." The minister always lives in a triangle with God and God's people. No one knew this better than Moses. In one of the great complaint scenes in Exodus 16:8, Moses tells the people, "Your complaining is not against us but against the Lord." In other words, Moses remembered that there is more going on than "the congregation is upset with the minister." There is a third leg to the triangle.

I see this sermonic triangle when I watch Barbara Brown Taylor preach.[5] It is somewhat like Tai Chi. The preacher is present to what is happening between God and the listener—but the preacher is not responsible for that relationship.

Occasionally, I'll say something like, "I, as a preacher, don't know what to make of this difficult text, either. But it is my job to remind you that it is in our Bibles. Each of us is responsible for our response to God."

When the prophet Nathan confronted King David with David's sin, it was not a direct confrontation. It was indirect through the use of a story about sheep and farmers. David fell prey to the story's spell. Then Nathan delivered the punchline, "Thou art the man."[6]

Systemically, Nathan attended to a preaching triangle. A=Nathan. B=David. C=the issue/sin/story. "C" also could be the community's need for a spiritually healthy king. Nathan skillfully and lightly spoke indirectly to issue as David "overheard."[7]

Often our well-practiced defenses deflect both judgment and grace. However, a story/parable which doesn't come at the congregation between the eyes can sometimes invite the listener to lower his/her guard. From an BFST perspective, (1) Nathan connected with David; (2) Nathan addressed the issue through a parable; (3) Nathan let David connect with the story rather than forcing the issue.

When I'm at my best, this triangle is in my prayers as I prepare to preach. It reminds me of my task to be with the congregation as they sit with the text. That image reduces my anxiety about "making something happen."

Also, it frees me to encounter the text and to invite the listeners to do the same.

The Emotional Triangle Systems Snapshot No. 3:
"Back Attack"

I counseled a parishioner who was dissatisfied with his work for a religious agency. "I can do the work," he said, "but my heart is not in it." Meanwhile, he was pondering the possibility of a new job that was "closer to his center." Plus, he disclosed having chronic back pain for the last few weeks, and when he referenced his job, he always gestured as if it was distant from him.

Months later, he thanked me for telling the "box story." He said it got him unstuck and he became free to choose a new job.

The box story went something like: "It sounds that the job you're doing is like picking up a heavy box. However, it is not the box that is heavy; it is your position in relation to the box that makes it heavy. If the box were at your feet, you'd bend at the knees and lift. No problem. However, the box is on the other side of the table, away from your center, and you have to reach over to pick it up. Stooping over that far must be tough on your back."

See the triangle? I did as Nathan did. I cast an image alongside him, and he did the work of connecting the dots.

Friedman used to say that what makes for burnout is not overwork. It is not long hours. Most people work hard. The burnout results from the stress of the relationships (the triangles) within the work.

The Emotional Triangle Snapshot No. 4:
Parenting, Even If You Aren't Dr. Phil

A parent said one of the most helpful things she'd heard me talk about was about the emotional triangle. Yet, the context in which she learned it was leadership training. I had offered an optional, hour long, one-on-one conversation about leadership to church leaders. It included the concept of the emotional triangle.

The rules of the emotional triangle that had helped this parent the most were: Rule #1: You can only change a side (relationship) of the triangle to which you are connected. Rule #2: If you try to change the side to which you are not connected, usually the results will be opposite that you intend. Rule #3: If you break rule #2, you will end up with the stress of that relationship.

For instance, here's a mother (A), whose daughter (B), is dating a guy with green hair (C). If "A" tries to push "B" and "C" apart, the result may be the opposite and they will attract like magnets.

The Emotional Triangle Systems Snapshot No. 5: Staff Supervision

In supervising the part-time Minister to Students, I've found it helpful to have the Youth Committee chair present twice a month for supervisory times. Having him or her as part of the process completes the triangle. It gives me a more complete perspective on supervisory issues. It fosters my connectivity with both persons. It shortens the implementation/feedback loop. This has allowed the level of misunderstanding and anxiety to drop; and raise all our levels of functioning.

The Emotional Triangle Systems Snapshot No. 6: Missing In Action

All churches have MIA's: Missing in Action. These folk drop out or drop away. The issues precipitating the drop-out are both maturational and situational. An example would be a retiree going through the grief of transition following the loss of job while at the same time feeling disgruntled about "the changes in worship." Since the later is more visible and taps into a larger congregational anxiety, it would be easy for both laity and clergy to be defensive about the worship changes, rather than see this as a symptom of the retiree's maturational discontent about aging.

One evening a group of deacons discussed compiling a list of MIA's, followed by a discussion on how the deacons might get the MIA's back. One speculation was that the MIA's might have "issues" about "what's going on at church."

I responded, "Before talking about who and what and how, I'd like to address the topic from a different angle: the position of the Deacon Family Minister as a caregiver, rather than the perceived need of the MIA." I then drew a triangle on the board (A=deacon, B=MIA, C=issue). I described a few of the "rules" by which triangles work.

We then role-played deacon conversations. I encouraged the deacons to work at staying connected to the absent parishioners ("I wanted to call and tell you I care about you. I haven't seen you recently."). Also, I encouraged them to connect with any issue raised by the absentee ("I hear your concern about XYZ at the church and know that is important to you."). However, the deacon was not to attempt to fix "the issue."

The deacons appeared relieved of a burden. They could respond more joyfully in their job as care-givers, rather than caretakers. This case study raises the question of one's philosophy/theology of pastoral care? How is personal ministry evaluated?

I remember Friedman saying, "If the goal of ministry is to meet people's needs, then what do you do with someone whose need it is not to get his or her needs met?" The accent of his question helps keep the focus upon appropriate ministerial initiative, rather than visible benefit or appreciation by the parishioner.

.The Emotional Triangle Systems Snapshot No. 7: Impression Management

A colleague named a demon with which I struggle. The term comes from the vocabulary of Alcoholics Anonymous: impression management. One symptom of living out of a "low sense of self" is to be busy attempting to control/manage the impression that self has on others. In other words, this brother gave me a painful gift.

My genogram (the map of relationships among my family tree) reveals some trickle down expectations that fell my lot as a first-born and standard bearer in my family. It's my job to make A's. B's won't do. Part of making the grade can mean attempting to impress the grader. Though we all do this to some extent, for a few of us, the task feels more necessary. Clergy especially seem prone to this dis-ease.

When I feel a pain growing in my lower back (a symptomizing spot for me), I ask, "Where am I overfunctioning?" Often on the way to answering that question, I discover that I'm also doing impression management. That is, I not only want to adequately handle an issue, I want to come off looking good while handling the issue. The triangle is A=me, B=the issue, C=impression management or image control.

I have a greater chance of living more authentically and less anxiously if I can name this extra burden of "pleasing" that seems to rise so naturally in me. Also, when I'm busy managing impressions, I am more apt to be willful—covertly attempting to impose my will on others. And you can guess where that gets me.

One more thing. The paradigm of a research project as *modus operandi* of ministry helps me tremendously. You can't fail a research project. Even if you disprove your hypothesis, the goal is not to achieve a certain result, the goal is to learn and discover. The research project notion is one way I reframe my high expectations of what I need to "produce."

The Emotional Triangle Systems Snapshot No. 8: Stuck in the Mud

When I feel stuck (emotionally immobile), Job #1 is to locate the triangle. That is harder than it sounds, partially because the feeling of being stuck raises one's anxiety. Where there's high anxiety, there's usually low creativity and even lesser insight. When in a bottle, it is hard to see the bottle.

Freidman spoke of three indicators of stuckness.[8] The first indicator is when you are trying harder but only producing the same or fewer results, like tire spinning in the mud. The wheel is turning, the engine is burning fuel, and yet the car doesn't budge.

A second indicator is when you are thinking in either/or categories. Issues are either black or white, all or nothing, unable to search for alternative means.

The third marker of stuckness is a fixation on finding new answers to the same question, rather than changing the question. I watched the tenor of a room change when Rev. Brenda Dedmon, a Minister to Families with Children from Marietta, GA, said, "Rather than continuing to ask, 'How do we get children from our Weekday Preschool Program to come to church on Sunday mornings?' why not ask, 'How could we teach them about God's love while they are here during the week?'"

She named the triangle of our stuckness. A=The church's responsibility for children's ministry, B=Weekday Preschool attendees, C=A thriving Children's Christian Education Program. But, "A" was stuck in seeing "C" as something that happens primarily on Sunday mornings. Brenda helped us change the question from, "How do we get them here on Sundays?" to, "How can we teach them about God's love while they are here during the week?" That shift of questions unleashed new energy.

I've heard that Ted Williams, the great baseball player, said, "When you find yourself in a batting slump, don't swing harder, change your stance." In other words, Williams repositioned himself in the triangle: A=Williams, B=the desire to bat well, and C=the position of his feet in the batter's box.

Thinking through areas of my own stuckness is vital to my own maturity and my leadership of the congregation. This takes work. I try to spend time each week prayerfully and strategically pondering, "Where am I with the issues with which our congregation is struggling? What do I believe about my own resources and those of the congregation?" By wrestling and naming the triangles (with their problems and wonderful possibilities) and what role I play in them, I am less anxious while standing with the congregation in those triangles.

Self-differentiation is strategic in a leader's position in the Emotional Triangle. It is to this concept to which we now turn.

Self-Differentiation

Definition: *Self-differentiation is an organism's ability to "define itself" apart from, yet staying connected to its surroundings.*

Notice the two-fold part of this definition. The first component is the capacity to claim one's unique position or role in a system. An example is the pancreas and its function regarding insulin. It is distinctive in this way. However, the second part of the definition often is overlooked. On the street, differentiation is seen as disconnected, individualistic, and autocratic. This is incorrect. The pancreas—though differentiated from other organs in the body—must remain connected to the body in order to function and for itself to survive. In fact, there can be no self-differentiation unless one is connected.

All this said, there does seem to be an intentionality required for humans to work at their differentiation. When anxiety climbs, it brings with it a tendency toward globbing or "group think." Anxiety can push people together and a herding effect can ensue.

Anxiety attack describes an escalating angst swirling in a person, where the mind is unable differentiate itself from the fear "in the body" and cannot slow down the acceleration. It is crucial for me as a pastor to be committed to the life-long job of working at my self-differentiation; and to do so while paying attention to staying connected. These are the law and prophets of maturity. Differentiation without connection can result in cut-off. Connection without differentiation will become enmeshment. It is easier either to speak *ex cathedra* at a distance, or to blend in (enmesh) and be one of the bunch. The hard work is to stand apart as a leader, but not apart from the congregation.

The pastor's task is a blend of two roles: priest and prophet. Though oversimplified, priests are advocates for the people, to God. Prophets, on the other hand, side with God and speak God's Word to the people. Thus, priesthood, taken to the extreme could enmesh one with the people. Remember Aaron and the golden calf?[9] On the other hand, a prophet's vocation, intense in its focus on God, could live too distantly from the people.

Working at one's own differentiation helps the leader stay grounded in what really matters in leadership: position. This attention to position is much healthier than focus on technique. As Friedman said, "You can have a leadership theory on mustard seeds and it will work as long as the leader is self-differentiated." This is the flaw in much of the technique-driven leadership methods. It also explains why a technique works for one and not another. The answer may not lie in the technique at all; rather, it lies in the self of the person using the technique.

Differentiation is necessary regarding two functions of leadership. First, leadership must provide and encourage imagination.

Self-Differentiated Leadership and Imagination

Imagination is a close cousin to vision. Not accidentally, the eyes are near the top of the body—both near the brain and at a strategic vantage point. As a leader, it is my job to do what only I can do from my position in the body. It is my job to watch where the body is going and have a sense of where the body should/could go. A lot of other factors will weigh in as to where we actually go. But it is my job to say, "This is what I see; and here is the adventure to which I invite you."

Thus, I try to be a good steward of vision, praying over and pondering the terrain of parish ministry and my choices. Pragmatically, the result of this musing is to "define myself" to the church. If a committee is at work on a project, I will frequently say to them, "Where to go with this issue is your choice.

However, as I see this project and how it fits with the larger life of the church, here is what I think, and here is what I recommend." I am attempting to be clear about what I believe about an issue; but not take it on as "my" issue. Also, "where I stand" will be interpreted by the committee members, not only by their perceptions of the issue, but also by their perceptions of how I am connected to each of them.

Self-Differentiated Leadership and the Immune System

The second role of differentiated leadership is that of the immune system. The function of the immune system is to identify "what belongs to self and what does not." A virus is breathed into the lungs. The immune system's job is to detect it, scan it, and if it is a threat to the well-being of the body, destroy or quarantine it.

However, viruses are shrewd. They have a way of looking friendly, but behaving like terrorists. Thus, the immune system must constantly do its work.

Cancer, too, is an example of cells that violate the body's integrity. Friedman spoke of cancer cells as adolescent cells. Normal cells know when to quit replicating and where to respect limits. The human body only needs so many pancreatic cells. However, like adolescents who have trouble maintaining boundaries, cancer cells violate other organs. Metastasis results.

Here's an example of leadership functioning as the immune system. I received a call that began with a disclaimer, "I want to tell you about something, but I need you to keep it confidential." Ever had a conversation that began that way? You sense that you are about to hear something that you may need to act upon, but the confidentiality piece could tie your hands to address it later.

At that point I used a line Larry Matthews taught me years ago. I said, "I respect your request for confidentiality. If this is a personal matter about you or your family, I absolutely will keep it confidential and drop it in a well. However, if this information is something on which I may need to act in order to take care of myself or to do my job as pastor if this issue affects the health of this church, then I would not be able to keep it confidential. And I wanted you to know that in case it colors your decision to tell me."

You hear what is happening? Remember, maturity is taking responsibility for one's own emotional/spiritual health. The above statement gives that option to both the teller and the listener.

The caller said, "Well, I better not tell you, because...."

"I respect that," I said.

After a long pause, the caller then said, "Well, I love you and the church too much to let my fear get in the way." I knew then, I was talking to a person who was working on his own maturity.

The story was about a church member who had made some derogatory comments about me at a gathering of about a dozen senior adults; plus, this person called into question as to whether I should keep my job. The member had never said any of these things to me.

I thought through what to do. I have been known to overreact. Overreacting is like hurting yourself while running from a non-poisonous snake. You can do more damage than the snake could do. Do I let it go? Do I call my accuser? Do I meet with the whole group and "straighten things out?"

Every action, is a blend of motivations. For me, the questions were: To what extent is my response out of clear/healthy thinking? To what extent is it reactivity? Has this hooked my need for impression management? Is this about the health of the church?

I decided to notify the church moderator of what had happened. I said I was hurt and mad, but that I did not know yet what to do in response. I asked for his support to help me resolve the misunderstanding.

This gave the moderator information he needed to serve as a strategic piece of the immune system. I went to bed that night knowing that a reasonable leader was aware of the situation; and should anything come of this, he would not hear it second-hand.

Eventually, another church leader accompanied me to have a conversation with my accuser. I asked the leader to simply be a witness—because things can get skewed with just a one-on-one. (Triangle, remember.) Again, he was functioning as part of the church's immune system.

I listened and took notes on all that was said of "what I had done wrong." At the end of the list, I playfully asked, "Is there more?" And there was! I took a few more sheets of notes.

From my perspective, the content of these accusations were not nearly as consequential as the value of the process. For me, this practice was not on the sidelines of pastoring—it is the stuff of pastoring. It is people being present with one another, even in their pain, believing that there is a Presence that transcends us all.

Yes, I got to apologize for a few things. But, my position was: "I love you. I love our church. I believe you love our church. I believe that Christian faith is lived out by a community that treats one another with respect. And I ask that we handle these issues differently in the future. If you want to make a critical comment about me in public, I ask that you say it to me first. Will you do that?" The person agreed to do so.

Through this approach I was doing three things: (1) I was doing self-care by not participating in my own diminishment through silence (2) I was pastoring, because I saw this behavior as detrimental to the health of the church; (3) I was treating this person with respect and honesty. My request for covenant at conversation's end included the affirmation, "I am asking something of you that few could do. However, I know you to be a person of strength, so I'll put my request clearly on the table."

Whether or not the covenant would be kept was not my chief concern. My concern was that I do my job and have it witnessed by a trusted church leader.

The Non-Anxious Presence

The notion of the non-anxious presence arises as one aspect of self-differentiation. There is no such thing as a person who is non-anxious. However, there are persons who are working at lowering their anxiety. In so doing one is owing the responsibility of self-regulation.

This is a primary gift of leadership. As in a marriage counseling situation, the calmness of the counselor makes a difference in how the couple does their work. It keeps "the issue" between the couple, rather than taken on by the counselor as something he or she can fix. It is a powerful thing to work on one's life in the presence of another who can sit calmly with you while you do it (spiritual direction is about this style of relationship.)

This process of "being non-anxiously with another" goes on with the pastor and the church. Part of my job is to give the church back to itself. Pastoral burn-out begins at the point of taking on the responsibility for the church's health, rather than being present with the church as it works or does not work on its own health.

Franklin Duncan, to whom I go for monthly supervision, says, "The job of the pastor is to attend to the church as the church attends to its own processes."

One of the best ways to work on one's level of anxiety with the congregation, is to work on your anxiety within your family of origin. More on that later.

The Borrowed Self

I can't leave this topic of self-differentiation without naming the notion of borrowed self. This is the act of scrounging self from the identity of another. For instance, a spouse is known exclusively as the wife of Dr. Smith. She almost is without a first name. When Dr. Smith dies, she loses her identity.

Scan the religious advertisements in the newspaper and you'll see borrowed self at work. Perhaps it is inevitable. Churches frequently borrow the identity of the "strong" leader. However, there are at least two dilemmas in the wake of charismatic-dependent leadership. First, it personalizes all the issues while polarizing the results. To vote for a red carpet when Pastor Bob wants green is to vote against Pastor Bob. Second, this kind of leadership sabotages successors. Again, with the organization structured around the personality of the leader, then the vacancy requires the successor to be a custom fit.

No small part of my current pastorate has been tending to the congregation as it navigates its grief regarding a charismatic leader who served as the church's Minister of Music for seventeen years. In hearing the church's stories, many things worked together to make those years a fascinating time: the demise of the Southern Baptist Convention, the energy of the 70's and 80's, and the demographic wave that was washing through northwest Atlanta. Though this leader has been gone for over 16 years, I've observed few committee meetings where his name has not come up—recalling and illustrating how his vitality and the church's were related.

With almost boundless energy he revised the church's liturgy, organized lay groups, recruited new members, phoned folk if they were absent from worship, made major administrative decisions, designed the new sanctuary, and was a fund raiser extraordinaire. Obviously, a lot of the church's life orbited around and was choreographed by his ministry. The process was efficient and appeared visibly productive.

However, it seems his sudden death in 1988 left the church without a center, and the absence felt by the church was sizeable. As you can imagine, staffing has been an issue ever since. "It would take many to do what he did." Systemically, I see the church, to some extent, borrowing self from this minister.

Living with the church's generational history is the work of every pastor. As Friedman said, "Every minister is in a triangle with his or her predecessors." Certainly, it has required a lot of me to work at being myself, rather than give in to the gravity of "filling in the gap."

On the other hand, the exercise of pastoring a church I love as it lives with its grief has been a wonderful gift and a perfect laboratory for me. Loving people where they are, and loving myself as I am are muscles that need strengthening in me. The gymnasium of a local congregation grows me as no other exercise facility can. And my growth is a gift I give back to the congregation.

Emotional Field

Definition: *The emotional field is an environment of influence that is not material in itself but which comes into existence because of the proximity of matter to matter. However, once the field does come into being, it has more power to influence the discrete particles within it than any of those pieces of matter can influence the field they have, by their presence, caused to exist.*[10] Ponder that for a while if it appears too thick. It notes the power of the family/church/system and the collective strength of the whole exerting a greater influence on the pieces, than the pieces do on the whole.

The emotional field is one of the least glamorous, but most important pieces of BFST. Never underestimate this part of the theory. I hear pastors say, "I thought if we could just swap out the members of the board, all of the problems would be solved. However, we changed the members—and the new ones act just like the old ones!" Do you see how the role of the committee tends to override the personality of each of the committee members?

Let's say one committee has historically under-functioned. Finally, one year, they begin performing more highly, and guess what, another committee takes their place as under-functioner. Why is this? Remember the notion of balance, homeostasis. The pieces will arrange themselves (trading under-functioning and over-functioning roles) for the sake of the stability of the whole.

Our church is walking through a two year "research project." We modified the function of our Diaconate, so that they may focus solely on the care-giving ministry. I told the deacons just last night, "Though I anticipated this shift would be hard for the congregation, I underestimated how hard it would be. Thus, I am even more proud of your efforts at staying on track; and as you have, the church's reactivity has diminished."

Sabotage is an ironic compliment. It is a mark that progress is trying to happen. Resistance is just part of being human. Being aware of the emotional field helps me interpret church processes as pieces of the whole, not isolated within themselves. Is the inflammation around the discussion of a new hymnal really about the hymnal? Or, what is going on in the congregation that is manifesting itself in the anxiety about the hymnal?

The same is true about the stewardship drive, the chapel renovation, the playfulness of the marketing campaign, or the new staff position we are trying to create.

I walked out of a conference room following an up-beat meeting, and overheard a person comment, "It sure feels different to come out of that room and feel good." She was saying that the space itself was part of the emotional field. The walls and tables held memories of tough times. The same dynamics explain why we behave one way in our "new" sanctuary built in 1976, and a much less formal way in our chapel which is the church's original sanctuary built in 1954.

The Isaiah 6 passage where the prophet sees the Lord high and lifted-up, is an Emotional Field story. Notice the time: "the year king Uzziah died." And notice the place: the Temple. In other words, young Isaiah's vision occurs in the very room where his high-profile king was struck with a fatal disease; and the vision comes within a year of the king's death. Thus, at the intersection of time and space, Isaiah's experience makes more sense.

Here is a good place to pass along another Friedmanism. (and you might want to brace yourself). "One way a couple can keep their marriage together is by pushing their anxiety into their children."

You might want to pause around that one. Isn't it "more acceptable" to have acting-out kids than to be rumored as having marriage trouble? It makes me wonder about the rave diagnosis Attention Deficit Disorder. How much of it is about the lack of attention the parents give to one another? Does the child become the symptom of something lacking in the marriage?

This has an echo in churches. What about this: "One way a church can keep the congregation together is by pushing their anxiety into the staff." If a church could keep the focus on the staff as the problem, could this deflect the pain of focusing on the hard work of relationships within the church?

But, staff aren't minors. Thus, if staff is the focus of the church's anxiety year after year, one must ask, "What does the staff get out of swallowing the congregation's anxiety?" To the extent that the church's anxiety is borne by the staff, the congregation is cheated of the pain needed to be a motivator for change. And of course it goes without saying, that in some church systems it could be the opposite. The staff could get the church to take on the staff's anxiety.

The power of the emotional field reminds me how small I am. I have little power to change the church. But I am greatly empowered to change myself. Consequently, my mantras are:

Stay in my own skin. Think through what I believe. Work at staying connected. Take clearly defined stands on appropriately chosen issues, and enjoy living a large life. The minister's own personal and professional health is the greatest gift a minister can give a congregation.

The anxiety of a local church is only a small tidal pool of the vast ocean of anxiety that is white capping in society. Think of the anxiety boosters that are at work: the war in the Middle East, instant communications, global warming, hard-wired stock markets, population booms, post-cold war terrorism, 24 hour media with late-breaking news. These make for huge waves. All of this is happening before one gets to the front door of the church.

This is a graceful thing for me to remember. No matter how highly I function, and no matter how well the Church Council or Diaconate may work, there are tidal waves of anxiety rolling that will affect and infect us (also, there are healthy forces that will challenge us and grow us). But with all this going on, it brings home Job #1: stay focused on one's own functioning (and live by the Serenity Prayer!).

Multi-Generational Transmission

Definition: *Multi-generational transmission references the process of passing along relational patterns, resources, symptoms, strengths, and behaviors from individuals and groups to their successors. Thus, to observe only the present is to see only the tip of the iceberg.*

Friedman said that if you put five generations of your family map (genogram) on the table, you'll have all of human history. They're all there: from good guys to bad guys, from fundamentalists to flaming liberals. You'll see reactions to anxiety:

cut-off's, rebels, and the enmeshed. Also, you'll see those who seemed remarkably self-differentiated.

There will be triangles and symptoms. For instance, you might see cancer for a few generations, then it disappears. Or, heart disease. Or, substance abuse. Or strong women. Or, distant men.

By viewing five generations at once, you may detect some patterns—patterns supporting strength, others carrying symptoms. And who is to say—the strength exhibited in one generation of the family, may have evolved in response to the symptomology of the previous?

I believe that a minister can take no greater action toward becoming a better person and pastor, than to work on understanding and being present with his or her own family of origin. As the opening story demonstrated, that work "grows self" and impacts all of life.

My maternal grandfather was a gracious man. He also was an alcoholic. In the family lore, I got credit for his sobriety. He sobered up when I came along. However, it was my father who actually took the tough stand: "You'll never see your grandson again if you don't stop drinking." And Grandfather stopped.

There's more to the story that preceded him and followed him, like a tragic train wreck that killed two of his close uncles and two cousins. There is a shame factor that follows me to this day. But also there is a grace factor. I've noticed that alcoholics have a great capacity for spirituality.

There's much strength in my family's story, like when my grandmother took a strong stand. Or the peace-keeping efforts of my paternal grandfather who was the town marshal. I've learned from my father how to connect. He is a country politician and makes himself at home with everyone up and down the food chain. I come to adulthood, as do all, with a self that's both wounded and wealthy. It is the adventure of maturity to learn from both by working on my family history.

In pre-marital counseling, I push couples back to their families of origin. I spend very little time attempting to teach communication skills. Rather, I listen for pain and curiosity—for these provide motivation. I usually doodle a genogram while asking about the family relationships. I say to a couple: "I don't think pre-marital counseling does a lot of good, because nobody seems to be paying attention.

However, I think what you bring to the marriage from your families of origin is very important and I invite you to pay attention to that. I want to hear some of your stories and maybe explore some of those relationships. I might suggest some homework on those relationships—if you are up to doing it—that may make a difference in the depth of resources you bring to the marriage." By so doing, I am meeting the couple at their level of investment in the counseling process; and, I am inviting them to consider growing.

As we go along I'll ask, Why don't you talk with your father about that? Or, could you ask your sister for some coaching on relating to women? Or, do you need something from your mother before you could fully enjoy this marriage?

The questions keep me out of the "professional expert" role; plus, they give a challenge to the couple. Some take me up on the challenge; others don't. Either way, it is my honest attempt at being fully present with people at a major rite of passage.

With other forms of counseling my approach is similar. I am sitting with a person that is one part of a very large extended family and part of a multi-generational system—even if I am sitting with an orphan. I encourage the person to consider working on issues with spouses, bosses, colleagues, finances, sexuality, spirituality—by working on their families. For instance, "Sounds like you are having trouble keeping friendships. What if you asked your father how he handled friendships when he was your age?"

There's something about going back to talk with your family about your struggles and their struggles that can be life changing. However, I tell counselees that the "advice" they get from family members is not the main reason for going. The main reason is that being in the presence of family gives one a gymnasium to work on one's own anxiety. As a 40-something woman told me, "If I can learn to be less anxious with my mother, I can be less anxious with anyone!"

Churches have multi-generational processes. When I was in conversation with Northside Drive Baptist Church about coming as pastor, I tried to pay attention to the multi-generational process. Two of the groups with whom I wanted to meet were: (1) The charter members, so that I might get a flavor of the DNA that was part of the birthing; (2) the present day members who were most invested in the church's future. I wanted to see if the early spunk and tenacity was still in the bone marrow.

Through some of these conversations I learned of the severance package resignations of the sixth and seventh pastors. However, it was years later that a charter member told of the forced termination of the first pastor. "All of this trouble we've had recently, is an echo of the early years," she said. There it is!

Conclusion

These observations, jaundiced though they may be, are still photos of how I see parish ministry through the lens of BFST. This lens helps me in three ways. First, BFST helps me focus on my functioning, not everybody else's. Too easily, my anxiety, coupled with a first-born-standard-bearer-Superman-complex, dupes me into obsessing on the actions of others and thinking that I can change them. However, the serenity prayer reminds me that I can only "change the things I can." And that "thing" can only be me. On my best days, I'm able to be playfully present. On my worst, I am anxiously serious and reactionary.

Second, BFST is a constant invitation to work on my self-differentiation in my family of origin, while paying attention to stay connected. In other words, sometimes the best thing a parish minister can do to improve her or his leadership is to attend her or his family reunion!

Third, BFST affirms the important work of thinking through what I believe. Only I can do that. And to know where I stand helps lower my anxiety, and seems to encourage others to work on where they stand. Also, this echoes the power of position over technique. I can fret all day about what method or approach or technique I use in a certain situation. Should I write or call or visit? Should I tell the committee, or just the committee member, or only the chair? Should I mention the idea while it is green, or wait for it to ripen?

I will end up worrying over a thousand qualifications. And who is to say that the technique I've chosen is the right one? Thus, BFST reinforces that step one is working where I stand, not what I will do with it. If I can do that with confidence and with low anxiety, I've done a day's work.

One more thing: for a theory, BFST sure offers me a deep bath of grace. I can be hard on myself as I think about what I "should have, could have done." But BFST reminds me of how much I don't know. Layers and layers of life are happening around every committee table, within every pastoral call, and between the pews and pulpit of every sermon. And it has been so for generations. Friedman said that nobody gets this right more than 70% of the time. That's good news—it means we begin with 30% of grace in our tank every morning.

I still see myself as an alchemist; however, I am not as busy looking for secret formulas. There is no secret to leadership. It's just playful and ponderous work of growing one's self.

The greatest laboratory on earth is the local congregation. Amid its problems and possibilities, its exasperations and epiphanies, is the strange chemistry of grace. And for that discovery and that opportunity, I give thanks to God.

---

[1]Brown, Robert McAfee, *Creative Dislocation: The Movement of Grace* (Nashville: Abingdon, 1980), 107.

[2]Friedman, Edwin H., *Generation to Generation: Family Process in Church and Synagogue* (New York: The Guilford Press, 1985), 1. "It is the thesis of this book that all clergymen and clergywomen, irrespective of faith, are simultaneously involved in three distinct families whose emotional forces interlock: the families within the congregation, our congregations, and our own."

[3]This definition, like many thoughts in this article, are modifications of Ed Friedman phrases. I will be quoting Friedman frequently. Most of these quotations come from my memory of hearing Friedman on audio cassettes, a few video tapes, several lectures, or relayed to me by other "system thinkers."

[4]Friedman, Edwin H., *A Failure of Nerve: Leadership in the Age of the Quick Fix* (Bethesda, Maryland: The Edwin Friedman Estate, 1999) 264.

[5]Rev. Barbara Brown-Taylor is The Harry R. Butman Professor of Religion and Philosophy at Piedmont College in Demorest, GA.

[6]II Samuel 12:7.

[7]No one demonstrates or writes about this concept better than Fred Craddock. See: *Overhearing the Gospel* (Nashville: Abingdon, 1978).

[8]Friedman, *A Failure of Nerve,* 40-46.

[9]Exodus 32:24 (This is a great example of avoiding guilt and claiming innocence: "…I threw it into the fire and out came this calf!")

[10]Friedman, *A Failure of Nerve,* 169.

8

Long-tenured Ministry and Bowen Systems Theory

Israel Galindo and Betty Pugh Mills

Bowen Family Systems Theory (BFST) has become a helpful resource for many clergy and congregational leaders. Since the groundbreaking volume Generation to Generation, by Edwin Friedman in 1985, the theory continues to be an influential "theory of practice" for ministry. In this article the Israel Galindo, and long-tenured pastor Betty Pugh Mills explore to what extent BFST can be a resource to clergy for a long-tenured pastorate. Galindo directs the Leadership in Ministry workshops at the Center for Lifelong Learning at Columbia Theological Seminary. Mills is a long time participant in the workshops and for a time served on the faculty. First, selected key concepts of the theory that lend themselves to the issue of long-termed pastorates were reviewed. Second, the authors examined responses to a survey from clergy who are in long-term pastorates and who have been participants in LIM for several years. In the interviews respondents affirmed that BFST was a useful construct for congregational leadership in long-tenured ministry contexts.

Introduction

What makes it more likely that a minister will enjoy a long pastorate in one congregational context than fall into the pattern of moving from church to church every four to seven years? Is it personality? Is it having accumulated certain pastoral wisdom and professional competencies? Is it the happenstance of the particular context—landing in a "healthy" church versus one that was more dysfunctional? Likely, it is a combination of factors. This article explores the question whether adopting a particular interpretive framework, specifically, Bowen Family Systems Theory (BFST) can be a factor in helping a minister achieve a long pastorate in one congregational setting.

When studying long pastorates we may only "look back" at a generation that has served congregations largely born from the "builder generation." It may be the American congregational model is changing to such an extent that long pastorates will not be as frequent, or as possible, as they were. As such, the role of congregational clergy may also be changing. For example, the profile of the bi-vocational pastor has grown dramatically in the past several years, at the same time as there is speculation in some denominations about the decline of opportunities for full-time ministry positions.[1]

It may be that for congregations, the bi-vocational model of pastoral ministry may become normative, with fewer opportunities for clergy in traditional pastoral roles. Certainly, that seems increasingly true in certain denominations.

This trend toward bi-vocational ministry, coupled with the relatively short terms in the pastorate which has become the "norm" (four to eight years) makes the phenomenon of long-term pastoral tenures a speculative topic for investigation. Without a doubt, there are benefits to both clergy and congregations in the stability a long pastorate provides. Some significant things in congregational development only happen within the arc of a long pastorate.

Longer tenures allow for deep and significant ministry across the multi-generational context of families and the congregation. They may also set the stage for more deliberate, visionary change in the context of deeper trust in relationships that comes with time. Likewise, long pastorates have potential liabilities. In and of itself, a long pastorate may not be a sign of health; rather, it may be symptomatic of accommodation, for example. There are instances where long-term clergy have not successfully re-equipped themselves vocationally, resulting in both pastor and congregation failing to develop, mature, or risk ministry with courage and vision. In those cases, long years in one setting might be a sign of being stuck emotionally, spiritually, and professionally. As Edwin Friedman wrote, "chronic illness is an adaptation to a relationship."[2]

This article investigates and speculates on the long-term pastorate through the lens of BFST. Through interviews with long-tenured pastors, we explore to what extent BFST can provide a theory of practice to interpret the dynamics that facilitate a long-term pastorate.

The Theory

Bowen Family Systems Theory has become a significant resource for many clergy and congregational leaders. Since the groundbreaking volume by Edwin Friedman in 1985, Generation to Generation, the theory continues to be an influential "theory of practice" for ministry. As a bona fide theory, that is, one grounded in a field of study and practice, BFST provides a more rigorous framework as a theory of practice than devotional, romantic, or individualistic understandings of the role of clergy in a particular context, the congregation.

Author Ronald Richardson claimed that BFST has some similarities to biblical anthropology. He wrote, "In both cases, the individual self is always a part of several larger wholes. The self does not exist alone. In the biblical world, individual identity is nearly always derived in part from what he or she belongs to, whether it is occupations, places, families, or tribes. The larger context helps to define the individual. The individual is often a particular expression of the larger corporate group."[3]

Murray Bowen developed BFST, or "Bowen Theory," from the clinical therapeutic context. The theory provides a framework for interpreting the emotional process of relationships as they are manifested in the context (the "emotional field") of a particular family constellation. The theory has been applied to other relationship systems beyond the biological family unit, including institutions, government, social networks, and for over twenty years, congregations. Bowen and Kerr identified eight interlocking components which comprises BFST. The eight concepts are:

1. Triangles
2. Differentiation of Self
3. Nuclear Family Emotional System
4. Family Projection Process
5. Multigenerational Transmission Process
6. Emotional Cutoff

7. Sibling Position

8. Societal Emotional Process.[4]

Within those eight integrated concepts lies a framework that can describe and interpret the complex interactions of individuals in relationship systems. Each concept can, to some extent, provide a way to approach the question of the long pastorate from the perspective of the interaction between the functioning of clergy and the congregational context in which the relationship between church and pastor finds expression.

For pastoral leaders, BFST can inform three main therapeutic interventions for long term pastorates: (1) working to understand one's family of origin to gain insight on one's formation of self and of how one functions in relationships; (2) committing to the ongoing work of differentiation of self — working on one's maturity, being one's own self in the midst of relationships, clarifying one's principles and values, working on functioning non-anxiously during times of high reactivity, and staying emotionally connected and present in key relationships, and, (3) managing anxious relationships by functioning better in triangles.

For this article the authors interviewed clergy who are in long-term pastorates and who have been working with the theory for several years, chiefly through the LIM workshops. They were asked their thoughts about the relation between the theory and their experience as long-tenured pastors. Most of the pastors interviewed started working with the theory either early in their ministry, or, in the midst of a crisis.

Mike Winters, a Baptist pastor in Virginia, began paying attention to the theory in the midst of a crisis. He said, "My full-time ministry began in 1981. In 1991, I experienced extreme stress, to the point that I was unable to preach one Sunday. At that time, I did not have the understanding or internal resources to cope.

"Soon afterwards, I was introduced to Family Systems Theory. In a session led by Larry Matthews, who was a faculty member in Edwin Friedman's program, he told his story about how BFST helped him. I clearly remember thinking at the time, 'I do not understand much about Family Systems, but I do understand that I need this.'"

Elizabeth Norton, now a long-term Unitarian congregational music director in the Northeast, likewise started working on the theory during a crisis. She shared, "I was feeling worn down by interactions with parishioners during several conflicts and felt like there was so much I hadn't learned in music school about dealing with difficult people. A student ministerial intern recommended the chapter on triangles from *Generation to Generation*."

Dan Koger, a LIM faculty member, a long-term associate pastor, now a senior pastor, who has served several Baptist congregations and who currently is in a long-term context said, "I first encountered BFST in my seventh year of ministry, but it wasn't during a crisis time. Well, maybe it was and I was unaware. I heard Friedman speak and as I listened, all kinds of lights began to go off for me. Without really understanding what he was saying, on some level I connected with the theory."

Other long-tenured clergy interviewed were introduced to the theory in seminary. Lance King, a Baptist pastor in Virginia shared, "BFST first appeared to me early in seminary, around 1998. In my first ministry setting, BFST provided helpful lenses and new hope regarding long standing challenges which I was unknowingly fueling. I brought a growing awareness of BFST into my current setting in 2006."

Fred Lewis, an American Baptist pastor in the Mid-west said, "I began to take serious interest in BFST in my early 50's. I had been at my congregation for twenty years and completed a D.Min. degree. I did everything I thought a capable leader was to do, yet ministry still seemed very confusing. At that point, I began to explore Bowen systems theory. I also had a clear sense I wanted to make a move to a more robust ministry setting, yet I lacked the "centeredness" and "integration" required."

BFST as Theory of Practice

Asked to what extent BFST was a "primary lens" that informed their practice of ministry, the majority of those interviewed (all but one) responded that it was "The primary lens I use for ministry and understanding self."

King said, "BFST continues to help me grow in understanding myself. It has taken 20 years for me to start to naturally think "What triangle(s) am I in?" or to remember in a moment of elevated anxiety that my role is to get clear about myself, not to control outcomes. It has greatly shaped my perspective when parishioners bring their life challenges to me. Rather than getting hooked into the personal issues of others, I can have less skin in the game."

James Lamkin, pastor of a suburban Baptist church in Atlanta, GA, said, "In some ways, this is like asking a fish to describe water. The theory is THE way I look at life, except when I get anxious and become myopic. It informs the triangle I live with as a preacher between the text, the congregational context, and my own self. It informs thinking about my role and function as the pastor whenever a committee gets stuck and I am part of it; when that happens, I go to my study and draw a triangle so as to get some objectivity in the anxiety.

"Even being stuck or encountering resistance is different for me now, because where there is resistance, there is potential power. And it has really changed premarital counseling; for example, drawing a genogram of each couple's families of origin and allowing the genogram itself to be a part of the relationship."

One respondent appeared reluctant to identify BFST as the exclusive lens for her practice of ministry, nevertheless, the significance of the theory's influence was evident, as can be seen in the following responses. "[BFST is] the primary lens, the one I use first and most. At the same time, I think the theory integrates well with other perspectives. Two examples are Goleman's Emotional Intelligence and Heifetz' work on leadership."[5]

One said that claiming BFST as primary ". . . sounds strong to me, but I realize that I do use the BFST lens in viewing just about everything: my family of origin, the congregational system, our denomination, the political world, racial justice work, other cultures. I also use it when entering a new system, such as when I have done some music ministry transition consulting with congregations."

Another said, "I use BFST and the Bible to form my perspective. I also see BFST as consistent and complementary to many Biblical ideas. My perception is that people are a combination of body, mind, and spirit. I see BFST as applying to the mind, while the Bible applies to the spirit. That is a bit of an oversimplification, but is basically true." For one respondent, "Beyond the spiritual practices that inform and shape ministry,

BFST has provided the most consistent and adaptable lens for engaging ministry."

In the interviews, the following concepts of the theory were emphasized by the respondents: differentiation of self, anxiety and reactivity, multigenerational transmission, triangles, and sibling position.

1. Differentiation of Self

The concept of differentiation of self speaks to issues of identity, leadership, and the pastor's role and function in the clergy-congregation relationship. Defined simply, differentiation of self is the capacity of the individual to cope with circumstances, relationships, and life in general within a relative scale of functioning, with adaptation and resilience being two key qualities.

In the context of intense relationships, like a family or a congregation, differentiation of self mediates a person's capacity to avoid fusion with others in the system, to function better in the midst of acute anxiety in times of crises. Differentiation of self refers to the extent a person can think and act maturely and principled while in the midst of emotionally charged issues (a situation all too common, and frequent, for clergy). It is the capacity to be yourself while at the same time, remaining emotionally and mindfully connected to others, even in highly stressful circumstances. The concept of differentiation of self proposes that a highly functioning and mature person has the capacity to discern the difference between the experiences of thoughts and feelings, can manage their own reactivity better, and is able to choose thoughtful, principled actions even in the midst of reactivity.

In terms of long-tenured pastorates, differentiation of self can be related to other concepts of the theory. For example, the concept of the fundamental relationship dynamic of the togetherness-separateness forces in a congregation can play a significant role in the sharing of self and identity among and between the pastor and the congregation. To what extent has the pastor-congregation relationship become one of accommodation, or enmeshment? Are the pastor and the congregation able to differentiate what aspect of congregational life, ministry, and identity belong to the pastor, and which to the congregation? Two common scenarios provide illustrations for this dynamic. First, on the occasion when there is a pastoral transition congregations commonly struggle with answering questions of identity, vision, and mission in the absence of the personality of the pastoral leader. A second illustration is the difficulty that long-term pastors tend to have in "letting go" of ministry and of the church with whom they have shared self. For many, their sense of self is so intertwined with the role, persona, and identity of pastor to a particular congregation that retirement, or leaving, is as much an issue of identity, worth, and self as anything else.

Lamkin said, "The differentiation of self has been a continuous research project. I remember a turning point when I was feeling very attached to outcomes and results. My friend, Betty Pugh Mills, said, "What if you loved more and cared less (as in caring less about my expectations about outcomes)."

Norton said of this concept, "As a leader, the concept of differentiation of self has been very helpful to me. I have witnessed the impact that my own differentiation (or lack thereof) has on those I lead. As I get older, I find that getting clear on my own perspective and calmly owning it, helps me be more open to others' perspectives. I am less threatened by opposition and conflict than I used to be."

For pastor Lance King, differentiation of self has become a long-term project. He said, "Over a 20 year period, my getting clearer about myself has allowed me to shift my enmeshed and hostile relationship with my mother. These dynamics were mirrored in the two to three other most difficult congregational relationships I've experienced in 20 years. This concept has reminded me repeatedly of my primary task of being a self, instead of seeking to be popular, close, connected, appreciated, etc."

Being able to function from a stance of differentiation of self is important to any leader in the congregation, not just that pastor, as Dan Koger's response illustrated. He stated, "My ongoing research project in my current church setting has been the "dance" between my senior pastor and myself. I perceive that in some ways the church system observes the dance. The more I work to define myself in this system, especially in times of crisis or increased anxiety, the more I am aware that I become a target for the anxiety. Most often in my tenure, the anxiety has been aimed at the senior pastor, for a variety of reasons. In recent months, out of my own self-differentiation, I, as the associate pastor, have become more of a target than in previous years. The theory helps me understand and gives me perspective. So for me, right now, it is differentiation of self as a leader in the midst of heightened anxiety. Now, in terms of my ability to better understand the dynamics of the system, especially with church members who are troublesome, poorly differentiated, or the ones who act out the most, triangles and birth order have been helpful. I've focused more in the last couple of years in trying to see the interrelatedness of these two concepts as I try to relate to the people whom I really don't like, but know I have to have a connection with them at the same time. Given my wiring in my family of origin (distancing when the anxiety is high), this is very hard work for me. Lastly, our church is in crisis mode at present, for several reasons. Yet, understanding the system's deep need for homeostasis at least helps me "see" more of what's really taking place. And, to not take it personally or try to be a savior."

2. Anxiety and Reactivity

While not one of the eight foundational concepts, anxiety is a key concept in BFST that helps describe, and interpret, emotional process dynamics in a relationship system. In the theory anxiety is a natural part of any biological system and network of relationships, from families to organizations. The theory distinguishes between acute and chronic anxiety and how they can manifest in reactivity behaviors like sabotage, herding, attack, and group-think.

Long-term pastors come to understand that congregations by nature are chronically anxious systems. That is, they are defined not by an occasional experience of acute anxiety (e.g., a crisis of some kind), rather, they are structured for chronic anxiety. This can explain how common the emotional process of all congregations—as relationship systems of a type—can be so similar in so many ways. "Chronically anxious systems take form when the system is structured for it: when someone in the system (typically the leader, or, an identified patient (IP)) is made responsible for someone else's functioning. For example, when pastors are made responsible for people's faith or for the functioning of the staff; when youth ministers are made responsible for the behavior and spirituality of teenagers; when the staff is made responsible for people's attendance and participation in church programs; or, when a committee is made responsible for how much money people give."[6]

For Rebecca Werner Maccini, the pastor of a Congregational church in the Northeast, understanding how anxiety and reactivity affect the members of the congregation has been a significant part of the value of the theory. She provided an example that occurred early when she first learned BFST. She shared, "My husband and I were co-pastors at the time. The matriarch of the church died. She was also the matriarch of the town and her sons and daughters considered both their parents (their dad had died about 10 years before) valuable citizens of the area. The eldest daughter, who had come from across the country when her mother was dying, yelled at my husband in the hospital, telling him that he wouldn't have his job without her mother's support and that he never realized how sick her mother was. He let her vent and did not say much back to her except that he was sorry about her mother's mortal illness. When it came time to plan the funeral, the daughter met with me, and I recognized that this family was full of anxiety and intensity and that there was much more going on than what was on the surface. I spent four hours with the daughter planning for the funeral, basically being present to her. Plans that were made at that meeting were later canceled by the daughter, and the daughter claimed that I had made a promise to her during the meeting that I didn't keep (I experienced this as sabotage.)

"It seemed like an act of will for both co-pastors to stick to our vision—to provide a meaningful memorial service for the congregation and the community for a church member for whom we greatly respected. Keeping in mind that there was enormous anxiety in the family and that the eldest daughter was the primary one reacting to the anxiety was important to help us, the co-pastors, stay focused on our job and goal: to provide a meaningful service. A year later, the eldest daughter came to us and apologized for her behavior around the time of her mother's death."

King shared an example of how he was able to deal with an anxious situation as a result of having worked with the theory over the long haul. "The congregation I serve is 242 years old. I was called essentially to care for the 200 participants, preach, and coordinate ministries. As the congregation has grown to 600 participants, my role has grown increasingly uncomfortable and exhausting. Caring, teaching, and administering functions are now being shared by several new staff. It seems to me that the system needs more leading and visioning functions from me (not parts of my original call). This kind of leading stirs resistance by several of our longest termed parishioners. My BFST lenses help me understand what is happening."

King narrated an episode that illustrates the anxiety that can arise when a pastoral leader shifts how he functions in the system. "I had just returned from a three month sabbatical. I relished having time to think and the freedom to refresh, while being completely disconnected. On day three of my return, some newly proposed solutions to enduring challenges created an unusually conflicted congregational business meeting, the first conflicted meeting in eight years! This highlighted for me one of my patterned function(s) in this system. Not only was I chief coordinator, but effectively chief coddler, often working extra hard to "win" the favor of our least mature. The conflict led to an impasse. In preparing for the subsequent long range planning meeting, I took my "freshly returned from sabbatical" brain and did the hard work of getting really clear about what I thought we should do next (interestingly, I also noticed that very few folks had been asking me). I clearly, calmly laid out my vision for the next three big steps and remained unusually free from concern about what anyone thought, or how anyone might resist. It was fun! It was an entirely different experience than my usual attempts to convince, coerce, or otherwise be willful. With one exception, the response of the committee was favorable, even enthusiastic.

I don't feel especially concerned about how my vision will affect the concentric circles of the congregation in the months or years ahead. But I slept really well that night. Further, I still believe firmly in my vision. But I feel flexible enough to adjust to accommodate others' thinking."

Conflict can be the outcome of poorly managed or unresolved anxiety. BFST does not overly focus on the particular issue, or the "content," of conflict as it considers conflict to be merely symptomatic of anxiety. It also doesn't look at leadership in terms of the acquiring of leadership skills and techniques. Maccini shared how she brings that perspective to her ministry, "BFST gives me a great lens to look at what is happening around me. When there is conflict, I ask questions about 'Why now?' Has there been a change and is anxiety on the rise? Are homeostatic forces in play?

When times of anxiety arise and crazy things happen, I expect them and do not over react to them. I most often seek to get clarity when conflict occurs or when something happens that I feel extremely strong about, I use the constructs of the theory to think about my own reactions. I also believe that through BFST I have learned to 'hang in there.' I take time to observe, process, and recognize that change does not happen immediately and that people need time also to think about what is going on around them. I intentionally tell church leaders what I see happening from my perspective as leader."

Lamkin said, "Regarding anxiety and sabotage, the theory helps me focus on encouraging health in the immune system, rather than on viral behavior. The viral behavior changes from crisis to crisis; the immune system is in place regardless of the challenge."

Koger shared how the theory helps in working with difficult people, "The theory gives me the ability to be present with some of our most difficult church members, those who are the most immature. An example: one church member is constantly critical of things at church, all the time. I also supervise her in her work as a part-time employee.

In my conversations with her, as she talks about her anger at some things at church, the theory helps me approach her in ways that allow me to "hear" differently. I know that whatever is going on inside of her is not about the church, but she's not able to have that perspective. This allows me to work at conversing with her from a different direction and on a different level."

Tim Schrag, a Mennonite pastor in the Midwest, shared an example of how BFST can help interpret a conflict. "After 17 years in my current congregation, I (and several other leaders in the congregation) came under attack by a particular person who sought to enlist allies and 'spread the virus.' BFST helped inform me in ways of a) noting what might be going in the family of origin of the critic; b) reminded me to stay in touch with him and all 'sides'; c) guarded me against overreacting, recruiting allies, and thereby amplifying the potential toxicity of his actions; d) at several crucial points, gave me the insight to take a stand and say, 'enough is enough'; and e) understanding his responses as natural reactivity and sabotage by the system to some proposed changes."

Lamkin shared, "I 'became' the pastor of my current church about my seventh year. The church had been doing a visioning process which included a survey of over 200 questions (an example of anxiety?). Plus, narrative comments were encouraged. The narrative comments were directed at the staff, and particularly at me.

My first response was to not even read them; however, the Personnel Committee demanded that I meet with them and offer a response. The meeting was intense. One co-chair said the survey revealed that I had done poorly as pastor my first seven years. The other co-chair said that I had a lot of proving to do if I was ever going to be his pastor.

"I'm not very good at moments like this, but I remember being surprised at how non-anxious I was. I said calmly, but directly: 'Certainly there are some interesting comments on the survey; however, I've had seven solid years as pastor of this church and I will stand on that record.

And regarding the need to prove something, I want to be clear that I will spend zero time attempting to prove anything.'" Lamkin concluded, "Oddly, that was that. And that was the day I became the pastor. Some more "self" grew in me. Friedman said that "criticism is a form of pursuit." Perhaps so."

3. Multigenerational transmission process
in congregations

Perhaps one of the most "mystical" of the eight concepts is that of the multigenerational transmission of emotional process in biological families. This concept describes how patterns of emotional process are passed down generation to generation in family systems. The same phenomenon can be seen in congregations. The concept offers a way of understanding how relationship patterns in a congregation go beyond the personality and individual qualities of a pastoral leader, or, of the members that make up the congregation during a particular time in the lifespan of a congregation. The focus of the theory is upon the spaces of interaction between different parts of the family, not the individual family members. Everybody enters in the middle of the story, and in becoming part of the relationship system, they take up the relationship patterns passed down in the system. This includes new ministers to the church as well as new members. The functions remain very similar down the generations, no matter what kind of family or organization is being explored.

For example, it can explain why no matter who is placed on a particular church committee, that committee will always follow the functioning pattern or role "assigned" by the system (underfunctioning- and overfunctioning-reciprocity, scapegoating, etc.). For the harried pastor, it can help explain why some things will never be "fixed" in the congregation, no matter how long she or he works at it. It can explain why no matter who responds to the call of a staff position, that person will find he or she will need to work within boundaries set by the congregational emotional patterns transmitted through generations. Long term pastors may find they will forever be dealing with behaviors, issues, and reactivity patterned under a founding pastor, no matter how long ago those were set in place.

BFST describes some of the patterns that can be passed on from one generation to the next. These include relationship triangles, anxieties about particular issues, ways of handling crises or relationships (e.g., cut off), patterns of reactivity in response to threat or crises, etc. These multigenerational transmission repertoires are not too difficult to identify in congregations (reactivity is not imaginative, so in one true sense, a congregation can say, "we've always done it that way"!). In some congregations, these patterns may be closely aligned to the multigenerational transmission patterns of biological family units that make up the congregation.

Related to the concept of multi-generational transmission is the concept of homeostasis. This concept refers to the "balance" a system achieves to help maintain the emotional process patterns that help ensure its functional perception of viability (though not necessarily its vitality), identity, and functioning. The concept is not "static"—it is a dynamic. As congregations adapt to changing environments and to the arc of its lifespan, sometimes including traumas, resilient congregations are able to modify or modulate homeostasis. This requires adaptation not only of the congregation, but of a long-term pastor who can accept that change is the norm over the course of a long ministry, and that real leadership is the capacity to manage the anxiety about the change.

One implication for long term pastoral tenures may be the necessity of finding a right "fit" in a congregational-pastoral relationship, but also, one that can negotiate the "fit" over time as both pastor and congregation move through the arch of both personal (pastoral and vocational) and corporate (organizational and institutional) changes over time. It is worth noting that BFST does not assume "health" in terms of these concepts. Of greater challenge, for example, is providing pastoral leadership to congregations where homeostasis is more rigid and less amenable to resilience and adaptation over time. Multigenerational transmission and systemic homeostasis can serve a function in systems whose homeostasis is dysfunction. That is, long term pastoral tenures can be found in unhealthy and dysfunctional congregations as much as in healthy ones. Again as Friedman wrote, "Chronic illness is an adaptation to a relationship."[7]

Pastor Mike Winters' thoughts illustrate how the concept of multigenerational transmission yielded insight that became a resource for him. He shared, "Many previous generations have helped shape me. Strengths and weaknesses in my life did not just show up out of the blue. Patterns were in motion and seeds were planted in previous generations. As I became aware of them, I tried to respond to and embrace them. For example, shame is an issue in my life. As John Bradshaw says, 'Guilt says I made a mistake, while shame says I am a mistake.'[8] My personal sense of shame has always been out of proportion. This raises the question, "Where is it coming from?" As I have worked on my genogram, I detected a clear pattern in previous generations. This awareness has lessened the impact of the shame."

Winters continued, "Another theme in my life and my family system is curiosity. Curiosity is the ability to step back from a situation and see it more objectively. It is about openness to new possibilities and positions me to learn and grow. It also re-positions me to take appropriate responsibility, which allows room for others to do their own part. Stamina in my larger family is a significant resource. This stamina has a physical, emotional, and spiritual component. It is that ability to find a way to keep going. It means reaching down and finding resources and resilience that I did not know I had until I really needed it." It is interesting to note that Winters is an avid runner.

For Fred Lewis, "Multigenerational transmission is also helpful in uncovering the hidden, yet persistent story that spans decades and the generations in congregational life. What seems to be so traumatic becomes less so when you can start to connect the dots that suggest this congregation has been here before, so let's see how they moved forward or remained stuck. In the mid-1970's my congregation had a church split that left the congregation weakened, disillusioned and hurting. The presenting problem was a desire for the church to maintain theological orthodoxy and retain a more conservative interpretation of scripture. When a strong and vocal group of folks called for my preaching to embrace a more theologically conservative view, I could see the church had been here before. Interestingly, it was the more progressive side that remained in place in the 70's and then again, in support of my leadership forty years later. I think many looked back in order to see what they wanted for their future."

For Elizabeth Norton, "BFST has helped me avoid taking things personally and, on good days, to observe the upheaval with some healthy detachment and curiosity. The concept of multigenerational process as it continued to manifest in these crises helped me keep perspective. Remembering the long history of our congregation and observing its resilience through political revolution, schism and a devastating fire instilled confidence and hope in our future. BFST has helped me stay less attached to outcomes and more focused on process. It has helped me be a calm(er) leadership presence as anxiety in the system manifest itself in bizarre behaviors among lay and professional leaders."

A major benefit for these long-tenured clergy has been how using BFST as a theory of practice has helped them focus as much, if not more, on how they are functioning than on how others are acting. Winters shared a dramatic example of this. "In one church setting, I had already been there about nine years. That year had been the most successful year to date in terms of worship attendance, baptisms, offerings, etc. However, a small but vocal group emerged as a disruptive force. A sincere effort was made to address their concerns. Myself, as Pastor, a committee, and then the Deacons all met with them at different times. There was a sincere attempt to listen to and address their concerns. These attempts were only met with more demands, finally resulting in a petition this group circulated to force the resignation of a staff member. One person in the group even composed a twenty page notebook of complaints!

"Family systems helped me to see that you cannot reason with someone who is being unreasonable," Winters continued. "A point-by-point conversation about twenty pages of complaints is absurd. The moment you grant credibility to such absurdity, you find that the list of complaints continues to grow even more. Family systems thinking helped me to stop catering to such blatant selfishness. I also learned not take to take on this group by myself. This was not just my issue as Pastor, but was a church issue. My responsibility was to appropriately involve the church. This meant to include, empower, and equip the church to deal with such difficulties. BFST enabled me to survive the most difficult time of my entire ministry. Without this resource, this crisis would have caused me to leave that church and the ministry. Instead, I remained at that church for another five years."

Baptist pastor Steve Crommer, of Myrtle Beach, SC shared how the theory helped him shift his functioning in the midst of emotionally-charged situations. "I labored for the first 10 years of ministry with the assumption that my role was to help others become closer to God and to grow in faith. The burden for the growth and health of the church was something I shouldered as well. That led me to a physical and emotional crash. Working with the constructs of BFST became a means to freedom (and recovery) – that I could simply be "with" the church and the individual members – sharing my thoughts and offering pastoral care – without being responsible "for" their development or well-being. Bottom line: I can participate in the on-going activity of Jesus Christ in His church and this world without feeling responsible for the outcomes. Those I leave to Him."

4. Sibling Position (Birth Order)

Sibling position, a concept originally from researcher Walter Toman[9] but which comprises one of the eight basic concepts of BFST, describes how one's birth order position can affect aspects of self and of functioning. For example, it can inform functional levels of differentiation of self, and can be seem in its manifestation of how an individual functions in relationships, individually and in groups. The concept describes how oldest, youngest, and middle children tend toward certain functional roles in families, influenced also by the particular mix of sibling positions, as well as by the sibling positions of parents and other significant persons in the family. In turn, these "formatted" and learned family functional roles carry over in an individual's own future families, and, in other contexts—work, church, etc.

To what extent may a clergy's birth order influence the capacity to stay in one place for the long haul? For example, Friedman pointed out that all famous explorers were second born. Might it be, then, that first-borns have a greater predilection and capacity for staying put longer? Can a clergy's birth order fit one congregational context better than another and thereby contribute to a longer pastorate? For example, middle children tend toward patterns of "peacekeepers" and mediators. For a middle child, finding a church that desires a "peacemonger" may help make for a longer tenure—albeit a perpetually stressful one.

For example, Mennonite pastor Tim Schrag observed, "My position as a middle child, in the midst of a very large and 'close' clan have made me a natural peacemaker. I have learned that this makes me an excellent politician in the congregation, yet averse to 'being out front' in the lonely position of leadership. I have learned to understand my anxiety when 'out front' scenarios occur, and have been more able to opt for courage and principle in how I function."

Pastor Lance King offered this example, "Sibling position has been key in understanding how I function in a system. As an oldest brother of brothers, I discovered that my "sister deficit disorder" was a consistent factor in my very painful struggles with all three "difficult" females in my ministry tenure. Having learned how to more freely share leadership, I less frequently get hooked by their living out their own birth order (oldest sister of sisters). I've learned to thoughtfully respect strong female leadership instead of feeling so threatened by it."

5. Triangles

The concept of triangles is the "building block" of emotional process, according to the theory. Acute anxiety brings instability in any two-person relationship. Very quickly the way to manage the experience of anxiety is to triangle a third person to relieve some of the stress, to seek allies, or to diffuse anxiety among three persons. In complex relationship systems, like congregations, triangles can become part of the structure of the system, at which point several interlocking triangles help distribute anxiety and create patterns of relationships. As with all concepts in BFST, triangles are neither "good" not "bad." They are merely a natural functional dynamic in any relationship system. Persons who become part of a dynamic anxiety triangle may function in it to the extent they have capacity to differentiate within its structure—remaining neutral but connected, or becoming part of the reactivity that drives the triangled relationship. Understanding one's position in the triangle is paramount to one's leadership function.

Elizabeth Norton explained how helpful the concept has been for her. "Triangulation has been the most helpful concept for me personally and in helping others to navigate roles and conflicts. I now automatically hear triangulation when folks say, for instance, "people are saying," or "I've heard . . ." and I encourage folks to speak for themselves and ask others to do the same. I can also help others recognize triangles. I find that describing an open triangle, where no one is "on the outside" sometimes helps me, my colleagues, and parishioners, to work for more healthy patterns of communication and emotional process." She explained, "The triangle is probably the BFST concept that is most well-known and most misused in common organizational thinking. Triangles are often portrayed as "bad." I find it helpful to remember with folks that triangles are always there, it is how we manage ourselves within them that makes the difference."

Mike Winters shared how his understanding the concept of triangles helps in marital counseling. He said, "Recognizing and responding to triangles has been very helpful. Triangles help me see what is on the playing field. This has enabled me to avoid many landmines. Even when I do step on a landmine, it helps me to learn from the experience. Triangles also help define what my role is and is not. One example of emotional triangles shows up in marriage counseling. My role is to listen and help them think through their situation, not to fix or save their marriage. The moment I slip into the "savior" role, I overstep my role and actually interfere with the couple doing their part. My role is to walk with them as they carry their burden, but not to carry it for them."

Lance King shared, "this concept has very frequently saved me from meddling outside my jurisdiction. For several years, I announced from pulpit my pledge to not keep secrets when told about one parishioner by another (I simultaneously pledged my confidence in matters folks shared/confessed about themselves). I think I learned this from Israel Galindo. The congregational members occasionally remind me of this, and they resist telling me stuff about others. I don't know what they're doing with that information. But I know I don't have to deal with it."

Tim Schrag shared, "My default lens for preaching, administration, and pastoral care has become triangles. Understanding triangles as beneficial in helping distribute anxiety, and as detriments when they become stuck, has informed me in how I function. The idea of triangles has also given me perspective on what I am, and am not, responsible for when conflict and disagreements arise. More recently, I have seen the intentional formation of triangles as a way of releasing positive energy in the right direction! Being able to see reactivity and anxiety in situations, and interpreting them as a symptom of process (thinking process rather than content), has been very helpful."

Can BFST Be a Resource for a Long-Tenured Pastorate?

As to the question, "In terms of your current ministry setting, to what extent did BFST aid in being able to remain in place for a long tenure," most of those interviewed claimed, "To a great extent." (all but one, who indicated, "To some extent").

Fred Lewis reflected, "A pastorate of ten years or more provides dozens of opportunities to think the problem will be solved by moving to another congregation, latching on to another or better program, or isolating or eliminating loud opponents, or other panaceas. These efforts do not lead to more healthful functioning or a more faithful congregation. The harder work has been continuing to learn BFST theory, staying connected yet self-defined (in both church and family) and being less reactive to all the hooks that hang in the air of congregation life. In the end, you find you can actually stay in place and enjoy it, having deeper relationships and a more healthful ministry."

King, in Virginia, stated, "Identifying generational patterns and ongoing systemic triangles in this 242 year-old congregation has helped me interpret individual and congregational resistance less personally. Presenting case studies twice annually to colleagues and coaches has created the regular discipline of applying BFST to my actual challenges. This exercise has very frequently informed and shaped my functioning in my most challenging situations. While understanding challenging situations in BFST framework rarely made them feel any better, it helped me untangle what was mine and what was not mine, and resist acting out of my feelings."

For pastoral associate Koger, "It has enabled me to navigate the waters of my current church setting when the waters have been smoother and when the waters are turbulent. I've been here long enough that church members who "get it" now understand some of what I often say ("the issue is never the issue" and "the system adapts to the weakest link"). It's more than just words they use; they understand the concepts of theory. It gives me perspective in terms of my own functioning, an awareness of when I am functioning in a healthier and more self-defined way. And, I'm more able at times to know when I am "hooked" by something taking place. That's when I get out paper and pencil and draw the triangles. When I am "hooked" and oblivious to what's really going on, an email or phone call to one of my BFST cohorts helps me gain the perspective I need in the moment."

Norton, serving in the Northeast, said, "I would have burned out long ago. I was feeling so responsible for everything! And I would not have been able to weather recent transitions in leadership, or lead through some difficult times in the past few years without the BFST "lab coat." BFST gives me tools for analysis, a way to monitor my own emotional response, a language to describe emotional process and, often, a sense of humor about it all!"

Rebecca Maccini, responded, "I am fortunate to be in a very positive ministry, a 'plum' as Ed Friedman might put it. I have done my best to use BFST during the challenging times and the times when conflict has arisen. I have also grown in emotional maturity and I credit learning about triangles, multi-generational family process, reactivity, and emotional process as giving me very good tools for my own personal growth. I think that if one can get clear about what are a pastor's responsibilities and what are a congregation's responsibilities and also learn to be more flexible and light, it goes a long way toward being able to remain in a pastorate for a longer period of time."

Finally, Winters shared, "My first two church ministries each lasted three years. In my next church, I began to burn out. Then I began participating in the Leadership in Ministry workshops on BFST and ended up staying almost ten years in that church. In my next pastorate, I stayed almost fifteen years. There is no question, BFST understanding and application was a game-changer that equipped me with important internal resources to grow as a person and as a minister."[10]

When asked specifically if BFST contributed to their longevity as a pastoral leader in their contexts, three of those interviewed had this to say:

James Lamkin: "I think the theory consistently emphasizes that the best gift a clergy person has to give a congregation, is a healthy self. The theory offers a life-long structure for growing self, from work on one's family of origin, to exploring one's function given the eight aspects of the theory. It has mattered to me from pulpit to committee to pastoral care."

Elizabeth Norton: "I credit my deepening understanding of BFST with my longevity. It has provided me resources to remain relatively clear-headed in anxious times and given me a framework in which to understand and interpret events in our congregational system and in my family of origin. There is no denying that my functioning in my family of origin and my functioning in my congregational system are analogous. My older siblings have looked to me for leadership and insight in coping with our father's death and our mother's declining health over the past decade. During that same time, my supervisors have looked to me as a resource in training the rest of the staff in the concepts of BFST. I would say that one of the biggest differences it has made in both systems is strengthening my capacity to let go of blame; to look for systemic causes for events and behaviors. This has truly changed my own perspective, which is really all I can control."

Mike Winters: "BFST is not just an "add-on." It is a way of thinking that informs how I do relationships, ministry, and life. The theory helps me think through how I need to position myself in a variety of settings. This could be in a one-on-one relationship, a committee setting, or as I relate to the whole congregation. It helps me to only take or accept responsibility that belongs to me. This has two benefits. It makes me less likely to burn out and it challenges the church, or anyone else involved to step up and do their part. It is very consistent with the Apostle Paul's "Body of Christ" metaphor for the church. I am one part of that body. Jesus is the Head, not me. I can only do my part. If I try to do the part of others, it sets me and the church up for dysfunction."

BFST As a Resource for Younger Clergy

The authors asked the long-tenured veteran ministers for their thoughts about to what extent BFST can be a resource for younger clergy in relation to achieving a long-term pastoral tenure in a congregation. While all asserted that BFST was an invaluable resource for ministry, they had reservations about to what extent the theory, as such, can be helpful to younger clergy. Here are their thoughts.

Fred Lewis: "There are just too many young clergy who do not survive the first three to five years of ministry. I would think an introduction to BFST would be invaluable. However, I think it takes time for people to really appreciate the tie between pastoral functioning and the concepts of emotional process inherent in family systems work. In my own case, I needed to have enough life experiences that took me into my late 40's and 50's in order to finally begin to appreciate the indelible influence of my family of origin and the framework BFST provided for healthier functioning.

"It may be that younger clergy are so anxious about skill development, that they miss the more subtle ways emotional process influences congregations and themselves. Younger clergy will especially need to have accessible and good resources to do this work."

Lance King: "Early in my ministry, I longed to exit from what I thought was simply a difficult and painful career. I think BFST offers very helpful lenses for any young clergy person to discover a self. Family of origin work was key to my remaining in ministry with some more objective self-awareness, and reduced domination by my feelings. Sibling position, triangles, multigenerational transmission all reveal that there is always more going on than appears."

Steve Crommer: "I think the biggest value that BFST had for me as a younger pastor (I was in my mid-thirties when I started working with the theory) is that it provides specific handles for minimizing willfulness with the congregation. As a young pastor I wanted to create change in congregational behavior, get people moving, help them draw closer to the Lord, get them to understand their calling, etc. As a result, nothing was really changing (at least underneath the hood), and I was quickly flaming out. BFST provided a way for me to actively be with the congregation and individual members in a less anxious ways – speaking into their lives, making observations, and asking questions – without willing outcomes. This helped decrease disillusionment, weariness, frustration, and made room for faith, patience and trust."

Tim Schrag: "I think BFST is of most value if one engages in it over a number of years. I am not sure that getting a small dose of it (reading a book, going to one workshop), is actually of value. I have seen too many pastors do what I did in my early years, use it as a quick fix or way to diagnose and 'manage' other people and situations.

"It took me a long time to start seeing my primary task as my own insight and maturity, and understanding that such maturation would have a positive effect on the system. I often feel like I am just starting to catch on! My unqualified advice to young pastors would be to find a venue for extended coaching in BFST, even as one is reading about the theory. Without a coach, there will be very little benefit, in my opinion."

Dan Koger: "It's one thing to read the books and use the language. I encounter lots of first-year ministers who have had exposure to BFST in their seminary training. They talk the talk and are simply unaware of their own naiveté at this point in their ministry.

"The shit has yet to hit the fan, and when this happens, the fan is an oscillating fan. The theory is a resource only when one works the theory in relationship – the hard work of staying connected in our church contexts, even with troublesome church members – and the hard work of being in some kind of a group context on a regular basis with others who understand the theory and can give us insight and help us to be more accountable to ourselves. Simply encouraging younger clergy to do the work and know that they really won't get it until they hit a crisis."

Rebecca Maccini: "It took me many years to engage wisely with the theory. Unfortunately, I have seen too many clergy use the theory to hammer their congregations. They seem to be great at talking about dysfunctional systems and dysfunctional people and all the family issues affecting someone else, but do not take much responsibility for their own behavior.

"That is the most challenging part of the theory for me. What is my responsibility in all of this? How has my own reactivity contributed to a problem? How can I act in a more mature fashion? It may be possible for young clergy to ask those questions of themselves if they have some emotional maturity already. I did not have the maturity or clarity of self as a young clergy."

Elizabeth Norton: "I think the theory is a valuable resource for a long pastorate—for longevity in any leadership position. Some understanding of the theory might be helpful to younger clergy, though a deeper understanding is gained through working the theory and observing it over time. As I said above, I believe it helped me to avoid early burn out. It makes sense that it could help young clergy to weather the storms of ministry with resilience. I think it is essential training for seminarians; continuing some kind of relationship with a BFST group is a valuable part of a pastor's support system. Informally, I have observed that many of my "healthiest" colleagues in ministry are well-versed in BFST."

Conclusion

In a day of transition with great swells of anxiety in local churches, it seems that the benefits of framing one's function as a leader using BFST as a construct of understanding emotional systems in families and congregations can be a significant resource. Clergy who make the intentional decision to immerse themselves in the readings and the contexts of accountability and feedback report positive results in their understanding of themselves and their development as leaders. Honest, collegial and safe conversations about local church challenges and local church resilience are continually helpful to those clergy in their application of BFST. Each of the clergy interviewed have made the commitment of being lifelong learners of the theory, and of themselves, through peer-learning and reflection on practice through the framework of the theory.[11]

Churches tend to function more like families than most groups and institutions, with only a little less intensity than the biological family. For ministers, the church context can feel as overwhelming and confusing as the personal battles found in their own family of origin and their nuclear family. The great benefit in the application of the theory is that work on one's self changes how one functions at home and at work. On occasion, working to define self while remaining connected might be easier at work, than at home. But at other moments, it can be the opposite.

The goals of ministers seeking to invest significant time in the life of one particular ministry context may be different than the minister who transitions from context to context. If long-tenured service is desired because of the ministerial and vocational values of the minister, then the BFST approach to leadership can be a significant orientation for proceeding in leadership. Applying the theory to one's function as a leader does not always produce great results. Sometimes, the anxiety is just too high and the minister and church will end the covenant relationship. But in other situations, when the church and the pastor are facing significant challenges, the way of seeing the emotional field and understanding one's position in the system can invite more thoughtful, informed decisions by the minister and the church. BFST cautions that differentiation of self is typically met with sabotage and resistance, but it also offers the real possibility for risking growth, effectiveness, and creative problem solving that the church needs more than ever.

Whether pastoral leaders are dealing with diminishing dollars, deferred maintenance on a facility, worship music and style battles, or micro-managing congregational leadership, those long-tenured clergy interviewed have acclaimed the role of BFST in their arsenal of resources for leading their churches over the long haul. Ultimately, the best gift that a long-tenured minister can offer to the church he or she serves, is the most whole, honest, and defined self that God created him or her to be.

Edwin Friedman wrote, "The basic concept of leadership through self-differentiation is this: if a leader will take primary responsibility for his or her own position as "head" and work to define his or her own goals and self, while staying in touch with the rest of the organism, there is a more than reasonable chance that the body will follow. There may be initial resistance but, if the leader can stay in touch with the resisters, the body will usually go along. This emphasis on the leader's self-differentiation is not to be confused with independence or some kind of selfish individuality. On the contrary, we are talking here about the ability of a leader to be a self while still remaining a part of the system."[12]

---

[1] See Leslie Scanlon, "Full-time called Pastor as an Endangered Species," *Presbyterian Outlook* (March 18, 2013).

[2] Edwin Friedman, *A Failure of Nerve* (New York: Seabury Books, 2007), p. 181.

[3] Ronald Richardson, "Bowen Family Systems Theory and Congregational Life," *Review & Expositor* (Vol. 102, No. 3, Summer 2005) 381.

[4] See, Michael E Kerr, "One Family's Story: A Primer on Bowen Theory," The Bowen Center for the Study of the Family, 2000. http://www.thebowencenter.org.

[5] See Daniel Goleman, *Emotional Intelligence: Why It Matters More Than IQ* (New York: Bantam Books, 1995) and Ronald A. Heifitz and Marty Linsky, *The Practice of Adaptive Leadership* (Boston: Cambridge Leadership Associates, 2009).

[6] Israel Galindo, *Perspectives on Congregational Leadership: Applying Systems Thinking for Effective Leadership*, (Richmond, VA: Educational Consultants, 2009), p. 55.

[7] Friedman, A Failure of Nerve, p. 181

[8] Paraphrased from John Bradshaw, *Healing the Shame That Binds You* (Deerfield Beach, FL: Health Communications, Inc., 1988), p. 21.

[9] Walter Toman, *Family Constellation: Its Effects on Personality and Social Behavior*, 4th Edition (Springer Publishing Company; 4 edition (1992).

[10]For information on the Leadership in Ministry Workshops Winters and others mention in this article, see www.leadershipinministry.org.

[11]This group of long-tenured pastors have been consistent and regular participants in the Leadership in Ministry Workshops, a clergy leadership training program focused on BFST as a theory of practice. www.leadershipinministry.org.

[12]Edwin Friedman, *Generation to Generation: Family Process in Church and Synagogue* (New York: Guildford Press, 1985), p. 229.

❖

9

Pastoral Care Triage: Bowen Theory and Leading with Heart and Mind

James Boyer

James Boyer, DMin, LMFT, PC, is a native of Portland, OR. After completing a D.Min. in family counseling at Colgate Rochester Divinity School he finished his clinical training in Scottsdale, AZ. He has facilitated Bowen Theory study and supervision groups in Portland since 1985. Jim is a clinical fellow and approved supervisor in the American Association of Marriage and Family Therapists and an Oregon State Licensed Marriage and Family Therapist.

When a therapist is fused or "stuck" to a family emotionally, he can be part of a family's emotional support system, but he cannot promote differentiation in the family. Kerr/Bowen

It is common for clergy to seek consultation around challenging pastoral care situations. A high percentage of people still prefer to talk initially with their clergyperson about a personal problem. The emotional process underlying these situations can have a common theme where the intensity of the emotions trigger instincts in the pastor to rescue, fix or otherwise will something to happen. Counterbalancing these instincts with a systems thinking perspective enables pastors to be emotionally caring while being objective and challenging, and as playful as needed. Maintaining contact with the intellectual system does not negate pastoral emotional support skills. Rather, it enhances them so that in practice pastors can lead with both heart and mind.

An example of this type of pastoral encounter might start with an urgent phone call from a parishioner, "Pastor we have to see you right away! Our marriage is falling apart and we don't know what to do! Please help us!"

Pastoral preparation starts before the couple shows up for an initial visit. You may begin by asking: What are the limitations of what I can offer? How can I show caring and clarity at the same time? How can I stay out of the triangle between the couple and their marriage while connecting to each?

After putting your thinking hat on it's time to meet the couple. For the first part of the consultation you provide emotional support. You listen, reflect, show equal interest to each, gather the facts and allow the power of an anxious system in proximity to an anxious heart and mind to take hold. Sensing a calming of initial anxieties you ask, "Now, what is anyone willing to do to make things better?" More blaming ensues. You name the feeling state, "You are both extremely upset, I can see that." You state a fact, "No positive changes will take place until someone focuses on themselves rather than the other person."

You listen to the mental wheels turning in the silence. The wife offers, "I guess we have been trying to change the other person more than focusing on ourselves." As they leave you add, "Give this some time. Think about what you might be willing to do to improve your relationship. Let's meet in a few days."

In this example the pastor did an excellent job of connecting with the couple, showing equal interest and support (heart). Then, once emotions had shifted she asked the critical question, "What is anyone willing to do to make things better?" The question is more important than any answer given at the moment. In fact unless the person(s) show an ability to entertain this question it is important to leave it with them for a period of time, respecting the need for their intensity to settle down prior to shifting into exploration of options mode (mind).

In this chapter I will explore the Bowen Theory (BFST) orientation to pastoral care where the clergyperson is connected to the emotional system of others (heart) while simultaneously standing outside of it (mind). I will first discuss how getting beyond the feeling system by means of the counterbalancing the intellectual system is critical to quality pastoral care. I will then demonstrate how BFST has redefined the helping role by putting learning and curiosity at the center. Next I will call on Ed Friedman to remind us how being a self supporting helper is rooted in curiosity about life as well as a firm belief in the regenerative capacities of all living things. I will conclude with a summary of guidelines for pastoral triage from a BFST perspective.

Getting Beyond the Feeling System

As Bowen said, "Systems thinking ... is directed at getting beyond cause and effect thinking and into a systems view of the human phenomenon."[1] He pointed out that the feeling and emotional systems are stuck in cause and effect, either/or, blame self or others, rescue/give me what I want mode when feelings are intense. Only the intellectual system is capable of recognizing the feeling system without being fused with it. I believe the importance of this process is equally critical to all areas of pastoral leadership. The better differentiated the pastor the more he or she is able to access the most recently evolved intellectual system as needed. Pastors tend to be naturally gifted with the emotional support side of pastoral care (the heart/feeling system). The need, then, is to develop their capacity to access the intellectual system (mind) especially when emotions are intense. Getting beyond anxiety, and the limited perspective it generates, is the responsibility of helping professionals who regularly work with people dealing with intense emotions.

With realistic expectations of themselves, their own family of origin work and clear boundaries around the number of times they would consult with someone, clergy can provide a missing resource in many communities of initial reflection and appropriate referral. Clergy are often "gate keepers" and first responders in times of emotional upheaval. Where then does pastoral care fit into the matrix of support and treatment of human difficulties? I suggest that pastoral care uniquely provides a valuable and timely resource of initial reflection or triage of human problems that precedes professional assessment and treatment. Both formal assessment and treatment of medical, emotional, relationship, financial and social problems are the purview of other professionals. Clergy do well not to function beyond the limits of their training. However, they have much to offer in the early hours and days of family, couple and individual crisis.

Redefining the Helping Role

BFST redefined the helping role, and care, more in terms of curiosity, understanding and learning than empathy, solutions or "getting it out." Those seeking assistance from a clergyperson have an expectation of receiving emotional support. At the same time emotional support alone is limited in its ability to assist people in developing and using the intellectual system associated with greater maturity and ability to intervene in their own problems.

Individual models of intervention tend to be based on the medical model, which in turn is rooted in cause and effect thinking. This mode of thinking is appropriate for a diagnosis, treatment, and curative approach to medical issues. Systems thinking, however, offer a different approach to the complexity of human emotional systems. The medical model asks, "How do you feel?" "What do you want?" and "How can I help?" In contrast, systems thinking asks, "What are you noticing, thinking or working on?" "What is your role in the problem?" and, "What are you willing to do to make a difference?" The shift could not be more profound. Curiosity, objectivity and learning seem to be the modes of care best suited for complex human systems. *Systems thinking shifts the meaning of triage from getting help to the neediest first, to supporting the most motivated in an emotional system and helping them in taking action to intervene in their own problem.*

The ability to think systems and to retain that theoretical perspective in an anxious environment makes it possible for a therapist (pastor) to be in emotional contact with a family and to remain "outside" the family's emotional problem. ... this is a quite different approach from that of a therapist (pastor) who tries to show a family that he cares or is sympathetic to their discomfort. Sympathy is available in a lot of places, but it eventually wears thin. Emotional objectivity, which is grounded in a consistent theoretical orientation, is less common and families never grow tired of it. Objectivity and neutrality are always attractive to an anxious family.[2]

In pastoral triage conversations the pastor is sometimes the only thinking person in the room. The persons seeking assistance are often flooded with emotion, unable to see the bigger picture, their brains operating under brownout conditions. They may be taken over by the "four horsepersons" of the anxiety apocalypse: quick fix, linear thinking, blaming and either-or-thinking. Staying calm is not the easiest advise to follow when the feeling system is dominating. Still, "objectivity and neutrality are always attractive to an anxious family." Heart and mind leadership can lend a thinking brain to an emotional system that has lost track of its own.

Learning at the Center

BFST grew out of the clinical observation of whole family units. In the 1950's Murray Bowen, with his staff and research families, formed a community of observation, understanding, and learning that was unique in the history of psychiatry. This effort to learn from the families themselves rather, than teaching them something from the outside, gave rise to the benefit of families becoming their own experts, with the staff serving as consultants and supervisors of their efforts.

This is how BFST redefined the role of helper: stay curious, respect the family's ability to intervene in its own processes and take the opportunity to learn as much as possible from each person and family. The theory shifts away from an individual model, which sees problems, and therefore cures, residing solely in the individual, to a systems model that emphasizes staying in touch with the emotional system. At the same time, helpers, stay outside of the emotional process to the best of their ability. This orientation towards curiosity and learning is, in my view, how emotional support and expression was transcended (not eliminated) by curiosity and understanding as the heart of the therapeutic/pastoral encounter from a BFST perspective.

Over the years, "research" families have done better in family psychotherapy than those for whom the primary goal was "therapy." This helped establish a kind of orientation which has made all families into "research" families. It has been my experience that the more a therapist learns about a family, the more the family learns about itself; and the more the family learns, the more the therapist learns, in a cycle which continues.[3]

Picking up the original example of a distressed couple, let's imagine a learning and curiosity orientation being played out. The second visit starts with the pastor noting the tone the couple is demonstrating, "You both look concerned yet a lot less anxious." She then adds, "I am wondering what your thoughts have been since our initial visit."

The wife responds, "I have thought quite a bit about your idea of focusing on changing my self rather than my partner." Turning to the husband, the pastor asks, "How about you?" He responds, "I thought we came to you for marriage advice not self advice!"

To which pastor replies, "I can't give advice about your marriage because I don't have the credentials for that. What I can and am happy to do is help you puzzle through your options and next steps."

Thinking for a bit the husband responds, "Oh I didn't realize we might have to talk with someone else. Well, in that case yes, I am willing to go and see someone to save my marriage." Pastor expresses curiosity with, "Have you considered talking with your parents about their marriages?"

Looking at each other they both break out laughing. Then the wife offered, "Of course not, both sets of our parents prefer to make war not love."

Pastor reflected, "Still, they could be a resource even though they seem like good examples of poor behavior. You might ask their advice and see what happens."

The husband replied, "That sounds very interesting. They care about us so much and do love to give us advice!" In sending them on their way with names to contact the pastor added, "I respect your efforts to find your way to healthier patterns. God bless you!" "Thanks pastor, see you Sunday," the couple said as they walked out of her office.

All pastoral triage encounters don't go this smoothly, naturally. But it illustrates the critical belief on the part of the pastor in this couple's ability to find their path forward. Family resources are often overlooked, especially between generations where one generation was not open to consultation while the new generation is open.

The weaving together of family of origin work and couple treatment is central to longer term couple work. This pastor did an excellent job of setting the stage for such work since she was leading from a BFST orientation of emotional support and thinking response. Good boundaries were maintained and she sent them off with a clear self chosen plan.

Warm Blooded Pastoral Care

The energy for doing the work of pastoral care comes from inside the pastor while the motivation to change stays with the person(s) seeking assistance. BFST teaches that we are not experts on anyone else's life. In fact, focusing on trying to understand and manage our own life rather than other peoples' makes us much safer and fun to be around. Self-differentiated consultants to human problems are motivated by their innate and ever expanding interest in the human condition. Willing change in others is the guaranteed burnout position. The chances of burnout in a self-differentiated approach are much less because this is a self sustaining, emotionally "warm blooded" approach to consultation. As Ed Friedman says,

> When the task of the clinician (pastor) becomes learning about life rather than imposing change, the challenge of therapy (pastoral care) lies no longer in the contest of will with the client (parishioner), but in satisfying one's own curiosity about what makes people tick.[4]

Religiously believing in the resources of the person or group is another legacy of a systems thinking approach to helping. This belief is based in nature and counters any notion that someone or some group is unable to help themselves. Human emotional systems are complex dynamic systems demonstrating the qualities of being self-organizing (seeking coherence), non-linear (small difference can make big difference) and simultaneously recursive and emergent (change emerges from stability). These are strengths built into families by nature. Staying curious and believing that change can come in mysterious ways respects the inborn resources of those seeking help. Pastoral care triage then is self sustaining, curious and offered from a consistent theory of human functioning while leading with both heart and mind.

Pastoral Triage Guidelines

Below are the pastoral triage guidelines I use in my work:

I connect with the individual or group by listening to their story while thinking about what systems dynamics are at play. I follow the facts, appreciate the feelings, and fill in the context. I am respectful of the chosen vulnerability involved in asking for help.

I believe in the regenerative forces of life at work in the person and the emotional system of which they are a part. I try to stay out of the way of those forces so as to assist rather than hinder the learning and growth processes rooted in nature.

I am prepared to explore all avenues of self improvement. If self study and peer support are what is within their means then that will be encouraged. I will also explain family of origin work and direct them to written guides for this.

I stay curious because that is who I am not as a technique to discover solutions. Being curious is its own reward. The more I learn about a person or family the more they learn about themselves and the closer they get to finding their way to adjustments that nature is attempting to teach them.

I pay attention to my body during and after pastoral triage visits. I look for connections to my family of origin noting any emotional triggers or parallel processes.

I have consultation resources to call on when I find it hard to stay in my thinking brain and as a regular practice to keep me sharp in applying BFST to my ministry.

My pastoral care curiosity is a natural extension of my self curiosity and the learning that grows out of my own family of origin work. This work is my qualification to be curious with others about their lives. This work helps me understand and regulate my emotional triggers, over functioning and anxieties so I can more readily move beyond them.

I observe without judgment. I try to focus more on emotional process and family dynamics than on the content of the problem or story. "Where are the triangles?" "Who is under or over functioning?" "Where is the fusion or cutoff?" "Can this problem be seen as a gift to this person or family?" "Who is motivated to learn/change?"

I expect resistance to my way of thinking about the situation. My gift to the person or group is my objectivity and neutrality not my agreement. Many folks are not interested in their world view being challenged. I intend to be helpful without needing to be.

I refuse to take any responsibility for people's lives, choices or wellness. I am responsible to connect and reflect via curiosity and objectivity to the best of my capacity. Anything further and I would have to draw up adoption papers.

I am patient with the growth process. Major transitions take two years to integrate into life. Typically I am supporting shifts within developmental processes over long periods of time more than solutions in the present.

I relate to the person behind their symptoms. I fill in their autobiographical narrative in such a way that a larger context for the presenting problem is established.

I think in terms of scenarios more than solutions. My anxious brain is a squeezed brain, not very flexible and not very far-sighted. Wondering about scenarios both positive and disastrous with neutrality can stimulate the thinking system.

Above all I stay playful. I think in terms of reversals and reframes that turn things upside down and sideways. When I find this difficult I am too much in my feeling system.

Conclusion

Pastoral triage from a BFST orientation then, is a self sustaining, curiosity driven, belief in regenerative qualities of all people, heart and mind ministry that occupies a vital place within the matrix of the helping professions.

> When people are neither depending very much on affirmation from others to enhance their own well-being nor feeling inordinately responsible for enhancing someone else's well-being, they are fairly calm – psychologically and physiologically. This calm ... is simply a way of being that is consistent with a way of thinking.[5]

In my thirty plus years in ministry as a pastoral psychotherapist one quarter of my clients has been clergy or other church professionals. They have, and continue to, teach me a great deal about the wonderful and challenging world of congregational life. What a great context to simultaneously support and challenge, care and learn; in a phrase, lead with heart and mind. I am thankful and curious and open and energized about past, present and future discoveries.

———

[1]Murray Bowen, *Family Therapy in Clinical Practice,* (NY and London, Jason Aronson, 1978) p. 420. Italics added.

[2]Kerr, Michael E. & Bowen, Murray, *Family Evaluation* (W. W. Norton & Co., 1988), p. 284. Parentheses added.

[3]Bowen, 1978, p. 156.

[4]Edwin H. Friedman, *The Myth of the Shiksa and Other Essays* (Church Publishing, 2008), p. 54. Parentheses added.

[5]Kerr and Bowen, 1988, p. 118.

10

Leadership is Easy – Or Is It?

Elaine Boomer

Elaine Boomer M.S.W., is a Licensed Clinical Social Worker in private practice in Vienna, VA. Prior to becoming a therapist, she worked in the corporate marketplace as a Bank Marketing and Training Officer. After receiving her Masters in Social Work in 1994 from Virginia Commonwealth University, she studied with Ed Friedman until his death in 1996. She has been on the faculty of Leadership In Ministry since 1996.

I never really thought of myself as a "leader," certainly not in my family. Over the years I signed up be a chairperson for various church committees in my church and I became a manager in my corporate job. In those days, I thought that being a leader meant organizing, running meetings, assigning tasks, over-seeing tasks, personnel reviews, inspiring people, etc. What naiveté! I had much to learn. It was only when I met and worked with Dr. Edwin Friedman that I learned what leadership really meant. It started with my family.

I was overly focused on my children and husband. I assumed responsibility for everyone's functioning and had little time or energy to focus on my own goals and my own functioning. I was stressed, unhappy, and tired, and it wasn't working for anyone. Dr. Friedman called this "over-functioning, " having goals for others that they don't have for themselves. The more I over-functioned in my family, the more my family functioned poorly. I learned to focus more on what I wanted, what I would and what I would not do. I had to learn to let go of the outcome of the things that weren't really in my control. It was difficult and anxiety producing, but slowly my children began to function more effectively. What I learned in my family was easily transferred to work systems.

According to Bowen Family Systems Theory (BFST), effective leadership involves being clear about your own goals, defining yourself, and managing your own emotional reactivity while staying in touch with the rest of the family or group members. Interestingly enough, when we do this, the group tends to follow. Systemic anxiety is reduced and more thinking occurs. In this way, we hold space for the vision and allow adventuresome creativity to take up residence. Anyone can practice leadership no matter what your position—family member, committee member, associate pastor, middle manager, lead pastor, CEO, or chairperson.

Working the theory by looking at our family and/or organizational history and patterns paves way for:

- Developing awareness of relationship patterns
- Decreasing cause and effect thinking
- Learning to relate to difficult others
- Increasing the repertoire of responses
- Considering multiple variables in any situation
- Clearing the path to develop knowledge and skills.

Without the investigation and study of these patterns we are subject to automatic functioning that cloud the vision we have for ourselves, church and family. We get tangled in reactivity such as distancing to avoid social pressure or addressing that which causes us discomfort. We capitulate or yield when we need to stand firm. We get into conflicts or try to force others to do our will. We engage in uncompromising triangles with others as a way of dealing with the anxiety in ourselves or others. This kind of reactivity goes from one member of the group to another in a chain reaction pattern. The total pattern is similar to electronic circuits in which each person is wired or connected by radio to all other people with whom he has a relationship. In other words, emotional reactivity is catching just like the flu!

None of us enters into a leadership position starting from ground zero. We inherit leadership positions in systems that are already "in play." We have to contend with past history, past leaders, societal pressures, set patterns, immature members and hidden agendas. The starting place is the investigation of your own family of origin patterns. Secondly, research the history of your church or organization. Thirdly, work on your own reactivity and have clarity about your own goals and values. Now what? We still have to contend with what is already there. Perhaps the next step is to put yourself in a place of potential by considering your unique gifts. Ask yourself what does this moment in time bring, what can I put in place right now, and where do I go from here. It's a matter of knowing what is on your watch and what you can attend to right now.

It helps to have resilience, a larger repertoire, and life balance. It also helps if you can learn to live with the disappointment of not getting where you want to be. Family patterns dictate who we are and how we have learned to function – both intentionally and automatically. It is the same with organizations. I find that it helps me to think about the qualities of leadership that are in me as a result of the people in my multi-generational family. Strengths are passed down through the generations both in families and in organizations. Here are some questions to ask yourself about what you bring to the table.

- What is my role if I'm the most powerful person in the group?
- How do I make others feel more powerful?

- How do I manage when the most powerful person is dysfunctional?
- What can I do when the "mission" is in jeopardy?
- How do I function when I bump up against authority?
- When can I allow ambiguity rather than rigidity?

11

Self-Differentiated Pastoral Leaders

Michael Lee Cook

Michael Lee Cook, ThD, LMFT is a licensed marriage and family therapist and pastoral psychotherapist in private-practice at Micah Counseling Services in Peachtree City, Georgia. He provides counseling to individuals, couples, families, and groups as well as congregational and organizational consulting. Dr. Cook is the author of Black Fatherhood, Adoption, and Theology *(Peter Lang Publishing, 2015).*

"Leadership has inherent power because effecting a change in relationship systems is facilitated more fundamentally by how leaders function within their families than by the quantity of their expertise."

— Edwin H. Friedman, *Generation to Generation*

A pastor accepted the pastorate at a local church seven years ago. During this time, he has regularly found it difficult to work with some members. Most of the tensions have been related to the direction and vision of the church, particularly over trying to find ways to meet the growing needs of the congregation on an increasingly dwindling budget.

In the past five years, the church has lost about thirty-five percent of its membership—primarily due to an aging congregation. These tensions have created an atmosphere of anger, anxiety, fear, loss, and mistrust in the church and within its leadership. The tension came to a head in a recent trustee meeting. During a discussion over the annual budget, the pastor got into an angry verbal altercation with a trustee.

He called the trustee "stupid" and said, "You are acting just like my stupid father who was terrible with money." This incident has deepened the relational tensions between the pastor and church leadership.

Introduction

Pastoral leadership is fundamentally about relationships. Indeed, ministry effectiveness is largely dependent upon the relational smarts and skills of pastoral leaders.[1] What is more, relational competence becomes far more crucial and important in times of high anxiety, stress, and uncertainty. It is in these moments that pastoral leaders must be sufficiently self-differentiated to achieve effectiveness in interpersonal relationships. In this short essay, I will explore the concept of self-differentiation in the context of pastoral leadership. Accordingly, I will briefly define and discuss self-differentiation; consider its implications for pastoral leadership; and propose several guidelines to help pastoral leaders develop and strengthen their self-differentiation. In the end, I hope to illuminate the need, importance, and usefulness of self-differentiation in effective pastoral leadership.

Self-Differentiation

Dr. Murray Bowen, a psychiatrist at Georgetown University, conceptualized the Bowen Family Systems Theory—a constructive theory about family structure and functioning within the field of family therapy. A major concept within his theory is differentiation of self.[2] In basic terms, differentiation of self (or as sometimes called, self-differentiation) is an individual's capacity to function independently while remaining emotionally connected to others—particularly when anxiety levels are elevated. This means that an individual can maintain control of his or her thoughts, emotions, and responses in relationships with others. In circumstances of emotional intensity, self-differentiated persons can remain connected and resist the urge to withdraw or cut-off relationships. Bowen theorized that individuals must experience sufficient self-differentiation from their families of origin to sufficiently self-differentiate in other interpersonal relationships. This emotional and familial shift is certainly necessary for those seeking to become effective pastoral leaders.

Implications for Pastoral Leadership

Congregations have often been characterized as families. Indeed, Edwin H. Friedman, suggested that in congregations "three distinct families" are present: "the families within the congregation, our congregations, and our own."[3] In the process of becoming self-differentiated, pastoral leaders are helped by viewing interpersonal relationships as microcosms of their own family systems and the "growing edges" they inspire. This is because interpersonal relationships, particularly stressful ones, will often awaken and stimulate experiences from our families of origin.

Therefore, in many ways, pastoral leadership can, and often does, take on the feel and process of family life. Case in point, the pastor above was impacted by this reality in his conflict with the trustee. Under intense anxiety, the pastor projected his unresolved issues around money with his father into his relationship with the trustee and within the church's leadership. Self-differentiated pastoral leaders are aware of the significant connections between their families of origin and leadership functioning. Consequently, they work to strength their self-differentiation to enhance their social-skills and interpersonal functioning.

Guidelines for Developing Self-Differentiation

Developing self-differentiation is a lifelong process. It must be worked on continuously and directly over the course of one's life and experiences. Notwithstanding, I believe there are several ways pastoral leaders can actively work on and strengthen self-differentiation, thereby becoming more effective in their lives in ministry. Consider the following guidelines:

Engage in Family-of-Origin Work

Early life experiences, particularly in the family of origin, largely sets the tone for the way we understand ourselves individually, and within relationships with others. This is particularly so when it comes to significant others (e.g., mother, father, etc.) who shape and influence us. Simply, family life is the primary site for personality development.[4] We often learn everything from politics to religion; education to marriage; and sex and parenting in and from our families of origin.

Sometimes the experience goes well. At other times, not so much. Thus, family of origin work entails closely examining and exploring our family experiences and understanding how they enhance or restrict our functioning in interpersonal relationships.

The genogram is a tool commonly used to map these relationships and connections, particularly the emotional aspects of them.[5] Family of origin work sets the foundation for self-differentiation and more effective pastoral leadership. Personal counseling/psychotherapy often serves as a key resource on this journey.

Cultivate Self-Awareness

Self-awareness is a cornerstone in the development of self-differentiation. Here, self-awareness is understood as the capacity to define one's commitments, goals, and values in a way that is consistent with who one wants to be in the world. Further, leadership theorist Daniel Goldman defines self-awareness as "the ability to recognize and understand your moods, emotions, and drives, as well as their effect on others."[6] Self-aware pastoral leaders have well-defined goals and values that order their lives. They also possess a deep awareness of how their emotions and behaviors impact those they lead and are sensitive to the emotional states of those they lead. Development of self-awareness is built on continuous critical examination of one's life experiences with the goal of moving towards greater self-differentiation and formation.

Develop a Theology of Pastoral Leadership

Pastoral leadership is fundamentally a theological and formation process. That is, it is grounded in a deep call of faith.[7]

Whether you are working in the role of a parish pastor; institutional chaplain; faith-based non-profit organization; or the like, you are engaged in the vocation of pastoral leadership. When pastoral leaders develop, understand, and root their vocations in clearly articulated theological terms, it allows them to better self-differentiate. Practically, they are better able to define themselves theologically in relationship to others as pastoral leaders. They know who they are in God and how this identity shapes the relationships with those they are called to serve. This clarity sets the tone for more controlled emotional engagement with others and oneself.

Conclusion

In this essay, I sought to demonstrate the importance and implications of the concept of self-differentiation for effective pastoral leadership and offer several guidelines to help pastoral leaders develop and cultivate self-differentiation. As noted, ministry is fundamentally about relationships. When pastoral leaders are sufficiently self-differentiated, they are often more effective in life, interpersonal relationships, and ministry. As author Roberta M. Gilbert noted, ". . . any change in the level of [self] differentiation makes for a radical difference in functioning in all areas of life, particularly relationships."[8] Thus, by sufficiently self-differentiating, we simply can become more of what God will have us be with those we are called to serve.

---

[1]Roy M. Oswald and Arland Jacobson, *The Emotional Intelligence of Jesus: Relational Smarts for Religious Leaders* (New York: Rowman & Littlefield), 119.

[2]Murray Bowen, *Family Therapy in Clinical Practice* (New York: Jason Aronson, 1978).

[3]Edwin H. Friedman, *Generation to Generation* (New York, The Guilford Press, 2011), 1.

[4]Ronald W. Richardson, *Couples in Conflict: A Family Systems Approach to Marriage Counseling* (Minneapolis: Fortress Press, 2010), 61-68.

[5]For an excellent resource on genograms see Israel Galindo, Elaine Boomer, and Don Reagan, *A Family Genogram Workbook* (Richmond: Educational Consultants, 2006).

[6]Daniel Goldman, "What Makes a Leader?" *Harvard Business Review,* November-December, 1998, 37.

[7]Roy M. Oswald and Arland Jacobson, *The Emotional Intelligence of Jesus: Relational Smarts for Religious Leaders* (New York: Rowman & Littlefield, 2015), 105.

[8]Roberta M. Gilbert, *Extraordinary Relationships: A New Way of Thinking About Human Interactions* (New York: John Wiley & Sons, Inc., 1992), 25.

12

Reciprocity in the Emotional Field

Israel Galindo

"Is there one word which may serve as a rule of practice all one's life?"
The Master said, "Is not reciprocity such a word?"

Confucious, *The Analects*, Book 15, Chapter 23

"A population can be very successful in spite of a surprising diversion of time and energy into aggressive displays, squabbling and outright fights. The examples range from bumble bees to European nations."

William Hamilton, *The Innate Social Aptitudes of Man* (1975)

Human relationships are governed by reciprocity dynamics. In a real sense, all relationships are reciprocal and transactional. These dynamics are a product of the system and are mediated by the emotional field of the system in which the persons, as actors, function.

Reciprocity is a phenomenon across biological systems. Reciprocity is a shared dependence, cooperation, or exchange between persons or groups for mutual benefit, or personal advantage. A common misunderstanding, however, is that reciprocity is "fair." The reality is that reciprocity does not have to be equitable.

Reciprocity and Evolution

Winterhauder and Smith help explain the role evolutionary processes have shaped reciprocity dynamics that impact us today. "Only with the evolution of reciprocity or exchange–based food transfers did it become economical for individual hunters to target large game. The effective value of a large mammal to a lone forager probably was not great enough to justify the cost of attempting to pursue and capture it. However, once effective systems of reciprocity or exchange augment the effective value of very large packages to the hunter, such prey items would be more likely to enter the optimal diet."[1]

Studies in natural systems indicate that there are biological and evolutionary influences, if not bases, for reciprocity in relationship systems. Robert Trivers, in "The Evolution of Reciprocal Altruism" provides an account for how natural selection can operate against cheaters in relationship systems. The details of the psychological system that regulates altruism were set by selection to set the tendencies at a balance appropriate to social and ecological environments. The reciprocity dynamic exists at multiple levels. Each level has emergent qualities and dynamics that do not exist in the lower level, or, do not apply to the same extent. The more complex the level, and the nature of relationships, the more complex the "rules" of reciprocity (e.g., differentials related to equity).[2]

DIAGRAM 1: Levels and Emergent Qualities

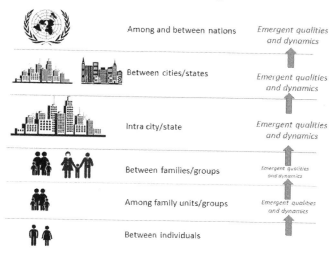

Bowles and Gintis argue that the reciprocity dynamics in relationship systems evidence in evolutionary history still guide us today. "The fundamental challenges of social living and sustaining a livelihood that our distant ancestors faced are in many respects not fundamentally different from those we face today. Modern states and global markets have provided conditions for mutualistic cooperation among strangers on a massive scale, but altruistic cooperation remains an essential requirement of economic and social life."[3] This implies that reciprocity is a dynamic that exists in all levels of relationship systems, from individual to global, each with emergent nuances of what reciprocity entails.

Richard Leakey attributed the very nature of humans to reciprocity. He claims humans survived because our ancestors learned to share goods and services "in an honored network of obligation."[4] Thus, the idea that humans are indebted to repay gifts and favors is a unique aspect of human culture. Cultural anthropologists support this idea in what they call the "web of indebtedness" where reciprocity is viewed as an adaptive mechanism to enhance survival.

Charles Darwin described the effect of reciprocity in individuals and society. "Selfish and contentious people will not cohere, and without coherence, nothing can be effected. A tribe possessing a greater number of courageous, sympathetic and faithful members, who were always ready to warn each other of danger, to aid and defend each other ... would spread and be victorious over other tribes. Thus the social and moral qualities would tend slowly to advance and be diffused throughout the world."[5]

Through the rules of reciprocity, sophisticated systems of aid and trade were possible bringing benefits to the societies that utilized them. Given the benefits of reciprocity at the societal level, it is not surprising that the norm has persisted and dictates our present cognition and behavior in relationship systems.

Reciprocity is not only a strong determining factor of human behavior; it is a powerful method for gaining one's compliance with a request. The rule of reciprocity has the power to trigger feelings of indebtedness even when faced with an uninvited favor and irrespective of liking the person who executed the favor.

In 1976, Phillip Kunz demonstrated the automatic nature of reciprocity in an experiment using Christmas cards. In this experiment, Kunz sent out holiday cards with pictures of his family and a brief note to a group of complete strangers. To his surprise holiday cards came pouring back from people he had never met. The majority of those who responded never inquired about Kunz's identity, they were merely responding to his gesture with a reciprocal action.[6]

Politics is another area where the power of reciprocity is evident. While politicians often claim autonomy from the feelings of obligation associated with gifts and favors that influence everyone else, they are also susceptible. In the 2002 election, U.S. Congress Representatives who received the most money from special interest groups were over seven times more likely to vote in favor of the group that had contributed the most money to their campaigns.

The Emotional Field

The reciprocity dynamics are played out in the emotional field. The position one occupies in the system has influence, if not determinative, of one's reciprocity functioning in a system. While universal principles apply to all relationship systems, systems of a type mediate how reciprocity dynamics get played out (e.g., family, school, work, political systems). Given this, it's interesting to hear the current chatter about "running Government like a business." This is something every clergy at some point faces: calls for running a church like a business.

As with all emotional process dynamics and functioning, reciprocity is morally "neutral." It manifests itself as a function of the emotional process in the systems. For example, reciprocity can express itself as competition or altruism. Conditions in the emotional field (shortages of resources, level of anxiety), or, multigenerational patterns may dictate the dynamics or "rules" of reciprocity.

DIAGRAM 2: The Emotional Field

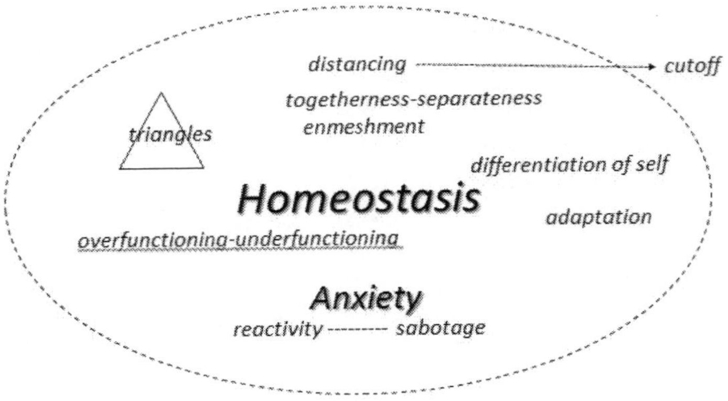

Reciprocity dynamics are played out in the emotional field. Reciprocity exchanges are a significant dynamic in maintaining homeostasis. Again, it does not have to be equitable. If someone who is not supposed to have "more" (more goods, health, influence, etc.) gets "more," the system introduces reciprocal forces to return to homeostasis. Religious systems use "social emotions" to effect reciprocity in behavior, often more effective than punishment. Know your system! Don't confuse one for the other (a congregation is not "family," and may not be "church"). That is, it's fine to "play politics" at a school board or housing association, but not in your family. For example, in religious systems, shame and guilt are "social emotions" used to influence reciprocity. They help enforce communal values and keep behavior in check in a system where togetherness is an important homeostatic force. Using the same reciprocity dynamic in a biological family, however (shame and guilt), will likely result in severe dysfunction and psychic harm.

Reciprocity and the Four Player Part

I have found Kantor and Lehr's four-player part schema helpful in observing reciprocity dynamics in the emotional transactive process during consultations, committee meetings, faculty meetings, and in boards. Kantor and Lehr observed a pattern of reciprocity in relationship systems in which a movement in the field (initiated by the Mover), solicited patterned responses from within the players in the system. Similar to small group dynamics these reciprocal responses were a product of the emotional field. These are universal reciprocal responses relate to change, and change, even the threat of change, poses challenges to a system's homeostasis.[7] Because this reciprocity pattern is universal, Kantor and Lehr claim, it can be a very helpful lens for a leader for interpreting the emotional process at play, especially when the leader plays the part of Mover.

Here is a description of each player in this dynamic schema:

THE MOVER

The Mover is the initiator of any action: an offer, a vision, a strategy, etc. Typically, the Mover is the leader in the system (the person in the "L" position), for example, the faculty dean who proposes a new policy or a change in curriculum, whether a schedule, room assignments, or a change in course distributions. Or a pastor who proposes a new vision, a new staff position, a new ministry, a change in the worship service. The Mover, however, can be another in the system who proposes or initiated an action. Indeed, anyone can become the Mover insofar as that person initiates an action, be it a proposal, challenge, complaint, invitation, or call to action.

Initially, the Mover seeks to gain access to a target within the affect, power, or meaning dimensions in the system. The Mover establishes the context for the others' response. Without a wide range of alternatives Movers can get locked into reenacting the same basic strategy over and over (reactive or unimaginative loops).

Movers, therefore, need a wide repertoire and imagination in anticipating the initial resistance to any initiation. For example, the family in which the parents only acknowledge children when they are "bad" reduce the range of options for interaction have limited their repertoire for reciprocity with the children. This also sets a narrow reactive pattern for the children as they learn that the way to get parents' attention is to disrupt family life by "being bad."

THE OPPOSER

The Opposer's function becomes to challenge the action of the mover. This person either obstructs the action of the mover (resistance or sabotage), or, pulls away from it (passive-aggressive, distancing). This creates a challenge by blocking the Mover's direction or intended goal. Again, these reciprocity dynamics are not "good" or "bad," they are systemically neutral. For example, Opposers may redirect the system and its members into more fruitful direction than those suggested by its movers. One can readily see that while this reciprocity position is "neutral," it can be positive or negative depending on the particular content, context, or intent.

Kantor and Lehr describe four possible responses from the Opposer: (1) the person's resistance can be global or specific in the challenge to the mover; (2) the person may redirect and teach, (3) may assault and attack, or (4) may become an ignored dissenter or a tyrant who consistently resists change in the status quo by systematically rejecting other member's mover initiatives without ever daring to play the part of Mover himself.

It may be helpful to conflict-averse leaders, when acting as movers and confronted by opposers, to remember that criticism is a form or pursuit, and that conflict is a form of intimacy or togetherness.

In rigid unimaginative relationship systems a person may be consistently relegated to the role of Opposer. If so, this person may become isolated, rejected, and in general made a victim (Identified Patient) by the system's unimaginative and reactive strategic process.

Opposers can make positive contributions to the system, however. They can help set limits on the energies and directions of the Mover, thus protecting the system from developing into a potentially tyrannical one by imposing checks and balances. By criticizing and dissenting, the Opposer can help the system engage in dialogue and to some extent, promote differentiation.

THE FOLLOWER

The Follower agrees with the action taken by the mover and moves in support of the center of action. According to Kantor and Lehr the Follower can respond out of three spheres: Affect, Meaning, and Power:

Affect: "Yes I am with you, sink or swim. because I love you."

Meaning: "Regarding this value, I believe the same as you." (acting out of principles and values)

Power: "Anyone who doesn't restrict my freedom has my support."

The Follower moves to support either the mover or the Opposer (therefore creating a triangle). This person is a prototype ally and joiner. Remaining in the role of Follower, this person has no potential for initiating his or her own movement. As with all reactivity reciprocity patterns, birth order functioning may apply to how the Follower (and all other players) react.

The Follower has potential for shifting his or her alliance from the mover to the oppressor. They can maintain independence by shifting alliance, or, lose autonomy by fixing support irrevocably on mover or Opposer. On the other hand these persons may maintain allegiance with both Mover and

Opposer (for example, supporting the intent of mover, but supporting the Opposer's rationale), but risks degenerating to double speak and losing credibility.

These persons have capacity to empower others in the system by granting them support and so are actively sought by movers and opposers. Kantor and Lehr stated "We believe that a system in which the mover and the opposer parts do not in principle have access to a follower's support will soon be in difficulty."[8] In some cases Movers and Opposers will seek to gain enough Followers to reach a tipping point for their advantage. It is worth noting, for example, the observation that in most cases of clergy forced termination the tipping point for ousting a pastor is ten people.

THE BYSTANDER

Bystanders often act as witnesses to the mover's action but acknowledge neither agreement or disagreement. They can be neutral or disengaged. Either way, they place themselves on the periphery of the action field. Bystanders are "watchers," being a witness to system's events, initially keeping what they think to themselves.

Witnessing itself, however, can be a force exerted on and felt by participants in the field. Those being observed will often feel unease and try to force the bystander to state what he or she thinks. By preserving neutrality this person maintains his or her options open.

The Bystander has three options: (1) remain as bystander, staying in place and continuing to be witness. He can remain silent, articulate his views in private, or, she can express opinions in public in a way that she does not move closer to other parties in the system; (2) leave the field to act as mover in a new sequence, or (3) move into action as opposer.

In terms of reciprocity, Bystanders stay out of the direct action in the field (de-triangles). This person makes no alliances with mover, opposer, or follower, though she or he may make bilateral alliances to maintain security of position. The bystander may shift from the periphery closer to the action. In doing so, however, runs the risk of being pulled into the conflict and relinquishing the role of bystander.

General Rules in the Four-Player Reciprocity Transactions

The following general rules apply to the four-player reciprocity dynamics:

1. These are transactive functions within an emotional field. They are neither "good" nor "bad."

2. Any social action initiated by one member in a system stimulates a reaction from the other members. This is a product of homeostasis in the emotional field, or, togetherness-separateness reciprocity dynamics.

3. These are reciprocal roles that facilitate or maintain emotional process. It is less helpful to see these are personality-driven or "individual" actions.

4. Any two or more people have the same basic options at their disposal in their roles relating to one another.

5. Kantor and Lehr contend "Even when there are only two persons present, there are four parts ready to be played, and if the relationship is to continue, all four parts most certainly will be played."[8]

6. The four basic roles encompass all potential moves individuals may make in an interactional relationship system.

7. These roles are in the context of two sets of opposing forces: (1) inner directedness vs. outer directedness, and (2) togetherness vs. separateness.

8. These forces create stress, if not anxiety, about defining self in relation to others, and the relation of others to self.

9. Individuals in a system are actors in relation to other actors in the emotional field. Therefore, any individual may play a different role given occasion and circumstance. In rigid systems, some roles may be assigned to one individual specifically, becoming an IP, foil, or scapegoat. "Consequently, as an actor in a social field, the individual may locate his participation at a level of unconscious, self-conscious, or system-consciousness. Consequently, the individual's internal feedback system can affect and even alter family process, especially in those situations in which the individual's psychopolitical decision is at variance with the system's expectations or demands, including the demands made by his own system-consciousness."[9]

10. Each individual seeks and negotiates for a place in the family or relationship system, in order that he or she may be affirmed by the family in ways that are compatible with his or her own needs, and optimally, with the goals of the family or relationship system. So, the individual consciously develops personal strategies in response to his family's strategies. These, then, are carried over into other relationship systems, like a work setting or a congregation.

11. As long as the initial action continues and a player maintains his position as mover, follower, or opposer, he or she cannot leave the field. Only the bystander can leave the field.

12. Individuals not only become familiar with the playing of certain parts, but also these parts continue to be played in social interaction far removed in time and place from the family of origin.[11] This is an influence of multigenerational transmission and the emotional projection process.

13. The advantage to leaders is that in relatively rigid systems the reciprocity of the players is predictable. You can anticipate who will always oppose a new idea or imitative, or, you can anticipate who the cheerleaders are, who the passive bystanders will be, and who the followers will tend to be.

Questions to ponder:

1. How does reciprocity manifest itself in your ministry context?
2. What four-player part role do you tend to play? Is it congruent with your position in the system? Does it replicate your family of origin functioning?
3. What were the four-player reciprocity dynamics in your family of origin?

---

[1]Winterhauder and Smith, *Evolutionary Ecology and Human Behavior* (Aldine Transaction, 1991), p. 60.

[2]Robert L. Trivers, "The Evolution of Reciprocal Altruism" in *The Quarterly Review of Biology*, Vol. 46, No. 1 (March 1971), pp. 35-57.

3Samuel Bowles and Herbert Gintis, *A Cooperative Species: Human Reciprocity and its Evolution* (Princeton University Press, 2011), p. 199.

[4]Richard Leakey, *The First Humans: Origin and Early Evolution of the Genus Homo* (Springer International Publishing, 2009).

[5]Charles Darwin, *The Decent of Man* (1873).

[6]Phillip R Kunz and Michael Woolcott, "Season's greetings: From my status to yours," *Social Science Research.* 5 (3): 269–278.

[7]Kantor, D. and William Lehr, *Inside the Family: Toward a Theory of Family Process* (Harper & Row, Publishers, 1976 (originally published by Jossey-Bass, 1975).

[8]Ibid., p. 181.

[9]Ibid., p. 187.

[10]Ibid., p. 179.

[11]Ibid., p. 240-1.

❖

13

Theology and Family Systems Theory
in Dialogue

Lawrence E. Matthews

This chapter is from a lecture presented by The Reverend Dr. Lawrence E. Matthews as the J. C. Wynn Lecture at Colgate Rochester Divinity School in Rochester, New York, on November 5, 1998.

We live in one of those historic moments when the forces of rapid change and the accompanying social crises cry out for maturity and informed judgment. At the same time, however, these same forces work in opposition to the very qualities so desperately needed. Viewed from the perspective of the human venture, ours is a familiar situation. To live relatively secure and satisfying lives on spaceship earth has never been easy. Yet ours is a new situation in so far as we are having to deal with the effects of a revolution in communication technology that immediately brings the major crises of the entire world into the living rooms of our homes.

The diagnoses and the prescriptions for cure of our situation multiply daily. A recurring theme is the need for (1) clearer understanding of the problems and (2) effective leadership to address them. There continues to be, however, a lack of agreement as to the true nature of our problems and of leadership itself. In this paper I will focus upon two resources which I believe offer valuable insights into these issues: theology and family systems theory—in particular the pioneering theoretical work of Dr. Murray Bowen and its application to leadership as taught by

Rabbi Edwin Friedman. I believe the understanding of leadership that emerges from a genuine dialogue between them can be a source of hope as we confront our present situation.

A Different Understanding of Leadership

According to Bowen, our moment in history can be understood as a period of what he termed societal regression, one of those times when the chronic, free-floating anxiety that is always present in societies spikes. Bowen understood the human venture as a constant struggle between two forces that compete for dominance in all persons. There is the togetherness force that moves us towards each other and the individual force that moves us toward distinct personhood. He observed that as anxiety heightens, the togetherness force becomes more dominant and results in a stuck-togetherness that subverts the individual force which moves us in the direction of less reactive, more thoughtful functioning. As a result, our anxiety-driven tribalism and reactivity defeat the very resources we need to get unstuck.

My mentor in Bowen Theory, Edwin Friedman, characterized our present situation as one in which:

> ... the focus shifts toward pathology rather than strength, safety becomes more important than adventure, adaptation is toward the dependent and empathy becomes more important than responsibility.[1]

Some families and individuals are able to respond less reactively and more thoughtfully to heightened anxiety in their surroundings, but these seem always to constitute a minority. The vast majority are caught up in the free floating societal anxiety and are, therefore, most vulnerable in times of societal regression. Their reaction is to displace their personal and family anxieties into institutions that are themselves caught up in the collective anxiety of the moment. The process is accelerated by a media that has both the technology and economic motivation to constantly raise the anxiety level.

At such times, problems surface in every human institution, but their presence is keenly experienced in those that are characterized by the most personal and intense relationships. Families and religious institutions are at the top of the list. Home may be where the heart is, but it is also the place where whatever is happening in the other organs of those who live there is shared, especially fear, anger and blame. And religious institutions are not far behind as members displace their personal and family problems into churches and synagogues already caught up in the anxiety of the larger community.

Now I turn to the other perspective in this dialogue: theology. Seward Hiltner, a pioneer in the field of pastoral care and counseling, taught me that the unique function of theology is to inquire into and rethink the faith in the light of all available data, and to do so on behalf of all believers. He cautioned that since this investigation must always be done in the light of revelation, there can be no simple baptizing of the point of view of any particular philosophy or science. However, his assumption was that these other efforts, and I include Bowen Family Systems Theory, contain accurate descriptions of "the way things are" from their perspectives. Likewise, theology brings to the dialogue with philosophy and science (and again I include Bowen Theory) a description of "the way things are" from a depth dimension uniquely its own.

I believe a theological diagnosis of our present predicament begins with a realistic view of the human situation and of God's activity in it. Created in the image of God, human beings are not gods. We are finite beings who share much in common with the rest of the created world, especially the capacity for anxious, self-destructive behavior. A theological word would also include the invitation to embrace this reality through faith in God, whose faithfulness alone can ultimately calm our frantic attempts at self-salvation. As always, this word of grace is mostly either unheard or unheeded. But in spite of such rejection, God persists in redeeming the beloved creation and the resources of grace and healing are always present. I am convinced that what we call "leadership" is one means by which these divinely offered resources can be present in our situation. To reflect theologically upon this concept is, I believe, to identify the phenomenon we call "leadership" as one of the built-into-creation means by which God can be creatively present in the life process.

A primary concept of Bowen Theory is the reality of what Bowen called the "emotional system." It is not an easy concept to grasp, but it is basic to this understanding of leadership. Dr. Michael Kerr, who followed Murray Bowen as Director of the Georgetown Family Center, understands the emotional system as " ... a naturally occurring system in all forms of life that enables an organism to receive information (from within itself and its environment), to integrate that information and respond on the basis of it."[2]

It extends beyond the individual to include relationship systems. One way Friedman conceptualized this was in terms of field theory.

In field theory parts of a system do not function simply according to their nature. Rather they express that part of their nature that is promoted or inhibited by their position in an overall set of relationships. One may apply this way of thinking to transistors, to genes, to the planets or to the members of a family or team.[3]

What we call leadership is viewed from this perspective as a natural phenomenon that fulfills an important function within an emotional system. It is an essential dimension of the emotional process of every relational system. The way the leader functions affects the entire system and the systemic processes themselves. It even has the power to modify the emotional processes transmitted from previous generations.

Since Bowen's initial focus was upon the family emotional system, his understanding of leadership emerged from his work with families. He wrote:

> Operationally, ideal family treatment begins when one can find a family leader with the courage to define self, who is as invested in the welfare of the family as in self, who is neither angry nor dogmatic, whose energy goes to changing self rather than telling others what they should do. ... A family leader is beyond the popular notion of power.[4]

To think this way about leadership requires nothing less than a paradigm shift. Rather than focusing upon others, leaders are challenged to focus upon self-care and self-expression as the keys to their influence upon the functioning of others. Such an understanding does not lessen the importance of the role of the leader. What it does is reframe that role. It shifts the leader's responsibility from how others function (over which he or she has little control) to how the leader functions, over which the leader has a great deal of control. Although the leader's functioning always affects the system, it becomes especially important in periods of high anxiety like our own. When understood within this systemic framework, leadership offers the possibility of creative response in times of heightened anxiety. I believe it makes possible a posture of hopefulness amid circumstances that easily result in reactions of despair and cynicism.

The operative word is possibility. If leadership is a naturally occurring phenomenon in all relational systems, the possibilities offered by the phenomenon are realized only through choices and actions. Therefore the possibility of incorrect choices and ultimately harmful actions is always present. Applied to family and religious institutions, the leadership position can be filled in ways that bring disaster to the relational system just as surely as this function can be carried out in ways that benefit it. Although Bowen Theory offers us a new way of thinking about relationships and relationship systems, it does not provide us with an automatic solution to the problems we face. It is not a quick fix. However, I believe it does provide a way to address our problems.

According to the theory, the way to more adequate and less reactive functioning is through a process Bowen called the differentiation of self. Simply stated, this concept refers to the life-long process of growing a self from the inside. From birth all of us are shaped by the relational systems in which we live. These outside emotional forces tell us who we are and what it means to be a person in our particular family and culture. We are literally defined from outside ourselves.

As persons "grow up" and increasingly choose their responses and act from motives that arise from within themselves, this inwardly determined functioning has the potential for affecting the emotional process of their relational systems. When persons are able to separate (differentiate) from the emotional processes that surround them, they stand a much better chance of providing the vision and challenge necessary for any system to change and grow. The inability to clearly see the way ahead and the lack of courage to make necessary changes usually result from being too emotionally fused with a system rather than from incompetence or any lack of ideas. The shift of focus to a person's functioning ("in here") rather than upon the reactions of the environment ("out there") can connect one to the inner resources needed to persevere and even thrive in a hostile environment. After all, is this not the key to the continued existence of human beings on planet earth?

Friedman was the most influential interpreter of Bowen Theory among leaders of religious institutions. His book, *Generation to Generation*, is now introducing a second generation of religious leaders to this way of thinking. When Friedman applied Bowen Theory to the broader concept of leadership, he spoke of leadership through self-differentiation. This is a description of the qualities and characteristics that enable persons in leadership positions to function in ways that are less reactive to the anxiety in their systems and, therefore, more likely to promote better decision making and functioning on the part of others. It refers to a process and not an accomplishment. It is a life-long work-in-progress that involves taking responsibility for one's thinking and actions and encouraging others to do the same.

Leadership through self-differentiation is a matter of being. It affirms the inherent value of the force that moves us toward individual 'selfhood', while at the same time stressing the importance of being connected to others in ways that truly enhance them and ourselves. It is not a cop-out on either responsibility for self or responsibility to others. Such a concept fits my understanding of the way God is at work in us and through us. And it is broad enough and basic enough to fit every human situation from families to congregations and nations and all the other institutions that result from our life in community.

To conceptualize leadership in this way requires some major shifts in our usual thinking about the subject. The first is a shift in context. As noted already, the emotional system becomes the context for understanding leadership, now viewed as an important dimension of a larger process. This means that one of the key functions of leadership is maintaining awareness of this larger process rather than focusing only upon content. It is amazing how much time and effort leaders spend on content rather than the emotional process, of which the content is only a symptom. Troubled families — and troubled churches –usually focus upon the individual or group designated as "the problem" and ignore the deeper relational dynamics that produced and sustain the problem person or group.

Second, there is a shift in focus. Much of the literature on leadership focuses upon the "others", those "out there" whom the leader is attempting to lead, their goals and their objectives. The assumption seems to be that the leader's major task is to understand and motivate others. Family systems theory reverses the picture. The needs and goals of others are not ignored, but they are prioritized differently. The leader's primary responsibility becomes paying attention to her or his own growth and ideas, realizing that even though you can't put motivation into people, you can challenge them with your ideas and vision.

When a pastor in one of our workshops began to teach this understanding of leadership to her Diaconate, an older life-long member revealed that she understood. She remarked: "This is different. Everything else we have done was to try to change the church. This is about changing ourselves." One of the most helpful analogies regarding this shift in focus is the instruction given to all airline passengers before takeoff: if you have another person you wish to assist in an emergency, put your oxygen mask on first and then help the other person put theirs on.

I know from experience that this shift is met with resistance and misunderstanding by many persons hearing it for the first time, especially those of us who live within a Christian tradition. It sounds selfish and, therefore, wrong. But self, in this sense, has nothing to do with what we usually intend when we use the term "selfish." Friedman maintained that the grammatical uniqueness of the word selfish reflects the ambivalence inherent in the reality of self.

> ... selfish is almost the only word in the English language where the addition of the suffix-ish turns an otherwise neutral noun, self, into the pejorative label, self-ish . Normally, adding -ish to a word only means "having the quality of." Book-ish is not necessarily negative; nor is blue-ish, red-ish, pink-ish, fad-ish, or Jew-ish. ... Why doesn't self-ish mean behaving like or having the character of a self, being "self-y"?[5]

Selfishness then, as the term is usually used, would point to just the opposite: taking from others out of a sense of personal deficiency; focusing upon self out of a sense of lack of self; attempting to fill up perceived inner emptiness by acquiring things or relationships. Bowen Theory assumes a difference between "self" and "pseudo-self". "Pseudo-self" refers to knowledge and beliefs that are acquired from others and are therefore negotiable in relationships with others. Created in response to emotional pressures, pseudo-self can be modified by emotional pressures. "Self", on the other hand, refers to knowledge and beliefs that are expressions of a person's own growth and development. Bowen used the language of biology when he named the process of growing as an emotionally separate human being the "differentiation of self". It is living life from the inside, having a "mind of your own", taking stands that express one's own commitments and ideals and allowing others to do the same. Self is non-negotiable. It simply is. It is who I am, really. It has to do with integrity, honesty and self-regulation.

During a 1987 conference on Bowen Theory and theology, Bowen stated:

> A major quality in the differentiation of self is complete selflessness in which "doing for others" replaces personal selfish goals. Jesus Christ has been a model of total selflessness. ... A well-differentiated self in families has to get beyond the selfish promotion of self. One has always to be aware of "the other". ... When selflessness becomes a thinking model, largely separate from the feeling process, it can become a vehicle for a special form of differentiation. With that orientation, true selflessness, devoid of selfishness, can become part of the differentiation itself.[6]

At the close of a monthly theory session's presentation on the subject of self-differentiation, Friedman, the rabbi who was also a therapist, defined it this way:

To self-differentiate is to be in touch with the universal force of all protoplasm that goes back to creation, is part of evolution and leads, not to narcissism, but to what is basic in all of us that enables connection to take place. It is spiritual.[7]

The more differentiated the self—and I include connection to others—the more natural concern for others becomes. Freed from the responsibility for others (excluding infants, young children and persons incapable of being responsible for themselves), one is freer to be responsible to others. In my work with leaders, from parents to congregational leaders and pastors, nothing is more basic than this shift of focus. Without it, I do not believe one can grasp the radical nature of leadership through self-differentiation. It seems to me that part of the difficulty is the paradoxical nature of the insight itself. Supposedly, the test of good leadership is the ability to focus upon the needs of others. But the assumption of a family systems understanding is that the ability to effectively fulfill the function of leadership in an emotional system requires that we begin with a focus upon the health, maturity and growth of the leader himself or herself. The leadership function is an expression of the "self" of the leader. How the leader functions is the crucial factor and this is understood as a matter of "being" preceding and finding expression through "doing." It has to do with who a person is, one's core responses to life and one's core belief system about life.

Leaders facilitate lasting change by focusing upon the modification of their own behavior and functioning rather than modifying the behavior of others. This understanding of leadership also avoids creating a polarity between leaders and followers. The emphasis is upon the functional position of the leader within the context of the system, not her personality or knowledge. The position of the leader is the leader's responsibility. The leader's task is to function in that position in ways that benefit the ultimate good and goals of the system. The personal formation of others is their responsibility and results from the self-actualizing process of response to challenge rather than imitation or cloning. Simply stated, self-differentiation promotes self-differentiation. The best evidence of an individual's change is the constructive impact it has on the functioning of others. Self-differentiating leaders know this and are better able to resist the temptation to attempt to will others into compliance with their ideas and goals. This is to say that a central ethical issue for leaders is that of coercion.

Leadership Through The Differentiation of Self

If this is what leadership looks like from a family systems perspective, how does one do it? If leadership has to do first with "being," what are the qualities of leaders engaged in the process of self-differentiation?

When Friedman applied Bowen Theory to these questions, he concluded that there are at least three dimensions to this phenomenon we call leadership. I label them "dimensions of a phenomenon" because it seems to me that they are inextricably bound to one another. To examine them individually may be practically helpful, but in doing so we should not forget that each one is a dimension of a unified process being lived out by unique human beings. These are not "three tips for would-be leaders" or "three simple steps to more effective parenting or pastoring". Rather they are three of the more visible signs of the presence of the life-long process of growing "self" from the inside, as contrasted to the pseudo-self we acquire from others. Much of Friedman's work focused upon the relationship between this process of self-differentiation and the phenomenon we call leadership. He spoke and wrote about leadership through self-differentiation, with "through" being the determinative word. Again, the emphasis is upon the direct relationship between a person's self-differentiation and the leadership function of that person within a system.

The first dimension of leadership through self-differentiation is self-regulation. Friedman often referred to this as "non-anxious presence." I prefer language that keeps us focused upon the difficult and challenging process of regulating one's own anxiety. (This was also Friedman's practice in our monthly theory sessions.) I've never met a non-anxious person. In fact, the term is in direct contradiction with a basic tenet of Bowen Theory. Bowen Theory is about anxiety! It assumes that the basic human issue is anxiety. And this is meant to include much more than the anxiety of which we are consciously aware. Anxiety, as used in family systems theory, encompasses the total human response to the perception of threat, real or imagined. It comes with human life. It may belong to all protoplasm. And yet basic to the process of self-differentiation is the task of consciously working at regulating one's anxiety. This includes acknowledging the anxiety and intentionally regulating one's reactivity to it. It is hard, daily work. It is never done in the sense of being finished. But the leader engaged in self-differentiation accepts the challenge. She knows that change is facilitated by focusing upon the modification of one's own behavior rather than the functioning of others.

Bowen Theory offers practical help in this endeavor by providing a "lens" through which one is able to view relationship systems. The concept of the emotional triangle enables one to actually observe the emotional process which—although always present and ultimately determinative –is in most situations outside of conscious awareness. To "see" the impact of others upon oneself, the impact one has on others and the impact others have on each other equips leaders with a valuable resource for self-regulation. This is why understanding the theory is so essential, why an integral component of this lecture is tomorrow's workshop on the basics of the theory and why the ongoing Leadership In Ministry Workshops are the main focus of my present ministry.

One of the most significant contributions of family systems theory is its awareness of the multi-generational nature of much of our anxiety. Not only does our anxiety come with the territory of being human, it comes in unique ways as part of the territory of being human in our particular family systems. This can be a source of despair as we find ourselves living out the reactive patterns of past generations, but it can also be a source of growth and change as we consciously face and rework those patterns. Therapy and healing in a family systems model involve such reworking and the freedom discovered through this process enables one to better regulate reactivity in the present.

I have learned from my personal experience and my experience with parents I have coached and pastors and other leaders who participate in our workshops that the people who are able to become less anxious and less reactive are the ones who are involved in reworking their relationships in their family of origin. Michael Kerr writes:

Learning enough about the multi-generational emotional history of one's family to change the way one thinks about the family and about oneself probably contributes more to the effort to 'grow up' than anything else a person can do.[8]

The theological word here is a basic one. Jesus often expressed the central human problem in terms of anxiety. He understood the human dilemma as one of lack of trust in the faithfulness and goodness of God. "Seek first the Kingdom" was his message. He taught his disciples to deal with their anxiety by trusting God's faithfulness as the core posture of their lives. And he warned that the failure to do this results in bondage to false gods and rewards a person with a life of fear and mistrust. Working at self-regulation—monitoring and regulating one's anxious responses to life—is a large part of the nitty-gritty work of differentiating a self. It seems to me that only the theological word of God's faithfulness can ultimately free us from the anxiety that comes with the territory of being human. Through worship, prayer and meditation the disciple is increasingly enabled to live life from a posture of trust in God's trustworthiness.

The second dimension of the process of leadership through self-differentiation is self-definition. Just as self-regulation is the internal dimension of this process, self-definition is the external dimension. Here the focus shifts to the communication of self to other selves, and I include all the various forms communication can and will take. To define self is to give expression to the thoughts, values and goals one holds dear. It includes taking stands. To use biblical language, it is self-revelation. I have come to understand this as one of my major jobs as a pastor. My task is to get clear about what I think and believe and communicate those thoughts and beliefs in words and actions—not to get others straight about what they should think and believe. It's a full-time job and a difficult one.

Self-definition has a powerful effect upon others and, when it is done by one who is working at regulating his or her own reactivity, it is an invitation to others to do the same. It enables dialogue and it causes things to happen. When a parent takes a stand that clearly expresses his or her true thoughts and values, family relationships change. When a pastor is able to preach the sermon that clearly and non-reactively expresses what the pastor believes about the emotionally loaded issue facing the congregation, the people are invited and challenged to do the same, and some will. And when the resistance of those who are most reactive surfaces, as it most probably will, if the pastor and other leaders are able to maintain that clarity of definition, the congregation stands its best chance of actually responding to the situation in faithfulness and obedience. It might even act redemptively.

I stated earlier that coercion is a basic ethical issue for leaders. It is my experience that leaders who are working at their own self-definition are better able to resist the temptation to attempt to will others into compliance with their own ideas and goals. To focus upon clarifying and communicating one's own ideas and goals is an invitation for others to do the same. Theologically, it is to affirm our belief that we human beings must respect individual freedom and responsibility just as God does. Whatever is meant by the phrase "the will of God", it does not mean that God violates the freedom and responsibility that is part and parcel of our God-created humanity. When willing others to be or do is present in a family or church leader, trust in self-definition has been abandoned and a coercion that can only lead to a conflict of wills has been chosen.

The third dimension of leadership through self-differentiation is connectedness. Self-differentiating leaders work at self-regulation and self-definition while maintaining connection to their relational systems. It is especially important to maintain this connectedness when sabotage or resistance is encountered because of the leader's self-differentiating behavior. At such times a leader is tempted to either give up or cut off. But if the leader persists, does not withdraw or quit and remains connected and on course, there is a good chance that the system will follow. Friedman referred to this posture of non-reactive persistence as "the key to the kingdom."

Which brings me to the matter of hope. Biblically understood, hope is the result—a by-product, if you will—of faith. It is possible because of faith in the faithfulness of God. It is not based upon faith in the human capacity to fulfill the modern "myth of progress," whether scientific, political, economic or technological. Biblically understood, hope is also related to the community of faith. There the stories of God's past faithfulness are retold and the reality of God's presence in the contemporary moment is celebrated in worship and experienced in the life of the community. Therefore the nature of the church's community, its togetherness, is always an issue in the faith journey. Family systems theory teaches us that what we call community can be an expression of either the fusion that results from fear and reactivity or a connectedness that expresses choice and mutual commitment. We need to be connected as well as to be separate individuals. The challenge is how to have both a connection that is not fusion and an individualism that is not isolated reactivity.

Jack Mills is the author of the Pulitzer Prize winning book, *God: A Biography,* and a visiting professor of humanities at Cal Tech. In a New York Times Magazine article titled "Religion Makes A Comeback (Belief to Follow)" he writes:

"Now, even people without faith are looking for God ... Despair, according to a study published in the American Heart Association's journal, is as bad for the human heart as a pack-a-day smoking habit. "Steps should be taken," writes one doctor in the study, "to try to change" the cardiac patient's situation."[9]

Mills raises the question, by whom should this attempt at changing the patient's situation be made? "By religion?" he asks.

In our day religion often begins in despair — in personal despair that hardens the arteries, in cultural despair that darkens the heart, in intellectual despair that humbles the mind — and moves from there to hope, not through argument but through affiliation. ... Just how anyone makes the decision to affiliate — to go it, but not alone, to be ... a joiner — is difficult to describe and impossible to recover, but it happens, this decision, and many such decisions can accrue to a movement. A movement toward hope? Perhaps. A refusal, at least, to despair.[10]

And there it is: the need for community if there is to be hope. But such community moves beyond the herding instinct of an anxiety driven togetherness. I believe family systems theory can help us understand the process by which such community becomes a reality and theology can clarify the divine initiative that enables it to become a reality. And I believe, viewed from both of these perspectives, leadership is a key ingredient in the process.

Leadership can provide marriages and families with the resources necessary to cope with rapid and unsettling change. Leadership can play a determinative role in helping to move the church beyond the polarized extremes of both the authoritarian "this is the answer" of religious fundamentalism and fanaticism, and the fuzzy "there don't seem to be any answers" of a so-called liberalism that can only celebrate the irreligion of the secular city. If there is to be a word of hope for either family or church, I believe it will be spoken by leaders. The theological language for such leaders would be: persons centered in God's love and faithfulness who are thereby set free to love and faithfully serve others. The family process language would be: persons moving towards self-differentiation who freely choose to be connected to others in ways that encourage their self-differentiation.

Christian theology assumes a posture of hope because of the faithfulness of God toward God's creation, supremely expressed in Jesus Christ. Family systems theory assumes a hopeful posture because of a belief in natural processes that are understood as moving towards new expressions of the life forces that drive creation. And both perspectives understand human anxiety as a barrier to such hope.

The late Paul Tillich understood anxiety as a central theological issue. He defined it as "the state in which a being is aware of its possible nonbeing" and he interpreted the crises of Western culture in terms of this anxiety. In *The Courage to Be* he wrote, "In our Western culture, the end of ancient civilization was characterized by ontic anxiety (the anxiety of fate and death), the Middle Ages by moral anxiety (the anxiety of guilt and condemnation) and the modern era by spiritual anxiety (the anxiety of emptiness and meaninglessness)."[11]

Viewed from a family systems perspective, the anxiety in our culture leaves us stuck in a reactive togetherness that inhibits our potential for the creative "out of the box" thinking that might enable us to get unstuck. Viewed from a theological perspective, our anxiety leads us to place our trust in the false gods of materialism and progress and the technology, political systems, science and economic theories that prop them up. Our need is for a spirit of adventure, but we pursue security and certainty. Our need is for genuine community that fosters personal growth, but we disintegrate into ever smaller tribal communities that stunt the development of personal responsibility to the neighbor at home and abroad. Our need is for a posture of hope, but our almost absolute trust in fragile political and economic systems barely hides the underlying posture of despair.

There is a long list of harsh realities that we face: a tribalized, conflicted world; Wall Street's extreme gyrations; voter apathy in every political arena; the church's frantic embrace of any program that guarantees numerical growth and easy success; and the family's involvement in divorce courts, drug rehabilitation programs, fearful flight to walled homogenized suburban enclaves or fearful banishment to decaying inner city ghettos. But if we are able to view these realities as symptoms—symptoms of deeper problems and not the basic problems themselves—then I believe we will have taken the first step along a more hopeful path to some viable solutions. And I view this as the basic understanding of both theology and family systems theory. An anxious family cannot move beyond a focus upon its symptomology. An anxious society functions in much the same way. According to family systems theory, in order for a family to break free from its 'stuckness' upon its symptoms, someone in the family must begin to function in a more self-defined way. From a biblical perspective, if the people of God are ever to break camp at Sinai or stop going in circles in the wilderness, a Moses or a Joshua has to point the way. In other words, what we call leadership is necessary if change is to take place.

The last time I heard Ed Friedman present a public lecture was at Virginia Theological Seminary in Alexandria, Virginia. After his presentation, I walked up to him and, before I could say anything, he asked: "What are you doing here? You've heard all of this." To which I replied, "No, I heard you say something tonight I don't remember ever having heard you say before." "What was that?" he asked. My reply was, "I heard you say that in order for a leader to move towards self-differentiation, the person has to experience serendipity." "I don't think I have ever said that before," he responded, "but I have come to believe it is true." "Just exactly what do you mean by serendipity?" I asked. He smiled and answered, "There has to be an openness to the not yet, a willingness to be surprised and have one's certainties rearranged."

That conversation took place a few months before his death and I never had the opportunity to pursue the matter with him. But months later, when I viewed the video "Rediscovering Leadership", there was Ed saying, "To unstick a system someone has to be willing to encounter serendipity, to be willing to adventure. The focus upon safety rather than adventure defeats this and leaves the system stuck."

Among the various dictionary definitions of the word "hope" is this one: "The feeling that what is desired is also possible." Hope deals with possibilities, not guarantees. Whether you describe it as an openness to adventure or an openness to the

Holy Spirit, it is a posture made possible by faith. It is the posture of self-differentiating leaders.

For the next to the last word, I turn again to Friedman: When a relationship system reaches that point (of gridlock), it can only get unstuck when it can bring forth leaders who can separate themselves enough from the emotional processes around them so that they can see things differently, who are hell-bent to pursue their vision, who can persist in the face of the sabotage of others, enemies and colleagues, who are challenged where others are made anxious and who value adventure more than safety.

This necessary condition for fundamental change is equally true for any relationship system, be it a family, an organization, a nation or even an entire civilization.[12]

And for the last word, I turn to the unknown author of the New Testament letter to the Hebrew Christians: To have faith is to be sure of the things we hope for, to be certain of the things we cannot see (Hebrews 11:1).

---

[1]Edwin H. Friedman, "Reinventing Leadership". The Guilford Press, 1996. Videocassette and Discussion Guide.

[2]Michael E. Kerr and Bowen, Murray, *Family Evaluation* (W. W. Norton & Co., 1988), p. 27.

[3]Friedman, op. cit. Discussion Guide, p. 34.

[4]Kerr & Bowen, op. cit. pp. 342,343.

[5]Ibid., p. 28.

[6]*Systems and Spirituality: Bowen Systems Theory, Faith and Theology,* The Papers and Proceedings of a Conference on Theology. Washington Theological Union, July 1987, pp. 14-15.

[7]Friedman, Unpublished lecture presented in Bethesda, Maryland, December 11, 1992.

[8]Kerr, op. cit., p. 309.

⁹The New York Time Magazine, special issue, "God Decentralized" (December 7, 1997), p.59.

¹⁰Ibid.

¹¹Paul Tillich, *The Courage To Be* (Yale University Press, 1952), p. 57.

¹²Edwin Friedman, "The Challenge of Change and the Spirit of Adventure." Unpublished essay, p. 4.

❖

14

The Possibility of Change

Carla Toenniessen

Carla Toenniessen LMFT, M.S., is a family systems coach, educator and practitioner in Fairfax, VA who explores Bowen Family Systems Theory and its applications to life and living. In 1993 she began a more intentional journey with BFST after hearing a presentation by Ed Friedman.
Carla joined the faculty of LIM in 2008.

I hear a lot of talk about change and transformation these days, some compelling and hopeful, other scenarios sound unrealistic or heavy handed, or both. And yet isn't change the very essence of life itself? What then does positive change entail? Is there any evidence that enduring change for individuals, families, communities, and organizations is obtainable and if so, how might we go about fertilizing the soil?

What Does the Theory Say?

According to the Merriam-Webster Dictionary to change is "to make a shift from one to another. To become different." One of the most attractive aspects of Bowen Family Systems Theory (BFST) for me is the theory's perspective on change. A review of the writings of Edwin Friedman indicates certain factors that foster the possibility of change along with those that favor maintaining the status quo. Friedman admitted that change presents what he calls a "dilemma" in that some of our best attempts can keep change at bay when at other times it may come in the back door totally unexpected.

Apparently, as much as we hear about change, it is an ever evasive and perplexing creature. To be honest, when did any one of us "change" as a result of a New Year's resolution or good intentions? As I consider the changes I have made in my life, usually the change occurred out of necessity, i.e. stimulated by a crisis or motivated by pain or unwanted consequence pushing me in a new direction.

It was such a situation that drove me to begin and continue the hard work of researching my family of origin and practicing the new way of thinking and responding that I was learning from BFST.

To speak quite plainly, what motivated me to persist in applying the theory was my desperation with the family-quagmire in which I found myself and the hope that perhaps systems theory offered me a chance to live life better and differently. However, that meant that I would have to stop doing what no longer worked; I would have to change.

The Black Box Theory

Bowen Family Systems Theory originated during the rise of technology and computers in the 1950's. With the information explosion making data and problems more complicated, systems theory came into focus presenting a new focus on process rather than content. Without having to know causes or how to fix everything, by just adding one new input, a completely different outcome could occur. "The possibilities of change are maximized when we concentrate on modifying our own way of functioning, our own input, into the family "black box."[1]

How to Promote Change without Trying

According to Friedman, knowing what gets in the way of change is as important as knowing what promotes its possibility. If you are on the side of change, watch out for the following.

- Feeling responsible for others
- Emotional triangles, they can sabotage change and keep things stuck
- Willfulness, trying to control or make things happen
- Emphasizing empathy and understanding over responsibility
- A lack of differentiated leadership.

If the theory is correct, the presence of any one of these factors tends to keep patterns stuck and block change from occurring. On the other hand, the following ideas may provide just what is needed to shift matters in a new direction.

- Questions are more powerful than answers
- Challenge and pain help us grow
- Awareness of who's responsible for certain things
- Pay attention to the emotional triangles
- Humor and play lower anxiety and promote clear thinking
- Clarity about one's own life, purpose and goals benefits everyone
- One can only have influence through connection
- Love the quest.

The Most Important Factor: Differentiated Leadership

It probably goes without saying that the most important contribution Friedman made to the field of family systems theory was in terms of how well-differentiated leadership affects the emotional process of relationship systems. Friedman recognized the organic nature of leadership and expanded the notion that all systems ultimately need such a leader in order to function well. In fact, the theory "locates the power of change in those who assume the position of family leaders."[2] Thus, the position and functioning of the leader becomes key to facilitating the possibility of change in any system whether it's a family, organization, or a nation.

Leadership That Makes Change Possible

What then constitutes differentiated leadership? What leadership qualities are necessary in order for a system to experience change and renewal? A differentiated leader has the capacity for the following.

To see things in new ways
To show up, be vulnerable
To be clear about principals and goals
To be aware of emotional process
To ask good questions
To be persistent
To endure
To promote maturity in the system and maximize its strengths
To value imagination, adventure, and integrity.

This is not an exhaustive list. And yet perhaps it can all be summed up in what I think is the theory's greatest gift: the hope for change and new life through the power and presence of differentiated leadership.

———

[1]Friedman, *Generation to Generation,* p. 18.
[2]Ibid., pp. 3-4.

❖

15

How to Let Go of the Outcome

Margaret Marcuson

Leaders need to let go of outcome. It's difficult when we care so much about the ministry and want to make it work. We can imagine that vision, and the potential impact on our community. However, letting go can be the best way to make room for something new to happen. "The wind blows where it chooses, and you hear the sound of it, but you do not know where it comes from or where it goes. So it is with everyone who is born of the Spirit." (John 3:8) The work of the Holy Spirit is unexpected, unpredictable. If you cling to a specific outcome and try to control it, you may get in the way of God's work in the world.

Here are four ways to let go:

Pray. First of all, pray like Jesus. This is part of the Lord's Prayer: "Thy kingdom come, thy will be done, on earth as it is in heaven." Praying the Lord's Prayer daily is not too often.

Second, you can pray for yourself. Pray for your own ability to persist, to be patient, to be courageous, to let go, whatever God is calling you to in this moment in your ministry.

Third, pray for others. I have a list of people I pray for every day. I've quit asking for specific things for them, mostly. I simply mention their name to God. I figure God knows better than I do what they need. I notice it's when I'm more anxious about someone that I get caught up in specifics.

Accept. Multiple forces are at work in your church, in the community, and in the wider world. Carol Howard Merritt, author of *Tribal Church* and *Healing Spiritual Wounds*, says this: "I really wish churches would stop blaming individual pastors for national trends. Older givers are passing away. Younger generations don't go to church as consistently and they have more debt... If these things affect your attendance and budget, it's probably not the pastor's fault. Pastors were not *that* much more awesome fifty years ago..."[1]

I'd add that I really wish pastors would stop blaming *themselves* for national trends. I know from experience how easy it is to think, "If I were just a better leader, everything would be going much better/the church would have more people/more money/more ministries." You do the best you can and recognize how many things are out of your control—not only the big trends in church life right now but decades or more of history in your specific congregation.

If you cling to a certain outcome, you will be constantly exhausted and frustrated. I don't believe making things happen is your call as a leader.

Claim your work. Your call is to show up and do the work that God has called you to do, to occupy your role of leader with as much grace and creativity as you can. Live out your call, in the place where you are, just for today.

Margaret Wheatley in *So Far from Home: Lost and Found in Our Brave New World* talks about the challenges of working for good in the world we are faced with now. She suggests that courage is vital, and she talks about what she calls "warriors." She means by this "those who have the courage to keep on, without knowing what the result will be."[2]

Wheatley also says later in the book, "As our hearts are wholly engaged, we experience ever more compassion for others, ever more confidence and energy that we can do our work. Our human heart seems capable of infinite expansion when we find the work that is ours to do. And that's a delightful feeling."[3]

It is a deeply spiritual practice to open our hearts to those we serve, without judgment, without a sense that it is all up to us, and to let go of saving the world, or even our church. You can do important work, the work that God has uniquely gifted you to do, without a Messiah complex—in fact, you can do the work better. Without the intense pressure to make things come out the way you think they should, you will have more freedom to be creative—and to be yourself.

What are you called to do, and can you simply wake up every day and do it?

Finally, take the long view. Everything of value takes time. I was reflecting recently on Adoniram Judson, a Baptist missionary in Burma. He labored for decades winning only seven converts. You might call that failure. And yet, now there is a thriving Baptist community in Burma (now called Myanmar). Not only that, Burmese immigrants to the United States are revitalizing old white Baptist churches when they migrate and immediately find a Baptist church to take part in. That's an outcome Judson could never have predicted. You never know what the impact of your work will be tomorrow, a year from now or two centuries from now.

---

[1]Carol Howard Merritt, Facebook post, December 15, 2016.
[2]Margaret Wheatley, *So Far from Home: Lost and Found in Our Brave New World* (San Francisco: Berrett-Koehler Publishers, 2012), p. 125.
[3]Ibid., 149.

16

Five Necessary Shifts in Thinking

Israel Galindo

Edwin H. Friedman's *A Failure of Nerve: Leadership in the Age of the Quick Fix,* marks a seminal shift in thinking about leadership. In a real sense, that work was the culmination of years of thinking on the part of Friedman on Bowen systems theory applied to leadership. In it he redefined leadership in contrast to traditional, and current, understandings of the nature of leadership.

The work challenges leaders to rethink assumptions about leadership. Rather than believing leadership is about power, personality or expertise, Friedman's perspective suggests it is more about courage, nerve, grit, imagination, and differentiation. Here are five shifts in thinking required of leaders in the age of the quick fix.

1. A shift from linear to systems thinking

Friedman argued that leadership in the age of the quick fix requires a different way of thinking. Leaders must think systemically, embracing the interconnectedness of the whole network of relationships in an organization, institution, or in any relationship system. The ways any member in a system, including the leader, has an influence, to a varying extent, on the other members of the organization.

Leadership is a functioning position present in all relational systems; all systems need a person in the leadership position. However, systems theory suggests that leadership is a product of the system, rather than of individual traits, characteristics, or even competencies. The most beneficial systemic reciprocity is when a leader can provide the leadership functions a system needs. At the same time a system needs to be able to find and support that leader, despite the discomfort of being challenged toward increasingly mature and responsible functioning.

2. A shift from personality to understanding motional processes

Freidman suggested that leadership relies heavily on the cumulative effect of the emotional process in a system. That includes the dynamics in the emotional field—homeostasis, multigenerational transmission, how the system responds to anxiety, reciprocity dynamics, etc. Contributing dynamics include the collective level of maturity of individuals in the system, and the patterns of how individuals and groups manage or self-regulate their emotions.

As important as understanding the emotional process of the system, leaders need to be aware of how emotional process affects them. Leaders are intimately connected to the emotional processes in the interlocking systems of family of origin, their current family, and the emotional field of the system they lead. The interaction of their thoughts, feelings, emotions, biases, patterns of reactivity and their past experiences in relationships all affect to some extent the system they lead — to positive or negative effects.

3. A shift from expertise to imagination

Friedman argued that emotional systems have a tendency to become "imaginatively gridlocked," that is, they become unable to think their way out of their problems. To Friedman, imaginatively gridlocked systems cannot change on their own merely by getting more information or data. What is required is a shift in the emotional processes of that institution. Imagination and curiosity are at root emotional, not cognitive, phenomena. In order to imagine the unimaginable and envision beyond limited perspectives and biases, people must be able to separate themselves from surrounding emotional processes before they can begin to see things differently.

According to Friedman imaginatively gridlocked systems as characterized by three interlocking characteristics: (1) an unending treadmill of trying harder; (3) a continual search for new answers to old questions rather than an effort to reframe the questions themselves, and (3) thinking in dichotomies: either/or, black or white, all-or-nothing ways of thinking.

Friedman concluded that "The great lesson here is for all imaginatively gridlocked systems is that the acceptance and even cherishing of uncertainty is critical to keeping the human mind from voyaging into the delusion of omniscience. The willingness to encounter serendipity is the best antidote we have for the arrogance of thinking we know. Exposing oneself to chance is often the only way to provide the kind of mind-jarring experience of novelty that can make us realize that what we thought was reality was only the mirror of our minds."[1]

4. A shift from conflict resolution to appreciating chronic anxiety

Friedman deemphasized a focus on conflict and conflict resolution and argued that relationship systems tend toward chronic anxiety. That type of anxiety (as opposed to acute anxiety) not only hinders the development of the system but also perversely operates time to derail leadership—the very resource it most desperately needs. Chronic anxiety is the "emotional and physical reactivity of all life" generated by individual and group reactions to disturbances in the balance of a relationship system—like change or threat.

Friedman described five characteristics of chronic anxiety: (1) reactivity (intense unthinking emotional reactions of individuals and/or groups to events and to one another), (2) herding (a process through which the forces for togetherness triumph over the forces for individuality and differentiation and move everyone to adapt to the least mature members), (3) blame displacement (in which members focus on blaming others, or forces, take on a victim mentality, rather than taking responsibility for their own being and destiny), (4) a quick-fix mentality (developing a low-threshold for pain, an inability for disciplined and purposeful actions, and thus seek symptom relief rather than fundamental change), and (5) a lack of well-differentiated persons in leadership positions leading to a failure of nerve in leaders that both stems from and contributes to the first four characteristics. Friedman often argued that leaders can recognize chronic anxiety by the absence of playfulness, which reflects both intimacy and the ability to maintain distance. With the absence of playfulness organizations lose hopeful perspective, things always appear dire, and their repertoire of responses to problems becomes myopic.

5. A shift from technical competence to differentiation of self

The best response to imaginative gridlock and chronic anxiety in organizations, according to Friedman, is the presence of well-differentiated leaders. Differentiation of self in the leader refers to the capacity of a leader to define his or her own goals and values in the face of surrounding pressures. It includes the capacity to maintain a relatively non-anxious presence in the midst of anxious systems, to take maximum responsibility for one's own, thinking, emotions, and emotional being. Friedman described it as:

> The basic concept of leadership through self-differentiation is this: If a leader will take primary responsibility for his or her own position as "head" and work to define his or her own goals and self, while staying in touch with the rest of the organism, there is more than a reasonable chance that the body will follow. This emphasis on a leader's self-differentiation is not to be confused with independence or some kind of selfish individuality. On the contrary, we are talking here about the ability of a leader to be a self while remaining a part of the system.[2]

According to Friedman, the number one crisis in leadership today is not technical competence, but a failure of nerve—the inability to define oneself clearly and function out of a differentiated stance with courage, nerve, grit, and imagination. It is a leader's self-differentiation, not empathy, which will encourage differentiation and responsibility in others. When a leader can be clear about his or her principles and values, be present in the midst of emotional turmoil, actively relate to key people while calmly maintaining a sense of the leader's own direction will a system have its best opportunity to meet challenges in imaginative and principled ways.

Lawrence Matthews, founder of the Leadership in Ministry workshops, suggested the following qualities of leaders who function out of self-differentiated stance: self-definition or clarification, self-regulation, connectedness and response to resistance or conflict. According to Matthews, those leaders consistently do five things:

Work on differentiation of self

Differentiated leader give expression to the thoughts, values and goals they hold dear. They have the capacity to take a principled stand in the midst of challenges. This quality has two dimensions: an internal and external. Mature leaders work toward clarity of what they believe and they let others know where they stand. The accept that their responsibility as a leader is to get clear about what they think and believe and communicate those thoughts and beliefs in words and actions.

Practice Self-Regulation

Differentiated leaders consciously work at regulating their anxiety. This includes acknowledging the ways anxiety affects them and mindfully regulating their reactivity. They acknowledge that influencing the emotional process, in self and in the system, is facilitated by focusing upon the modification of one's own behavior rather than the functioning of others.

Stay Connected

Self-differentiated leaders work at self-regulation and self-definition while maintaining connection to the relationship systems of which they are a part—family of origin, nuclear family, work system, etc. They realize they are influenced by all these systems, and that they cannot affect an emotional system of which they are not connected in significant ways. The central dilemma for leaders is how to remain emotionally close while maintaining a differentiated self?

It becomes especially important to maintain this connectedness when resistance is encountered in the emotional field of any one system because of the leader's self-differentiating behavior. During such times a leader may be tempted to either give up or cut off. But if the leader persists, does not withdraw or quit, and remains connected and on course, then a system stands a better chance of dealing creatively with challenges.

Expect Resistance

Friedman referred to a leader's ability to maintain a posture of non-reactive persistence in the face of resistance and sabotage as "the key to the kingdom." Leaders can expect to be consistently surprised and disappointed by the reactivity from others to creative, even common-sense, leadership efforts. But they can also realize that resistance is systemic in nature—the common, first response to any challenge to change. Leaders must be prepared for resistance, and be able to recognize it (not often that easy to do), and be ready to practice persistence of vision.

The paradox is that resistance is a product of the leader's own making. Any leader who needs to bring about change will disturb the homeostasis, the sense of balance, of an emotional system. Resistance and sabotage are reactive systemic forces to a loss of balance—even if the original condition is dysfunctional and stuck. Leaders expect resistance to any challenge toward change and to the unfamiliar and uncomfortable readjustment that are necessary to move to a new state of balance, new ways of functioning, different ways of relating, and new practices.

Avoid Peace-Mongering

Friedman coined the phrase "peace-monger" to describe the conflict-averse leader who lacks courage, grit, nerve, and differentiation and desires peace at any price. This leadership failure of nerve, says Friedman, reflects the epidemic in today's culture that favors false harmony and good feelings over progress and integrity. He explained,

> In any type of institution whatsoever, when a self-directed, imaginative, energetic, or creative member is being consistently frustrated and sabotaged rather than encouraged and supported, what will turn out to be true one hundred percent of the time, regardless of whether the disrupters are supervisors, subordinates, or peers, is that the person at the very top of that institution is a peace-monger. By that I mean a highly anxious risk-avoider, someone who is more concerned with good

feelings than with progress, someone whose life revolves around the axis of consensus, a "middler," someone who is so incapable of taking well-defined stands that his "disability" seems to be genetic, someone who functions as if she had been filleted of her backbone, someone who treats conflict or anxiety like mustard gas—one whiff, on goes the emotional gas mask, and he flits. Such leaders are often "nice," if not charming."[3]

In conclusion, Friedman challenges us to consider that it is when the leadership position is filled by a leader (or leaders) who is moving forward in his or her own process of self-differentiation, when any system stands the best chance of dealing creatively with, rather than simply reacting to, change and challenge. The presence of self-differentiated leadership offers the greatest opportunity of such a possibility happening.

———

[1]Edwin H. Friedman, *A Failure of Nerve: Leadership in the Age of the Quick Fix* (New York: Seabury Books, 2007), p. 46.

[2]Edwin H. Friedman, *Generation to Generation: Family Process is Church and Synagogue* (New York: The Guilford Press, 2011), p. 229.

[3]Friedman, *A Failure of Nerve,* p. 13.

17

Herding in the Bovine and the Human

William T. Pyle

This article will explore the way anxiety affects bovine and humans. This introduction will provide background information on my herd of cattle in Franklinton, NC and hopefully raise your awareness of the cow/calf operation. As we explore the way that anxiety affects cattle, we will explore similar ways anxiety travels in our families and work systems.

Our Niche

Ours is a small seedstock operation that provides breeding animals for commercial cow-calf operations in our local area. Most of our customers have small herds (25-100 cows) which produce feeder calves that will end up in a feedlot in the Midwest. Most of our buyers will purchase a single bull at the time. The heifer calves that we do not keep for replacements are sold to a small group of farmers who regularly add our surplus females to their herds. We use artificial insemination (AI) to provide access to superior genetics from bulls that we could not afford to own or are not available. Most of our cattle are Sim-Angus hybrids, a cross between Simmental and Black Angus.

Like most cow/calf operations, the reality is that as much as we want to think we are "cow people," we are really "grass people." We manage an integrated operation where we must balance the raising of grass with the harvesting of the grass using four-legged herbivores. The triangle is operator, land (grass), and cows. Prior to their domestication, cattle roamed in search of grass when they finished grazing one area. Now, the operator is responsible for rotating the cattle between paddocks or fields.

Our Goals

There are specific goals that guide our operations and practices. They are:

1. To raise grass and grain in an environmentally responsible manner;
2. To market the grass and grain through seedstock to commercial cattlemen within a 100 mile radius;
3. To produce seedstock that will genetically improve our customers' herds;
4. To raise cattle in a humane and safe environment;
5. To operate the farm in a fiscally responsible manner;
6. To enjoy a rural lifestyle.

The Annual Cycle

The annual cycle on our farm has four quarters, or seasons: Calving (September to November), Breeding (December to February), Growing (March to May), and Resting (June to August). The calves are born in the fall, the cows are rebred in the winter, calves continue growing with their mothers during the spring and are weaned from their mothers at the end of May. The cows rest and gain weight through the summer as they prepare to begin the cycle again. We can think of the "liturgical colors" of this cycle as green from March through November, brown from December through February, with white occasionally.

Lessons Learned from the Farm

Over the years we have learned many lessons on the farm, but here are just four:

1) All changes and modifications have unintended consequences.
2) With a multitude of counselors comes a variety of advice, most of which have some basis in fact or theory.
3) Learn from early-adapters; watch for the unintended consequences that they did not anticipate.
4) Adopt a middle-adapter posture; be open to modifications in practices that are consistent with our guiding principles and are beneficial to the operation.

In the pasture and free from threat, cattle graze as a group. They generally will graze as a single unit or divide into smaller groups within sight of each other. Under stress, however, their natural inclination is to move closer together. They will crowd together in a closer proximity than they are normally comfortable with. And when they flee, they flee as a group. In most herds, a few animals fill a leadership position as an "early warning system" for potential threats. Other animals function as a "brake" and have a calming effect on the herd.

Herbivores' natural responses to threat are fight, flight, or freeze. Some—like deer, rabbits, and squirrels—freeze but their natural colors blend in with their environment, and so they may avoid detection. For many herbivores, in contrast, the first response to a threat or perceived threat is to flee. The flight response has been formatted as the initial response through millennia of conditioning. To stop and think about the threat and possible responses is dangerous for an herbivore. Time is of the essence when a predator is near. So, the natural response to threat is quick, immediate, and unthinking. This has served the species well as demonstrated by their survival. The fight response is a last resort that is used when they are cornered.

A stampede occurs when anxiety over a perceived threat reaches a point where the group grows so uncomfortable with the anxiety that the group is spooked and they begin to run. The destination seems to be inconsequential. Escape from the anxiety is the goal. The togetherness force runs amok and individuality evaporates. Conversely, the stampede begins to abate when a small number of individuals begin to slow down. It is as if they look around and think, "What are we running from?" And as they begin to slow down, it has a calming effect on the group

Modern cattle operations utilize a species whose innate response to threat is counter-productive to the production of beef. The production of adrenaline requires calories that must be diverted from other functions such as maintaining weight/body condition, reproduction, and lactation. Individuals that maintain a high state of alert compromise their productivity; they burn calories through hyper-vigilance and consume less forage. The natural evolutionary instincts that were essential to life in the wild are now counter-productive to domestic production.

In our herd, we select for docility (and cull for poor disposition). The infectious nature of anxiety means that an easily agitated individual has an exaggerated impact on the over-all disposition of the herd. The mere removal of an easily agitated individual cow does not remove anxiety from the group, however.

Another "early warning system" will arise within the herd, because the function has been evolutionarily important to the herd. But the removal of a highly anxious group member may result in a slower (lower) response to threat.

Michael Kerr recognized that individuality is present among animals as well as among humans. "Family systems theory assumes that the concept of differentiation can be extended to other animals. Humans, however, appear to have more capacity for differentiation than other species. . . . Some individuals are so reactive to even routine life stresses that their functioning is undermined. Others are better able to maintain competent functioning under the usual conditions of their existence."[1]

Our herd has been developed over 25 years. As seedstock producers, it is important select for traits that will enhance the genetic potential in our customers' herds. Most the cows in the herd descend from three cows, from which we bought daughters and granddaughters. Docility is important both in our herd and in the herds of our customers. The majority of cattle farmers who purchase livestock from our herd are 60 years old or older. Most of my customers do not need to run from a hostile bull or cow!

Because we are working with the cattle daily, it is important that the cattle learn to follow consistent patterns of movement. The cattle learn to come when I call them to move to the next pasture, or when I need to move them to the corral for routine health vaccinations or for the treatment of a sick animal. Nature and nurture are important in the development of the group's norms. Heifers who are weaned from their mothers at nine months of age and are kept as a group separate from the herd for six months. This is the one time in their lives where they are fed grain each day. They learn to come running when I call or when I drive in the field with the truck or the four-wheeler. It is during this time that they learn the pattern that we will use for their entire time on the farm.

Later as a cow, each time they are called to the corral, there will be feed waiting for them, and they will race to get in the corral. Cattle like to feel that what they are doing is their choice, so I give them the opportunity. I call them to the gate to a lane that leads to the corral. When they are gathered at the gate, I open the gate and follow them to the corral and close the corral gate behind them.

Most of the cows weigh between 1200 and 1500 pounds, so it is difficult to make them go where they do not want to go. If I try to push them where they do not want to go, they just scatter; they know that I am not a predator, so they just scatter. Trust is built over time in this relationship, and there are no short cuts.

"In animals, there is a tendency for anxiety to ripple instantaneously through a herd when there is danger. The herd functions as an emotional unit. The anxiety moves from one individual to the next, causing all the individuals to push closer together. The predictable ways in which the group handles anxiety (such as the herd moving closer together) are characteristic of the togetherness force."[2]

One of the difficult management decisions is the decision to cull a genetically superior individual because of disposition. As the leader responsible for the over-all health and productivity of the farm, the responsibility to make difficult decisions goes with the position. Another management decision is required when an animal does not reach the potential that her bloodline suggests she will have. In my experience, at least 50% of the heifers that we retain as replacements fail to reach their genetic potential. In the quest to keep improving the genetics of the herd, it is necessary to keep culling the low performers in the herd.

Anxiety appears to be a natural part of life on planet earth. While it may be important to regulate one's anxiety, anxiety serves a useful purpose. Jeffrey Miller describes it this way, "In everything that lives, anxiety is a fundamental expression of the survival instinct. . . . . Anxiety is the instinctive response of any living organism to a perceived threat. . . . Anxiety is simply a state of alert, of heightened readiness to respond. . . . In and of itself, anxiety is neither functional nor dysfunctional. It is a keen state of readiness to do something or other that may or may not be appropriate in response to a threat that may or may not be accurately perceived."[3]

Humans, like other mammals, evolved their response mechanisms as a survival instinct. Faced with a threat, we automatically reach into our stockpile of natural responses. Flight, fight, or freeze are automatic instinctual (emotional) responses. Roberta Gilbert adds a fourth response for humans; caretaking. Examples of caretaking include having all the answers, dominating, doing all the talking, and worrying about a third person.[4]

We do not have to think for these instinctual responses to activate. When you are at a Deacons' meeting and your alert system activates, your body automatically prepares to race out of the room or to punch back at your perceived attacker. You might even freeze and be unable to move or think. Even though a grizzly bear has not suddenly appeared, your emotional system has been activated. Your heart begins to race, adrenaline begins to be secreted, your pupils begin to dilate to let in more light and increase your peripheral vision, you are prepared to scream. Your body is ready to react to a physical threat. You are, to use the lyrics of the rock star Meatloaf, "all revved up with no place to go." Even when the mind knows that these instinctual responses would be counter-productive, if not disastrous, adrenaline has already been dumped into the blood stream, and it takes time for those neuro-chemical levels to dissipate.

One way that the rational system can calm the instinctual responses is to use breathing exercises. Breathe deeply and slowly exhale, repeat. Do not respond to the threat. Pause, relax, send the message to your entire body that this is not an emergency. Personally, I do not find it effective or helpful to try to use my reasoning or rational mind until I have been able to calm my body. I am not able to do my clearest thinking when I am reacting to a threat. When I am reacting to a threat, real or imagined, my repertoire of responses is limited. In those situations, my thinking will usually reinforce the instinctual responses instead of my principles.

Human groups, like other mammals, transmit anxiety throughout the system until each individual member is impacted. The herd's first response is normally flight. They run from the perceived threat. The threat to the herd is normally external to the herd and they attempt to distance from the perceived threat. Human groups are also threatened by external forces; and when there is a clearly identifiable external threat, we are often able to close ranks and cooperate to find a response to the threat. One of the differences in the sources of threat in human groups and a herd of cattle is the addition of other sources of perceived threat that spawn anxiety in the humans: (a) threats to the group from individuals within the group and, (b) threats to the individual from the group. While individuals in human groups may experience the anxiety that is pulsating through the group, they rarely agree on what the actual threat is or what they should do to respond to it.

My observation is that humans instinctually want to share their anxiety when they feel it. It is instinctual in that we do not have to be aware of what we are doing; in fact, most of the time we share the anxiety we are experiencing without naming or being aware of what we are doing. It is instinctual or natural for us to "share" our anxiety. When someone shares their anxiety with us, we instinctually look for someone to whom we can pass it on. That seems to be the way that anxiety works its way through a system. As members of the system, we are emotionally connected to the other members. This emotional system works to diffuse and spread anxiety among the members. It is as if we are connected by some invisible electrical current. Anxiety is systemic; each part of the system plays a part in how anxiety makes its way through the system. Each part is affected by the group and each part affects the group. The particular route that anxiety uses as it moves through the system is dependent on each member following their patterned response to anxiety.

The typical patterned responses to anxiety that humans employ is not an extensive list. Humans appear to be much more creative when we are thinking clearly rather than just being swept along by the current of anxiety. When we are reacting with our instinctual evolutionary emotional responses, our repertoire is limited. The patterned responses that humans use when faced with stress or anxiety applies whether the context is family, church, or business. Since they are a part of our evolutionary inheritance, we carry them with us wherever we go.

Blaming

One response to anxiety is blaming. Rather than taking responsibility for one's part in a conflict or problem, blaming seeks to place the responsibility on someone or something else. Often there is a focus on trying to get the other person to change in order to stop the offensive behavior that is causing the problem. Normally blaming occurs within a reciprocal conflictual pattern where no one in the system takes responsibility for the problem and no one feels the need for personal change.

In a system where there are multiple players and multiple factors contributing to the "problem," clearly identifying the problem and finding solutions is difficult. And when the problem cannot be clearly identified, a vicious cycle of blaming ensues. The focus is on getting someone else to change.

Blaming may diffuse responsibility for a time, but it fails to provide an environment where change is realistic. More often, when an environment becomes characterized by reciprocal blaming, members take a defensive posture where they are risk-averse and creative thinking is penalized.

A natural mammalian response is to freeze. "If I don't do anything, no one can blame me for it." The system remains stuck in a pattern of reciprocal blaming, unless a member of the group begins to get clear about his own responsibility and role in the system and then begins to change his functioning—whether anyone else changes or not. That kind of self-differentiating response can provide an opportunity for change within the system.

Scapegoating

Another instinctual response that is a form of blaming is scapegoating. Scapegoating is a focused form of blaming where members of the group identify one member as the cause of the group's problem. While blaming is more reciprocal, scapegoating is more focused. With blaming, multiple people may be identified as the problem: scapegoating allows the group to channel its anger and attention toward one member. Ultimately, the group is often surprised that the problem resurfaces even after the scapegoat has been sacrificed.

Distancing and Pursuit

One other instinctual response to conflict and anxiety is distancing. It is important to get some emotional distance from the group so that as an individual you can do your own clearest thinking. And sometimes, it is important to get some physical distance. Distance can be an important intentional strategy for clarity in determining one's own principles. Notice the difference in distance as a temporary, occasional, intentional strategy and distancing as an instinctual, reactive response to threat. The reciprocal response to distancing is pursuit. The togetherness forces are always aware of the subtle moves in perceived distance and closeness. When we move farther away, either physically or emotionally, the system knows. And the homeostatic forces will activate to restore the balance. Pursuit is the instinctual unthinking response to a "feeling" of abandonment. Pursuit can become willful when it attempts to force a distancer to return. And predictably, pursuit is counter-productive. Distancing and pursuit, like other reciprocal functions continue because (a) both parties maintain their part of the dance and (b) through the attempt to change the behavior of the other person. Predictably, the dance is changed when either party takes responsibility for their part and changes their functioning.

Overfunctioning

Another instinctual response to anxiety is overfunctioning. Overfunctioning is taking responsibility for that which belongs to someone else, and includes thinking, acting, feeling, or worrying for someone else. Like other reciprocal behaviors, it requires an underfunctioner, a person not taking responsibility for themselves.

Triangles

You may have noticed the ways that triangles developed in each of these instinctual responses to anxiety. But, we shouldn't be surprised since triangles form to disperse anxiety and spread it around. Triangles are by nature a shifting relationship. Two people occupy a close relationship and a third party occupies the outside position. Normally there is some fluidity and flexibility in the ways that triangles form and mutate in a living system. Involving a third party is a natural instinctive reaction to anxiety. As a third party moves closer to one of the two occupying the close positions, something changes between the two. The homeostasis shifts and evolves.

Most relationships are living and moving, they are dynamic. A system like a church or a family is a living system.

People are being added and people are leaving. Scapegoating is one of the times that a triangle becomes rigid and inflexible. The identified problem is placed in an outside, distant position and may be the subject of every conversation without being a participant in the conversations. Scapegoats are talked about; not talked to. Most systems develop their own patterns for how triangles develop and how they evolve over time.

One of the advantages of a long-term pastorate is the opportunity to watch triangles develop over time. Often the patterned response is the same regardless of the content or issue involved. Conversely, the down-side of a long-term pastorate may be the way that the pastor has become a part of how triangles evolve and mutate in the congregation. Triangles are neither good nor bad, they are just a part of how we handle anxiety. And while triangles spread the anxiety around, anxiety doesn't diminish by being spread around. That will take someone with the courage to separate from the herd enough to recognize the role they have been playing in keeping the anxiety moving.

Conclusion

One starting point in learning more about the way that anxiety travels in your group is to diagram or map its movement. Who is the first responder to a perceived threat? Who do they share their anxiety with? What are the natural alliances that emerge? Who gets the blame? What part do you play in the dance? If you can detach yourself from the emotional swirl enough you may begin to see some of the ways that anxiety travels through your group, and you may begin to see some of your own instinctual patterned responses. These patterned responses are always contextual. The responses that you use at home may be different than those that you may use at church. You may be a distancer in your primary relationship at home and a pursuer when anxiety increases at church. Different settings may bring our different patterned responses from you. As you begin to see the ways that anxiety travels in your system, you may calm yourself enough so that you can begin to envision changing some of your patterns which have allowed the system to function in predictable ways. And that is all that you can do. You can take responsibility for yourself: your functioning, your principled positions. And while anxiety is catching; calm and collected composure is also catching! You make a difference in the system when you can change your patterned instinctual responses.

Questions for reflection:

1. When anxiety increases in your family system, what is your typical response?
2. When anxiety increases in your work system, what is your typical response?
3. What strategy do you use to calm your mind, so that you can think clearer?
4. How do you recognize when you are being guided by your clearest thinking, rather than using your intellect to rationalize following your patterned instinctual responses?

---

[1]Kerr and Bowen, *Family Evaluation,* p. 93-4.

[2]Roberta Gilbert, *Extraordinary Relationships: A New Way of Thinking About Human Interactions* (Wiley, 1992), p. 13.

[3]Jeffrey Miller, *The Anxious Organization: Why Smart Companies do Dumb Things* (Facts on Demand Press, 2008), pp. 16-18.

[4]Roberta Gilbert, *Extraordinary Leadership: Thinking Systems, Making a Difference* (Leading Systems Press, 2006), p. 8.

18

Exploring The Ninth Concept: Faith and BFST in Dialogue

Israel Galindo

"In building a theory of the world, it helps if one's vision is a little blurry."[1]

"Any effort to explain the world must begin with a leap of faith."[2]

"A man can read Darwin and the Bible but it doesn't mean he's trying to integrate the two."[3]

Introduction

One question often asked by persons beginning to explore BFST is, "Where is God in it?" While they grasp how the theory is helpful in explaining the dynamics of relationships in religious systems—and in their families—they find the lack of an overt religious orientation insufficient for their need to legitimize a way of thinking they wish to apply to their ministry. For those who claim a faith perspective the questions linger: "What's theology got to do with it?" or, "To what extent can we reconcile the theory with our beliefs?"

The answer to the question, of course, is, "God's not in the theory;" although one answer to that question from Murray Bowen is found in a letter dated Christmas 1965:

> But I do believe in the principle of believing in God! Does that make sense? It does to me. Another way of saying it is that I believe in the usefulness of the concept of God, without which man would be less than he is. . . . Where would Man be without God? God is man's continuity. Better said, God is continuity for man the individual."[4]

The Ninth Concept: A Proposal

Bowen offered the idea that it should be possible to eventually construct a scientific systems theory from functional facts about spiritual phenomena. Reading his description, it seems Bowen was hopeful for a "theory of everything."[5] Bowen was considering if there are ways to verify the function of subjective experience (e.g., spiritual experiences) into natural systems in "factual" ways.

The concept originated from Bowen's experience with individuals dealing with cancer. Michael Kerr wrote that in his interaction with these persons Bowen "was impressed that what they believed about their cancers, what they believed about their ability to survive them . . . were factors in their staying healthy. He said that what they believed may not be factual, but the fact that they believed it could be having some favorable psychological effect."[6]

While Bowen was impressed that experiences of spirituality, faith, hope, and prayer were sometimes to be positive forces on people's lives, he discovered a need to avoid a misunderstanding that the emerging concept was about "spirituality," or particular beliefs, or faith, or even religion. He therefore framed the concept at "a systems concept of supernatural phenomena."[7]

It is not a fully developed and integrated ninth concept in the theory, it is more of a proposal that acknowledges the impact of spirituality on emotional process. It speculates on the ways systems theory can be used to think about and interpret supernatural phenomena. The idea of the ninth concept was to consider whether the function of belief and faith could be integrated into a natural systems theory. Bowen "was not trying to integrate the content of beliefs. In other words, the ninth concept is about the function of belief in the emotional process of relationship systems. The concept is about the observation and interpretation of phenomena, not the thing itself."[8]

James E. Smith clarified, "While acknowledging the fact of religion, as well as other supernatural phenomena, Dr. Bowen took great pain in consistently distinguishing clearly between what can be learned by studying supernatural phenomena scientifically and the subjective experience of them."[9]

For some, the expansion into the natural sciences as an additional facet for thinking about religious systems, spiritual experiences, and leadership in congregations can feel like a stretch. For theologically-trained clergy, this often requires acquiring a new language from fields of which they have had little exposure: evolutionary biology, neuroscience, etc. The perspective of the proposed concept also does not seek to affirm particular beliefs, doctrines, theologies or confessions.

But as Randal Frost challenged, "theological claims are not exempt from the rigor or evaluation by available evidence."[10] One assumption of BFST is that "Humans are members of a multigenerational, emotional family system which radically influences all human behavior. Bowen theory focuses on the same emotional processes operating within and between humans that evolutionary biologists have discovered all life forms have in common."[11]

One challenge in the dialogue between BFST and faith is that the fundamental orienting question each asks is as different as their approaches. Religion and faith ask "Why?" as questions of meaning. Science asks questions of "How?" based on inquiry, with the "Why?" question only as to cause. Nevertheless, there is common ground between BFST theory (as science-oriented) and faith, religion, and belief.

Feverston stated, "Simply put, materialists want to research the how of existence. Spiritualists, on the other hand, search for the why. Semantically, the polarities are reflected in the difference between 'knowledge' and 'faith' and between 'perception' and 'speculation.'"[12]

The Challenge of Language

Let's begin by defining some of the terms we'll use in exploring the dialogue between the key spheres of thought.

Theory

First, we can define theory as *"A set of statements or principles devised to explain a group of facts or phenomena, especially one that has been repeatedly tested or is widely accepted and can be used to make predictions about natural phenomena."*

A theory is not an ideology nor a doctrine. BFST is a bona fide theory in that it has all the characteristics that makes up a theory: (1) it describes phenomena as it is experienced; (2) it is open to being disproved; (3) it is internally consistent; (4) it is universally applicable to the subjects of its focus.

"To move towards a theory that fits the criteria of the accepted sciences, it is essential to build it on proven or provable facts. Such a theory can only be changed by facts alone, not by personal opinion."[13]

Theology

When we use the term theology we mean "a set of intellectual and emotional commitments, justified or not, about God and persons which dictate ones beliefs and actions." Theology is metaphorical and confessional, and not primarily about truth (that's the realm of philosophy) or observable fact. Further complicating the matter is the tricky issue of schools of theology (Biblical, systematic, anthropological, process, historical, apologetics, historical, mystical, contextual) in addition to theologies that fall under the un-orthodox camps (if history teaches us anything, it's that the winners of debates get to name what constitutes orthodoxy).

Spirituality

Spirituality is a bit more difficult to define. Here's a working definition for our purpose: spirituality *is "…an emotional state of being and an emotional force that moves among humans who are aware of its presence, within themselves and within others. Like anxiety, it can be contagious."*

Spirituality is an instinctive part of humans which operates primarily as a function of the emotional system, as opposed to the feeling and intellectual systems as described by Bowen. Glenn Kellerman-Fischer stated, "In my opinion spirituality is a part of the evolutionary force described by Darwin as the force for survival."[14]

It is not too great a leap to deduce a biological brain-based basis for spirituality. The primal emotions, earliest to develop in the deep brain, are: fear, rage, panic/grief, lust, anger, play, care and searching.[15] With the development of the cortex we can extrapolate that the biological searching impulse we share with animal biology develops into an existential seeking impulse. "The process of searching for connection to the universe, the sacred or holy or the source of all life; that is, the supernatural or what is beyond human observation."[16] In a real sense, the search for the sacred is a never-ending experience for humans, because the seeking pleasure is satisfied in the experience of seeking, not by finding what it seeks.[17]

Religion

Religion is an observable aspect of human functioning. Religion is about content; about how persons order the individual in a relationship system (a culture, a tribe, a church) and in association express and consolidate beliefs about a perceived Transcendent of human existence. Spirituality is not religion; it is about the process that informs some religious content. It concerns the quest of persons to appropriate and understand foundational ("primal") forces that inform and direct life. In contrast to religion, spirituality "is not necessarily religious. And on many (most) levels, it is not about religion at all."[18]

Sometimes our language does not help in the dialogue between science and faith, or theories and belief. Our primary resource for talking about faith and spirituality is religious language, which tends to be metaphorical. Both Descarte and Ricoeur, for example, illustrate the dualism of religious language:

Diagram 1: The Dualism of Religious Language

| A cognitive description of objective reality | ← Descarte → | An affective expression of subjective experience |

Religious Language

| A hermeneutic of proclamation | ← Ricoeur → | A phenomenology of manifestation |

For Descartes religious language is a cognitive description of objective reality and an affective expression of subjective experience ("God told me to…"). Paul Ricoeur's dualism claims a hermeneutic of proclamation (e.g., doctrinal confessions) and a phenomenology of manifestation. These sufficiently illustrate the challenge of language in and dialogue between religion and science.

In response to the psychoanalytic reductionist views, however, theologian Alister Hardy claimed that spiritual experience is the experience of an actual objective reality and as such cannot be dismissed as mere illusion. Far from being a pathological aberration, religious experience is natural to the human condition, claimed Hardy, an integral part of our normal biological makeup.[19]

Further, in opposition to behaviorist psychology Hardy argued that our biological makeup does not constitute reductive cause of our spiritual experience, but rather that we possess a biologically determined openness to transcendent reality. He challenged modern hermeneutic suspicion directed against objective spiritual reality: human beings are spiritual by nature. Demitrius Dunim argued, "The spiritual world does not tolerate the kind of human control that is suggested by rigorous scientific methodology. This does not mean, however, that its reality and effects cannot be validated by careful human observation. It means, rather, that human scientific study must be modest enough to allow for the existence of a world that it cannot observe or evaluate directly."[20]

Starting Points for a Dialogue

According to Daniel Papero, "Scientific fact requires subjective agreement among scientists that the facts are reliable and reproducible. To apply Bowen's suggestion to the study of the function of the supernatural in the family would be difficult requiring access to people and families or other relationship systems regularly with systematized protocols for observation.

"It requires careful inter-observer reliability and meticulous attention to details of the interactional process. Until such a study can be conducted, or perhaps several such studies, any discussion of a ninth concept for the Bowen theory is premature."[21]

The subjective element remains a thorny matter. Paul McLean asserted that "A person working in the brain-related sciences . . . cannot avoid the realization that in the final analysis, everything reduces to subjectivity and that there is no rigorous way of defining the boundary between the subjective and what is regarded as objective."[22] According to Kerr, Bowen was seeking examples of how human subjectivity can function in ways that can be verified factually. "Verifying the function of subjectivity is one way to include supernatural phenomena in a natural theory."[23]

A Starting Point

Where might we then begin the dialogue between BFST and the realms of religion, faith, and spirituality? Both theology and theory place focus on three foundational issues: (1) describing and exploring the nature of human beings; (2) the explanation of "things as they are" and the description of "things as they appear"; (3) defining and interpreting the nature of relationships.

Bowen theory is built on the idea that all human existence is essentially and fundamentally relational (a fundamental assumption in theological anthropology and in theology in general). Differentiation is concerned about the togetherness and separateness in relationships. Religious systems, likewise, share the same idea: human existence is essentially and fundamentally relational. They are concerned with togetherness and separateness in varied ways, including mystical togetherness with the Holy, unity in the Body, separateness among people, people's relationship with God's creation, and the tragic separateness from God that results in a less than fulfilled life of meaning.

These three areas comprise points of commonality between theology and theory. In the case of BFST these relate to persons in their primary and sustaining relationship systems. In the case of theology these relate to the context of God, persons, and the relational systems of Church, world, and self. In other words, one natural starting point for dialogue between theology and theory is in striving to understand and define the nature of persons and the nature of relationships.

BFST and theology have different starting points in their epistemology. BFST strives to be grounded in the "scientific" and relies on inquiry (findings from the natural sciences based on the scientific method and other science-oriented fields), observable phenomenology ("functional facts"), and theoretical assumptions about the "self" in its approach to answering perennial questions.

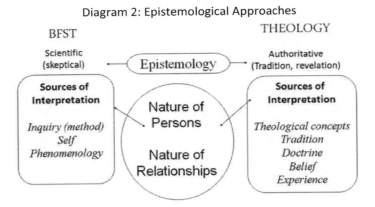

Diagram 2: Epistemological Approaches

Theology's epistemological starting points, its source of interpretation, includes theological concepts, Tradition, doctrines and beliefs, and experience (a subjective phenomenology). These are merely by way of example. Depending on the theory and the theology the function of epistemology and interpretive sources, the elements will vary.

Differentiation of Self

The concept of differentiation of self is considered by many the cornerstone of BFST. Differentiation is a function and a behavior in the context of an emotional field and the relationships within it. We all have a normal range of emotional functioning (seemingly, as do emotional systems). This range of functioning exists within the emotional field of which we are a part. Positive conditions or states are resources that help us function better within our range in the field. Anxiety, poor emotional and physical states, lower levels of psychological and emotional maturity, or toxic conditions, influence the field, and our functioning, toward less-differentiated levels of behavior and thinking.

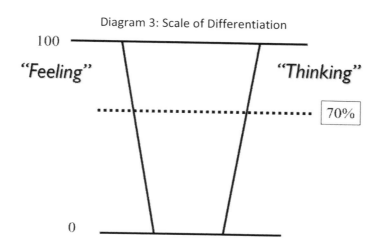

Diagram 3: Scale of Differentiation

Bowen's scale of differentiation is an illustration of a "continuum" of functioning, not a scale of static concrete stages or states. It illustrates the breadth of emotional functioning in a manner that is continuous. The metaphor of a scale is not intended to illustrate or hint that there is a way of achieving a "stage or state of differentiation," as there is in some religious traditions. More specifically, the concept identifies people's functioning according to the degree of fusion or differentiation between emotional and intellectual functioning. This characteristic is universal, the theory claims, and therefore can be used as a way of characterizing all people on a single continuum.[24]

Our level of differentiated functioning falls within the homeostatic range that is normal for us. "Given the same objective circumstances, families or individuals are more likely to dysfunction or develop symptoms 'to the extent that' their differentiation is low, and to tolerate more intense symptoms, or rebound better from intense crises, 'to the extent that' their differentiation is high."[25]

Victoria Harrison states that at lower levels of differentiation of self, fusion between members of a relationship system (a family or a congregation) produces higher levels of reactivity. "People react with and for each other. Relationships are more tense and more demanding. People will tend to depend more upon each other, or, become more reactive to each other.[26] In episodes of acute anxiety, a lack of differentiation among the members of the group heightens the occurrence and manifestation of reactivity. The most basic and universal reactive response (due to biological dynamics) are: fight, flight, frenzy, fornicate, feeding, and herding.

With higher levels of different of self, says Harrison, individuals are better able to maintain close relationships with various family members well dedicating energy toward independent pursuits. Reactivity is balanced by perspective, focus facts, and awareness of self and others. There is more flexibility to adapt to challenges of life. While depending more on self, family members are a resource to each other.[27]

Differentiation and Faith

In addition to describing the togetherness-separateness dynamics in religious bodies and relationships, Bowen theory's idea of differentiation helps us interpret two pervasive struggles with religious communities: superstition (seeing patterns that are not there) and denial (not seeing patterns that really are there). To this end Bowen theory presents objectivity, not as a delineation of the way things really are, but rather as the capacity of an observer to know where one stands inside an emotional system, and to engage the system with diminished reactivity. "And it represents subjectivity not as a delineation of idiosyncratic individualism, but rather as one standing inside an emotional system while thinking and behaving as if one is in fact outside and not affected by relationship forces."[28]

Is the concept of differentiation as spiritual concept? Marilyn Barton argued "holiness is, in fact, the top level of human functioning, that 75-100 level that Bowen could never quite pin down; no ninth concept is necessary to state that the human being is spiritual."[29]

She continues, "So, if holiness is at the top level of human functioning, then at that level we transcend completely the instinctive part of ourselves that we share with the lower forms of life. The need to attack, defend, or avoid is replaced by the selfless concern for the well-being of others (altruism) and the availability for self sacrifices. People at this level break completely free of instinctive and emotional level. They become so concentrated a self that they embrace a universal good that even frees them from being a self."[30]

Friedman described differentiation as direction in life rather than a state of being.[31] Kerr cautions that "The problem rests in viewing differentiation as a set of principles for living one's life as opposed to viewing it as a way of being that grows out of the way of thinking."[32] For Kerr differentiation is a behavior—a way of functioning in the moment in the context of a relationship system (with its emotional field). It is the ability to maintain a self in relationship to others, to be present and accounted, to function out of one's principles and values, without intruding into the life space of others.

Perhaps there is no better example of differentiated functioning than an anxiety-charged church business meeting. Every clergy is too familiar with this experience. A controversial and emotionally-charged issue in the church heightens reactivity. At a church business meeting people come out of the woodwork like cockroaches to speak to the issue. Members who have not darkened the doorstep of the church to months, even years, show up to demand a voice and assert ultimatums. People attack the pastor, the staff, and each other—making the issue personal. They question others' motives, function out of emotional reactivity, feed on conspiracies rather than facts, and generally lose their religiosity.

In the midst of the swirl of that reactivity, the pastor and others, as the leaders in the system, must stand front and center, remain non-reactive in the midst of toxic reactivity and personal attacks, and provide the function of the leader in a system gone insane with emotionality. Leaders must remain emotionally present while speaking out of their principles, the corporate values of the community (when it is at its best), and the framework of the religious beliefs the community confesses. This is differentiation in the context of a relationship.

Randall Frost said it this way, "One test of differentiation is the ability of a person to take a more principled position and hold it against the opposition of important others."[33] How is this different from stubbornness? In contrast to reactivity, differentiation is based on clearly held principles and values that serve as a guide to life, dealing with relationships, and practice.

Thomas Kelly said, "An adequate life …is one that has grasped intuitively the whole nature of things, and has seen and felt and refocused itself to that whole."[34] There is opportunity for dialogue between BFST, the concept of differentiation of self, and various stage theories, including Fowler's Stages of Faith, Piaget's cognitive theory, and Kohlberg's moral development theory. Those developmental theories describe a qualitative difference in lower and higher ways of thinking (cognition), or between naïve and immature ways of thinking. We see similar in the concept of differentiation of self, and in the realm of spirituality. For example, we don't expect spiritual maturity from the emotionally immature; and we don't expect capacity for a higher level of functioning in differentiation from a person lacking the capacity to think critically, clearly, and systemically.

The concept of differentiation of self is highly application to religious systems, perhaps most helpful to clergy and other religious leaders—if only because of its focus on functioning. It helps us understand that a highly differentiated person can function in healthy ways in a highly emotional system.

Differentiation can help religious leaders move healthily between boundaries: between I and ours; between "We" and "us." It can help leaders stay within appropriate boundaries and avoid being willful or invasive—both forms of spiritual abuse in religious systems. It helps clergy avoid trying to create others, or the system, in his or her own image—a form of idolatry.

Differentiation of self can help clergy maintain clarity between function, role, and identity. It is extremely helpful to clergy to not confuse being a "Pastor" with personal Self, and accept that most congregational members will have a relationship with their role than with them personally. Differentiation can help pastors (who often are at a different place theologically, and a different stage of faith than their congregations) authentically share the corporate values of the systems they lead. They can navigate the necessity to differentiate corporate values (which are negotiated) and personal ones, and can reconcile the difference. They can share to an appropriate extent their pastoral identity with the emotional system, without losing their own.

Religious Communities as Emotional Fields

So here's a question: to what extent does a religious systems (e.g., a congregation as a community of faith) serve to provide a Pseudo-self to the undifferentiated, at the expense of the promotion of a Real-Self? This is an important question when one accepts the idea that the best we can do both in families and in any relationship systems is the promotion of differentiation of self which enables individuals in the system to take responsibility for self. Given the following characteristics of faith systems (like congregations), to what extent is it possible?

- Religiosity
- Togetherness forces (seeking the unity of the Body)
- Shared corporate identity (the Synthetic-literal faith of the majority in a congregation)
- Group think (us vs. them. If religion is about anything, it's about who is "in" and who is "out")
- Uncritical belief and magical thinking
- Reinforcement of community bias
- Rigidity in beliefs and perspectives (fundamentalism, dispensationalism, Rapture-theology, cults).

One fundament challenge for clergy is to what extent can a congregation foster growth and development of a real-self, of differentiation, in its members? How can a religious leader work to promote differentiation and spiritual maturity given the dynamics of the togetherness forces in a faith community? The responsible dialogue between BFST and religion, spirituality, and faith cannot ignore that question.

BFST, Spirituality, Religion, and Faith

There is a limit, of course, to what BFST can address in matters related to faith, spirituality, and supernatural phenomenon in religious systems. Kerr confessed, "There is a supernatural plane that will never be explained by science. . . . The key is acknowledging what we cannot explain, and incorporating into theory only those aspects of what cannot be explained that are proven or provable."[35]

Bowen theory is built on the idea that all human existence is essentially and fundamentally relational—a concept shared by most religious systems. Differentiation is concerned about the togetherness and separateness in relationships. BFST offers questions on two sides of the same coin: (1) understanding how the function of a belief fits into the emotional system, and (2) understanding how the functioning of the emotional system influences the development of belief.

E. O. Wilson claimed that people need a sacred narrative. They must have a sense of a larger purpose in one form or another, however intellectualized. "They will refuse to yield to the despair of animal mortality. They will continue to plead, in company with the Psalmist, "Now Lord, what is my comfort?" They will find a way to keep the ancestral spirits alive. Man would rather believe than know, have the void as purpose, as Nietzsche said, than be void of purpose."[36]

John Bonner, says, however, that science "is about things. It is about all those things that surround us and which used to be called Nature with a capital N. Furthermore, it is about the relation of things; science is concerned with order. There are two ways we can deal with these things. The first and most obvious is to describe them. But description itself is dissatisfying and insufficient. It is a large heap with no order to it. Finding the order in the descriptive facts is the great purpose of science. The making of generalizations—sometimes called theories, or laws, or principles—about facts is always considered the greatest triumph in the human pursuit of science."[37]

While E. O. Wilson was correct in saying that religion "will possess strength to the extent that it codifies and puts into enduring poetic form the highest values of humanity consistent with empirical knowledge. This is the only way to provide compelling moral leadership"[38] One major benefit in the dialogue between BFST and spirituality is that "the idea of 'functional facts' is crucial for "extracting facts from the morass of human subjectivity." As Bowen described, whatever love is, it is factual that people react to statements regarding it. Seeing the function of the statements in a relationship permits the observer to discern knowable and predictable relationship patterns."[39]

There are facts about the way beliefs function in emotional systems claims Kerr.[40] What, then, might be the functional facts of spirituality and faith on emotional systems? Here are a few.

1. To reduce anxiety

Religion and other belief systems have been and are powerful binders of human chronic anxiety.[41] Modernism, claims Douglas H. Ort, attempts to resolve its anxiety about religious fragmentation and animosity by promoting what is essentially amounts to an unregulated "togetherness" naming it "spirituality." Postmodernism, facing the same social anxiety promotes a relativism that essentially amounts to an unregulated "individuality." Why not also name it "spirituality?"[42]

Ona Cohn Bregman, also claims, "Belief systems develop to manage the instinctive existential anxiety which humans have about mortality. They are built on selective assumptions. The assumptions may be personal and/or communal, part of a religion, or not. It cannot be proved that any are 'right.'"[43] In other words, whether religious beliefs are true or not, they serve the same function: to reduce anxiety.

2. To provide a frame of meaning

Belief systems developed manage the instinctive, existential anxiety which humans have about mortality. They are built on selective assumptions. The assumptions may be personal and/or communal, part of the religion or not. It cannot be proved that any are right, however, states Bergman.[44] Beliefs provide a moral code for ethical behavior in relationships systems, thereby mediating functioning and emotional process among its members. They also provide a "center" for the formation of corporate identity, which facilitates and perpetuates the togetherness forces.

3. Maintain Tradition, pass on the faith.

Beliefs help maintain and provide generative homeostasis. The generative nature of faith communities requires them to pass on beliefs, practices, norms, culture, and yes, emotional processes from generation to generation. In other words, the concept of multigenerational transmission very much applies to faith traditions, religious bodies, and faith communities (like congregations), as much as it does to biological families.

Conclusion

We can approach the dialogue through six theses and several framing questions:

Theses

1. Spiritual experiences and religious beliefs can be treated as "functional facts" which are open to exploration when they are relevant in the context of the emotional process in a system (e.g., a family, a congregation). The veracity (the "Truth") of those beliefs is subjective and is to a greater or lesser extent of secondary concern to an observer.

2. Religious relationship systems (congregations, synagogues, religious societies, etc.) function in similar ways to "family systems," and certain to a great extent, consistently, with relationship systems; they follow the "rules" of those systems and manifest universal emotional process dynamics.

3. There is a positive correlation between spiritual maturity and the capacity to function in a self-differentiated manner, though the concept of differentiation of self is not equivalent to emotional or spiritual maturity. Nor can the concept be defined by ideas of spiritual or mystic stages.

4. The practice of spiritual disciplines—including religious rites—and beliefs can have a mediating effect on anxiety in a relationship system. Feverstein claimed "there is gathering observable evidence that spiritual activities (meditation, religious practices and so on) change the nature and functioning of the brain."[45]

5. The theory provides clergy and religious leaders the ability to deal with spiritual religious positions, beliefs, and content without the anxiety-driven need to change the other, or keep the other from changing (avoiding willfulness that can lead to spiritual abuse).[46]

6. BFST can help clergy and religious leaders cultivate the ability to deal with triangles involving the people's relationships with their clergy: their own religious and spiritual unresolved issues and the congregation; triangles which involve responding to critics of religion; triangles involving church members' unresolved issues of spirituality and faith and the church; triangles involving parental anxiety about the spiritual condition of their children ("Make my child more religious," "Help me get my child baptized!"), etc.[47]

Questions

- What is the function of invoking religious belief in an emotional system?
- How does religious belief impact the emotional process of a system?
- What is the relationship between "functional facts" and religious experience?
- Can we be objective about subjective spiritual experiences?
- Can we observe spiritual process at work in individuals and families? What does it look like? How is it manifested?
- Is there empirical evidence for, or a biological connection to, supernatural phenomenon? Is there a "God gene"? Or a "God spot" in the brain? Is spirituality part of our biology?
- Can we articulate that which is thought to be spiritual as part of the functioning of the family as an emotional unit? Spirituality is a personal phenomenon. Does it extent to larger relationship systems? Can you have a "spiritual church"?
- Is that which seems to transcend nature still a part of nature? If we hold to the concept of "super-natural" phenomenon, to what extent is it part of nature? Is it something else that requires particular epistemologies, ways of sensing? (Gnostic)
- How do humans use the supernatural in their lives?
- What is the function of the supernatural in human processes?
- To what extent can one investigate how the supernatural functions in the human family?
- Who in the system invokes the supernatural, when and where is it invoked, and what happens when it is invoked?
- How does the invocation of the supernatural affect family emotional process and functioning positions of the individual, of various key relationships, and of the larger family system?

- How does the invocation of the supernatural affect family emotional process and functioning positions of the individual, of various key relationships, and of the larger family system?
- How does the invocation of the supernatural affect the patterns of family emotional process?
- How does the invocation of the supernatural enhance or hinder the family's adaptation to challenge?[48]

------

[1]George Johnson, *Fire in the Mind: Science, Faith, and the Search for Order* (New York: Random House, 1995), p. 44.

[2]Ibid.

[3]Charles J. Crotty.

[4]Murray Bowen. Correspondence dated December 1965.

[5]"In the past few months I have been saying that we will eventually be able to *think* systems 'all the way' and when that time comes we will be able to conceptualize the total of human existence within a single systems framework," Bowen, correspondence dated April 27, 1980.

[6]Kerr, "On the Development of a Ninth Concept," July 2004, p. 1.

[7]Ibid., p. 7.

[8]Ibid.

[9]James E. Smith, "Bowen Theory and The 'Wisdom of the Ages,'" a paper presented at the Wisdom of the Ages conference, 2004, p. 5.

[10]Randal Frost, "Faith and functioning," (1998), p. 4.

[11]Donald J. Shoulberg, cited in Ernst Mayr, *The Growth of Biological Thought* (Harvard University Press, 1982).

[12]Reuven Feuerstein, Louis Falik, and Refael S. Feuerstein, *Changing Minds & Brains* (Teachers College Press, 2015), p. 121.

[13]Michael Kerr, from a paper presented at the Wisdom of the Ages conference, 1998.

[14]Glenn Kellerman-Fischer, "Bowen Theory and Spirituality: A Look at One Aspect of a Broad Range of Supernatural Phenomena," a paper presented at the Wisdom of the Ages Conference, 1994.

[15]See Jaak Panksepp (1992). "A critical role for "affective neuroscience" in resolving what is basic about basic emotions." Psychological Review. 99 (3): 554–60.

[16]Ona Cohn Bregman, "Bowen Theory, Spirituality, and Judaism," paper presented at the Wisdom of the Ages conference, 1998.

[17]See Jaak Panksepp, "A critical role for "affective neuroscience" in resolving what is basic about basic emotions."

[18]Douglas H. Ort, "Differentiation, Spirituality, and Religion," paper presented at the Wisdom of the Ages conference, 1998.

[19]See Alister Hardy, *The Divine Flame* (Collins, 1976) , *The Spiritual Nature of Man* (Oxford University Press, 1979) and *The Biology of God: A Scientists' Study of Man the Religious Animal* (Taplinger Pub. Co.,1976).

[20]Demitrius Dunim, "Human Fulfillment from a Biblical Perspective," paper presented at the Wisdom of the Ages conference, 1998.

[21]Daniel Papero, 2014, pp. 17-18.

[22]Paul D. McLean, *The Triune Brain in Evolution* (Springer, 1990, p. 570

[23]Kerr, 1998.

[24]Bowen, "On the Differentiation of Self," in *Family Therapy in Clinical Practice* (Jason Aronson 1993), p. 472.

[25]Edwin H. Friedman, "Bowen Theory and Therapy" in *The Handbook of Family Therapy,* edited by A.S. Gurman and D.P. Kniskern, Brunner-Mazel (Routledge, 1991), p. 143.

[26]Victoria Harrison, "A Study of Prayer and Human Reactivity," 1998.

[27]Ibid.

[28]Douglas H. Ort, "Differentiation, Spirituality, and Religion," p. 3.

[29]Marilyn Barton, "The Complexity of Telling a Simple Story of Man," 2004.

[30]Ibid.

[31]Edwin H. Friedman, *A Failure of Nerve: Leadership in the Age of the Quick Fix* (Seabury, 2007), p. 236.

[32]Kerr, "On the Development of a Ninth Concept," 2004.

[33]Frost, 1998, p. 4.

[34]Thomas Kelly, *A Treatment of Devotion* (New York: Harper Collins, 1992).

[35]Kerr, 1998.

[36]E. O. Wilson, "Back from Chaos," *The Atlantic Monthly* 1998, p. 70.

[37]John Tyler Bonner, *The Scale of Nature* (Pegasus, 1970), pp. 18, 22.

[38]E. O. Wilson, "The Biological Basis of Morality," *Atlantic Monthly* (April 1998).

[39]Kerr, "On The Development of a Ninth Concept," p. 8.

---

[40]Kerr, "Towards A Systems Concept of Supernatural Phenomenon," 1998.

[41]Ibid., p. 14.

[42]Douglas H. Ort, "Differentiation, Spirituality, and Religion," paper presented at the Wisdom of the Ages conference, 1998.

[43]Ona Cohn Bregman "Bowen Theory, Spirituality, and Judaism: The Connection and the Self," paper presented at The Wisdom of the Ages conference, 1998.

[44]Bergman 1998.

[45]Reuven Feverstein, *Changing Minds and Brains,* (Teachers College Press, 2014), p. 121.

[46]Carl Jensen, "The Ninth Concept in Practice: Toward Models for Consultations," a paper presented at the Wisdom of the Ages conference, 2004.

[47]Ibid.

[48]See Nancy Gimbel, "On the Development of a Ninth Concept," paper presented at the Wisdom of the Ages conference.

19

Understanding and Being Understood: Positives and Perils

Rebecca Werner Maccini

In 26 years of pastoral ministry, Rebecca has been a pastor of young adults, co-pastor, bi-vocational pastor, and sole pastor. She attended workshops at the Center for Family Process, Georgetown Family Center, New England Seminar on Bowen Theory, and the Vermont Center for Family Process. She has presented several times about applications of Bowen Family Systems Theory in congregational settings at symposiums of the Vermont Center for Family Process, the Dartmouth Hitchcock Medical Center, the Vermont Conference of the United Church of Christ, and ATTach. Through the New Hampshire Conference of the United Church of Christ, she has been a consultant to churches, led small church vitality workshops, and currently leads a clergy

group and coordinates the New Hampshire School of Ministry.
Rebecca joined the faculty of LIM in 2015.

Providing pastoral care is an essential responsibility of clergy. Being understanding and helping parishioners to feel understood are basic aspects of pastoral care. What is the value of understanding? What are the pitfalls of understanding? How much understanding do we give to those whom we serve? How much understanding do parishioners really need? I want to explore understanding and being understood through two concepts of Bowen Family Systems Theory: (1) the nuclear family emotional process; and (2) the family projection process.

Every congregation is an emotional system, with its own relational patterns between clergy and congregation and amongst and within committees, methods of communicating, ways to hold or perceive the history, and secret-keeping. In a congregation, the nuclear family emotional process can be observed through ongoing relational patterns. It might be a conflict between the music director and the pastor, or the distance between the women's group and the church leaders, or constant anxiety and focus on the lack of youth, or the overfunctioning of the pastor.

When we observe common relational patterns in the emotional process, we can learn how people in various roles in a congregation commonly relate to one another, and understand the overall ways that a congregation functions. We can become aware of common patterns and where conflict is most likely to arise to impede or affect ministry.

Within the nuclear family emotional process is the family projection process. Murray Bowen defined it as "the process by which parents project part of their immaturity to one or more of the children."[1] I believe that this plays out in congregations as an intense focus on those who have the most needs or are the most immature. Clergy can easily become focused on the people who are the squeaky wheels, those who come to the clergy and demand the most time, the ones who most often criticize the clergy or the church, those who bludgeon the by-laws to get what they want. People who have an acute crisis come to the pastor with needs that often are fairly clear; and the pastor responds. This is not the projection process. However, there are people with chronic conditions (not always those who have the least financial or material resources) who constantly need our help and support. Often, these are people upon whom we project anxiety.

When I was in seminary, the concept of empathy was endorsed. If we could fully understand another, if we could feel what they were feeling, our pastoral care would be more effective. I was a very, very sensitive child, and empathy was highly familiar to me. However, serving as a congregational pastor for a couple of decades, I have learned several things about empathy. One is that always seeking to empathize can lead to burnout, and an overfocus on making sure that someone is understood, and on feeling what they feel, still leaves that person feeling misunderstood because we cannot ever fully understand anyone. If we strive for complete understanding, it fails to allow room for other people's growth because of the invasion into someone's space, mind, and feelings. Ed Friedman said, "An enormous amount of empathy is a disguise for anxiety. Caring is an unlimited concept. If you make the basis of the way you're going to deal with people caring, there is absolutely never a way to know when to stop or how much is enough, and it feeds into the hands of the unmotivated."[2]

What I seek to bring into my pastoral care work is perspective, presence, and principle. I want to listen to and learn how others see the world, gain their perspective; however, I do not want to think their thoughts or feel their feelings. I want to listen to their story, reflect upon what is important to them, and try to discern their real needs as best I can.

I also want to offer a loving presence that includes a sense of good will toward the other. As clergy, we often work with people who are handling life's challenges poorly. We are called to share God's love with them, but God's love is not to be equated with coddling.

I also want to keep in mind the principles that I have for ministry and what is integral to my call. One of my principles in pastoral care is to focus on and try to identify what strengths and resources someone may have and which ones are available to support them in their walk in life. If I have difficulty with this, I remain focused on being a loving presence, and a calm and thoughtful listener.

To sustain oneself in ministry, to do effective pastoral care, is always a matter of knowing and growing oneself.

---

[1]Murray Bowen, *Family Therapy in Clinical Practice* (New York: Jason Aronson, 1978), p. 477.

[2]Edwin H. Friedman, *Work Systems and Family Systems*, cassette recording (Silver Spring, MD: Seven Oaks Foundation, 1987).

❖

20
Anxiety Makes the World Go Round

Margaret B. Hess

Margaret (Meg) B. Hess received her BA from Meredith College in Raleigh, NC and received her Master of Divinity from Andover Newton Theological School as well as the Doctor of Ministry degree, with honors, in Pastoral Counseling. She is ordained by the American Baptist Churches, USA, where she served pastorates for twenty years in Massachusetts and New Hampshire. She has been an adjunct faculty in preaching at Andover Newton Theological School. Hess is a Pastoral Counselor with The Emmaus Institute in Nashua, NH, and a Fellow in the American Association of Pastoral Counselors.

My first introduction to Bowen Family Systems Theory was through reading Ed Friedman's book Generation to Generation. But I didn't begin to integrate the theory into my life and ministry until I took a Family Systems course as a part of my DMin in Pastoral Counseling. In the unit on Bowen Theory, Professor Earl Thompson wrote one word on the blackboard in all caps: ANXIETY. "If you don't understand that Bowen Theory is all about anxiety," he said, "then you don't understand Bowen Theory." My ears perked up at that point, because anxiety is a state of being with which I am very familiar. Now, after more than 25 years of studying BFST and working with anxiety, my own and in the systems where I live and work, I heartily agree that anxiety is central to the Theory.

A simple definition of anxiety is that it is the "response of an organism to a threat." The threat can be real or imagined; often the brain cannot distinguish the difference. Anxiety is hardwired into the human brain, a gift of evolution to keep human beings awake and alert to danger so that they may survive. Anxiety is expressed by physical symptoms in the body: elevated heart rate, increase in blood pressure, shakiness, feeling faint and wobbly, constriction in the throat and chest area, muscle tension, sweating; all signs that the body is on high alert. Anxiety also shows up in a sense of impending dread, fear, panic, confusion, or racing thoughts. Sometimes a normal anxiety response can escalate into a panic attack where the physical symptoms are so intense the person fears they are experiencing a heart attack.

The part of the human brain known as the amygdala orchestrates the anxiety response in the body. It alerts the automatic nervous system to kick in the physical responses named above and impacts the body's hormones. The result is increases of adrenalin, cortisone, insulin, and thyroid. When anxiety kicks in, the body and mind are on high alert and ready to engage in fight or flight behavior: stay and fight the threat or escape. All of this is designed to keep humans safe and to help us act quickly in dangerous situations.

We can add some other ways to the list of how we react to anxiety. I like to think of these as the "F" words. In addition to *fight* or *flight*, there is *freeze*, where the individual holds perfectly still in order blend in and not be seen. Feeling stuck or paralyzed in the face of fear or distancing from others may be expressions of freezing. *Flocking* engages the "herding mechanism" where the individual seeks safety in numbers. Going along with the thinking or actions of the group is an expression of flocking. Some have even suggested that care-taking or fixing is a response to anxiety. And then there is always *fornicate*, for those who engage in sexual behavior or acting out when under stress.

Anxiety and Systems Thinking

If anxiety is central to an understanding of Murray Bowen's Family Systems Theory, then it is rooted in his thinking about basic life forces. "The theory postulates two opposing basic life forces. One is a built-in life growth force toward individuality and the differentiation of a separate "self," and the other an equally intense emotional closeness."[1] Bowen posited that every dyadic, or two-person, relationship is inherently unstable. Two individuals in a relationship are always moving between the two forces of togetherness and individuality. Each dyad has a baseline of comfort with the amount of distance between them. If they move too close to each other, then their anxiety rises. If they move further apart from each other than their normal baseline allows, their anxiety goes up. There is a continual movement toward and away from each other as the dyad seeks to find a balance that does not escalate their anxiety. This understanding is foundational to Bowen's theory of triangles.

A triangle is formed when the dyadic relationship draws in a third person to stabilize the relationship, or to return it to its comfortable baseline of closeness/distance. Anxiety is the driver behind the creation of triangles. The triangle binds the anxiety as it helps the dyad return to its familiar level of connection.

And if you watch how interlocking triangles are formed, you can see how the anxiety is handed around the system. Triangles are both the binders and the distributers of anxiety in an emotional system. When thinking about your position in a triangle, you might wonder about whose anxiety you are holding in the triangle: yours, someone else's, or the system's.

One can apply curiosity about anxiety to all of Bowen's basic concepts. For example, use anxiety as a lens to explore the development of basic relationship patterns of the *Nuclear Family Emotional Process*. Patterns of distance, cut-off, conflict, accommodation, fusion, over/under- functioning reciprocity, or triangulation can all be framed as a response to anxiety. *The Family Projection Process* reveals how parents transfer their emotional anxiety to their children. One can trace how anxiety impacts levels of self-differentiation in the *Multigenerational Transmission Process*.

One generation's capacity to deal with the episodes of acute anxiety can raise or lower the next generation's ability to develop resilience- or not- in relation to stressful events. Events of acute anxiety can become chronic anxiety for future generations in a system. And the rise and fall of anxiety can be clearly seen in *Societal Emotional Process*, especially in the intense polarization of our current political process.

When thinking about the connection between anxiety and Systems Thinking, it is important to remember that anxiety is contagious. Anxiety is one of the most communicable of mental health states. As you become aware of your own anxiety profile, then your ability to choose your responses thoughtfully increase. Developing spiritual practices and self-care strategies that help you to down-regulate in times of high stress are vital to your effectiveness as a leader. Noting how your response to anxiety has been shaped by the multi-generational process in your family of origin can help you override reactivity with thoughtfulness.

Anxiety is What You Make of It

The temptation is to think of anxiety as "bad." When the amygdala hijacks our brain and we are flooded with anxiety it can be deeply uncomfortable. Not to mention that when anxiety gets triggered, we can react in ways that are counter to our goals, values, and guiding principles. But it is important to remember that anxiety has kept our species alive. The question for congregational leaders is: how can we make friends with our anxiety and learn to have a relationship with anxiety that serves our best functioning?

In his book *Finding Serenity in An Age of Anxiety*, Robert Gerzon suggests we think of three types of anxiety: Natural or normal, Toxic, and Sacred. Natural anxiety alerts us to real danger and helps keep us safe.[2] Paying attention to normal anxiety motivates us to do practical things to take care of ourselves and to make wise choices.

Toxic anxiety is where natural anxiety is no longer helpful to us, but rather keeps us stuck, dwelling on the future or ruminating on the past in ways that do not serve our best goals. Toxic anxiety has taken over when our reactivity is "driving the bus" of our choices and decisions.

Sacred anxiety is stirred up by the big questions of life: who are we, why are we here, what is our purpose, what is our connection to the Sacred or Divine? Attending to these questions can lead us to live more meaningful lives. Gerzon's categories help us to be more discerning when looking at our own anxious responses to life's challenges and opportunities.

Know Your Anxiety Story

Knowing our own anxiety story helps us to achieve self-differentiated leadership. According to Ed Friedman, the three key areas of this type of leadership are self-definition, self-regulation, and staying connected. Anxiety generated confusion can contribute to fuzzy thinking about our goals, principles, and values. Anxiety leads to reactivity, which also can result in poor leadership functioning. Relationship eroding distancing or cut-off can also be responses to intense anxiety. Promoting self-awareness around anxiety supports our efforts to define who we are, to self-regulate, and to stay connected in healthy ways with everyone in our relationship systems.

Managing our own anxiety, and understanding the impact of the anxiety of others on us can help us to lead in ways that are less anxious. Friedman suggests that the "non-anxious presence" of the leader can increase a system's capacity to function more effectively. I prefer to think of this as "less-reactive functioning" because I know it is impossible for me to be completely non-anxious. Again, anxiety can be a valuable source of information. But I can *feel* anxious and still *function* in a less reactive way. Our efforts to learn from and manage our anxiety more effectively can serve the health of a system.

In my work with congregational leaders, I invite them to make a research project out of studying their own anxiety. In exploring the following questions, one notes their internal level of anxiety and can track when it shifts up or down. Increased awareness of our own anxiety patterns will help us to know when we need to down-regulate our reactive responses.

- How do you know when you are anxious?

- What physical symptoms do you experience when you are anxious?
- How do you talk to yourself when you are anxious?
- What strategies help you to calm yourself and down-regulate when you are anxious?
- When flooded with anxiety, how can you get more thoughtful about your responses?

I also ask leaders to examine their role in their family of origin in relation to anxiety. There are a few roles that people play in a system around anxiety. Some are the *generators* of anxiety (think drama Kings and Queens.) Others are the *amplifiers* of anxiety. They take minor anxiety and exaggerate it (like Chicken Little.) The *dampeners* of anxiety play it down and make it seem less important than it is. And then there are the *absorbers* of anxiety. These are the people who soak up the anxiety in a system like a sponge, often developing somatic symptoms.

The role you play regarding anxiety may vary from system to system. For example, in your family of origin you might be an amplifier but in your congregational system you are a dampener of anxiety. Remember, in systems thinking this is not a function of personality but rather a result of the relational dynamics in an emotional field. Some questions to consider are:
- What role did/do you play in relation to anxiety in your family of origin?
- What role do you play in relation to anxiety in your work/ministry system?
- How might you become more mindful about these roles?
- When do you notice that you are taking on the anxiety of others?
- How might you hand the anxiety back to the congregation?

Exploring these questions provides prospective on how the emotional process is at work in a System. Getting emotional distance from the intensity of the System can help us to think more clearly about our goals and strategies as a leader. Assessing the anxiety levels in the emotional systems where we live and work helps clarify our leadership choices. Managing our own anxiety helps us to be "more at home in our own skin" as we lead our congregations.

Questions for Consideration:
- How do you assess the anxiety level in the emotional systems where you live and work?
- Whose anxiety are you likely to hold when the anxiety ramps up in your ministry setting?
- How can you tell whose anxiety you are holding?
- How might you "hand the anxiety back" to another person or system?

---

[1]Murray Bowen, *Family Therapy in Clinical Practice* (Jason Aronson Inc., 1990), p. 424.

[2]Robert Gerzon, *Finding Serenity in the Age of Anxiety* (Bantam Books, 2012), Kindle edition.

21

Leader Self-Differentiation and Team Empowerment

Brian Virtue

Brian Virtue is Leadership Studies Professor at the International Graduate School of Leadership in Manila, Philippines and the Director of Leadership Development and Human Resources.

Introduction

In response to an observation that the Indo-European word leith, for leader, means "to go forth, to die," Peter Steinke poses the question, "Is it foolish to ask, 'How can I lead and stay alive?"[1] Heifetz and Linsky similarly muse, "To lead is to live dangerously."[2] While Steinke's humorous yet sobering question reveals the extreme of the potential pitfalls of leadership, it also assumes as reality the age-old tension naturally inherent in the dynamics between those who have power and those who do not, between the leader and the follower. These tensions continue to be evident today and frequently present challenges to churches and ministries as well to the ministry teams entrusted with leading them.

The challenges of ministry leadership are numerous amidst the complex dynamics between leaders and followers, but the greatest challenge for the leader in his or her efforts to maximize progress towards the larger vision may very well be related to their own personal maturity in relationships.

Leadership does not occur in a vacuum. Where there are organizational or ministry leaders attempting to lead or who have been entrusted to lead, there are others that complete the relational backdrop of a team or chain of command. The leader's effectiveness will largely be based on their ability to lead these others towards effective and meaningful service towards their unifying purpose or vision.

A leader's level of emotional maturity has one of the greatest influences upon their ability to create the healthy and empowering environments needed to lead well. In fact, emotionally mature leaders will be able to sustain these kind of healthy relationships and team environments that are fruitful in ministry, while emotionally immature leaders will tend to produce unhealthy team environments as a result of embroiling themselves in cycles of emotional reactivity with or in response to those that they are entrusted to lead.

Emotional Maturity and Intentions

Most leaders in my experience recognize that their success is connected in large part to those that they lead and their team's collective health and productivity. They often have read the latest leadership books and have good and sincere intentions towards the people that are under their trust. The good intentions are there, yet progress towards the vision often gets derailed as a result of team or interpersonal conflict or low morale. Progress can also be hindered by the loss of highly valuable laborers, who rather than leaving "for" something else have chosen to flee "from" a situation that they perceive is harmful to their personal well-being.

These all too common realities reflect the sobering truth that despite good intentions, leaders cannot escape the fruit of their own character when it comes to executing the roles and responsibilities of a leader. Steinke agrees as he writes, "The way in which the leader functions arises out of who the leader is. The leader's being and functioning are twin to each other."[3] The character ingredient often missing from leaders who are failing to produce health and effectiveness in ministry is emotional maturity.

Emotional Maturity and Differentiation

Mark McCloskey, professor of transformational leadership at Bethel Seminary, identifies five critical factors that determine one's level of emotional maturity: (1) recognition and regulation, (2) resilience, (3) realism, (4) responsibility, and (5) resonance and relational connection.[4] First, an emotionally mature person has the capacity to connect honestly with his or her own emotional climate and exercise self-control over that climate in the context of relationships (recognition and regulation). Second, an emotionally mature person has a strong capacity for hope and sustaining motivation and drive amidst struggle and challenge (resilience). Third, he or she has a strong capacity to embrace the reality about themselves and about the external world or circumstances with honesty and humility (realism). Fourth, the emotionally mature person is able to assume responsibility for their own feelings, attitudes, actions, as the impact of their decisions (responsibility). Finally, the emotionally mature person has the capacity to stay connected with others in a meaningful way over the course of the ups and downs of work and relationships (resonance and relational connection).

All of these capacities reflect a central concept integral in family systems theory and made popular by theorists and practitioners such as Murray Bowen and Edwin Friedman. They describe this concept as self-differentiation. Leroy T. Howe writes,

> "Theologically construed, the capacity for self-differentiation is the capacity to be the persons God intends us to be, sharing with all human beings a common destiny to care for the earth on our creator's behalf....human beings are created with both the capacity and the calling to differentiate themselves as distinctive individuals even as they remain connected and contributory to the larger family which is humankind itself."[5]

Self-differentiation and the larger notion of emotional maturity have as their basis the capacity to stay separate, but stay connected relationally. Parker Palmer describes this capacity as being able to embrace the "profoundly opposite truths that my sense of self is deeply dependent on others dancing with me and that I still have a self when no one wants to dance."[6]

Emotional maturity is a broader concept than self-differentiation, but at the same time it is very much dependent on one's level of differentiation. Many of McCloskey's components of emotional maturity or even what Daniel Goleman identifies as "emotional intelligence" is anchored in a person's ability to have a healthy sense of their own limitations as well as the limitations of others. Can one really regulate one's own emotional landscape or empathize freely with the plights of others when there is emotional confusion about where one's significance and identity is anchored? Self-differentiation is a vital ingredient of identity that fuels one's capacity for self-control and internal harmony as well as the capacity to relate to others well without confusing the dynamic with unresolved personal identity issues.

Leader Self-Differentiation and Challenge

If one's sense of personal security is not resolved, they are going to be more vulnerable to being blown about by the storms of leadership and personal anxiety. Leaders have an immense challenge before them as their level of self-differentiation is challenged at every turn. Leaders are the "go to" people when team members have needs they want to have met, want change, have feedback, or disagree. Even if team members demonstrate great maturity in bringing these items to the leader, the leader who is insecure or poorly differentiated can still be overwhelmed with anxiety because poor self-differentiation opens one self up to confusion about what defines them and what does not. These leaders grow anxious because such feedback ends up having a disproportionate amount of power in their lives, serving as a catalyst for the destructive belief that their identity is connected directly to what people think or feel about them. Leaders caught in this emotional dynamic often swing to the extremes of either allowing themselves to be completely defined by the feedback as they lose sight of themselves or they completely disregard the input or the messengers themselves so that they can preserve their own sense of identity.

Emotionally immature leaders, especially young leaders, can have a difficult time discerning the difference between healthy community feedback that serves the greater good and the toxic pushback that flows from others' lack of emotionally immaturity. McCloskey writes that, "The leadership challenge is to distinguish between the two, and appropriately handle the constructive dissent."[7] Younger leaders who lack a secure sense of self can cave into the demands of toxic demands out of an effort to prove one's self or preserve one's status as the leader. Undifferentiated leaders may not always give into toxic demands, but again they often swing to the other extreme of guarding against all challenges or feedback. These leaders tend to get emotionally lost amidst feedback, pushback, and frustration. They then tend to throw the proverbial "baby out with the bathwater" as they are not secure enough to identify important feedback when it comes.

Emotionally mature leaders are able to look beyond their own anxiety to sift out toxicity and learn as much as they can from those that have worthwhile contributions to make to the greater good. Maybe even more importantly, emotionally mature and self-differentiated leaders have the capacity to stay in relationship with those messengers of feedback or push back, because they possess the personal security and the humility to continue to move towards relationship without the anxiety of losing their own sense of self in the process.

Anxiety is a key concept in modern family systems theory and it represents the general or specific angst that people carry around in response to change, differences, or an encounter with things or situations outside of their control. Anxiety is a mark of poor self-differentiation when we understand the concept in the context of relationships or relational systems. Anxiety reflects the condition of a person who needs factors in relationships external to them to change in order to be restored to a sense of personal security. From a leadership perspective, emotional fusion and emotional cutoff are two extremes of how individuals can respond out of their own anxiety if they are unable to preserve their sense of self in the face of the relational demands around them. In the context of leadership, both reactions are deadly to any hope of creating healthy environments that are empowering other leaders to action for the sake of the mission.

Emotional fusion in this context occurs when a leader's anxiety about being separate is so great that they become enmeshed with those that they are leading, ceasing to be able to effectively execute many of the duties of leadership such as thinking clearly and objectively, holding people accountable for results, and preserving directional focus to the team's efforts. Enmeshment is when someone chooses a limitless "togetherness" to avoid a sense of anxiety about alone or rejected. Steinke even notes that leader indecisiveness can be a form of this kind of emotional reactivity because it functions as a defense mechanism against having to take a stand that might threaten the perceived relational harmony of the group.8

McCloskey observes that these types of leaders "feel duty bound to respond to the 'need' of others, no matter the nature of the need (italics mine)."9 These leaders are unable to function as responsible adults due to the strength of their need for approval or emotional security. Emotional fusion takes place when the leader abandons a healthy sense of self for a form of peace and harmony, no matter how dysfunctional it may be. The emotionally fused leader is afraid and unable to be separate enough to lead. Rima issues the warning that, "We cannot expect to provide strong leadership if our self-leadership is so ineffective that we are unable to overcome our own fears and worries."[10]

Emotional cutoff is the other extreme reaction of the emotionally immature person or leader who is unable to stay differentiated. While the undifferentiated leader who becomes enmeshed with their followers essentially chooses relational togetherness to the complete neglect of healthy separateness, the leader who emotionally cuts off is choosing self to the complete neglect of togetherness. Emotional cutoff can manifest itself in many ways, but it occurs in leadership when leaders are unable to stay connected relationally out of their reactivity to others. Emotionally cutoff leaders end up withdrawing, disconnecting, ignoring, "scapegoating" or avoiding their followers and their followers' needs. Another way of putting it is that emotionally cutoff leaders go "all bad" on their followers to preserve their own sense of self.

Leaders who react to followers by cutting off emotionally add to the followers' anxiety by directly or indirectly communicating that the followers' well-being is secondary to the interests of the leader and organization. In these situations, follower anxiety will tend to rise in proportion to the degree that they feel objectified or used by their leaders. In addition to lacking both self-awareness and the capacity for self-regulation, leaders who emotionally cutoff from their followers tend to be especially deficit in that component of emotional maturity that McCloskey identifies as resonance and relational connection.

Neither emotional fusion nor emotional cutoff are acceptable alternatives for the ministry leader who is entrusted with stewarding a vision and direction as well a team of other leaders who also have been made in the image of God. Emotional fusion paralyzes the leader from leading. Emotional cutoff undermines the credibility and spiritual authority that the leader has. Both are a reflection of a lack of differentiation and emotional maturity in the leader. In both cases, "the anxious leader leaves the congregation without real leadership."[11] Having a healthy sense of self and a foundation of emotional maturity is necessary to helping leaders affirm the dignity and humanity of their co-laborers as well as getting the most out of their people for the sake of missional effectiveness.

Differentiation and Identity

Peter Scazzero, in *Emotionally Healthy Spirituality* describes three temptations common to mankind that are especially relevant for those in leadership. Jesus encountered these three temptations in the wilderness at the hand of Satan in Matthew 4. These temptations tested Jesus' own emotional maturity and level of self-differentiation and security prior to his public ministry. Scazzero summarizes that the temptations were centered on three alternative sources for Jesus' identity and sense of personal security. They are performance (I am what I do), possession (I am what I have), and popularity (I am what others think).[12]

These temptations are ever present in leadership as over-achievement, comparison, and people pleasing run rampant in society. Scazzero describes differentiation as, "The degree to which you are able to affirm your distinct values and goals apart from the pressures around you (separateness) while remaining close to people important to you (togetherness)."[13] In an effort to help leaders resolve this tension, Heifetz and Linsky stress the importance of distinguishing between your "personal self, which can serve as an anchor in stormy weather, and your professional role, which never will."[14] The leader who cannot differentiate his or her own personal value and significance apart from their professional role or performance is likely to respond with anxiety to the relational demands of those they lead. The leader whose sense of personal value is driven by their professional performance just simply has too much personal identity at stake in their own success to be truly free to listen to and absorb the many needs and wants of their followers and those around them.

The Apostle Paul documents an example in his letter to the Galatians of how one of the pillars of the early church, Peter, failed to lead out of a secure sense of self along with the resulting consequences of his failure in leadership. Paul writes that Peter was eating with Gentiles with a clear conscience until a group of Jews from James arrived. Paul writes, "but when they came he drew back and separated himself, fearing the circumcision party" (Gal. 2:12). In the face of follower expectations, Peter withdrew and separated from his Gentile brothers. It appears Peter's anxiety overwhelmed him as he temporarily severed ties with the Gentiles because of the cultural pressures of the Jews. The unity of the fellowship was broken because of Peter's fear and anxiety. Paul appropriately speaks into Peter's life in this situation, bringing the perspective of the gospel into Peter's leadership behavior. In this early church ministry scenario, Peter is exposed as being anxious in response to Jewish pressures while Paul shows himself to be secure enough to withstand these pressures and speak the truth of the gospel into a fellow ministry leader's life.

The benefits of emotional maturity for one's own peace of mind are great, but having the emotional maturity to differentiate who you are apart from the demands of others will also have a significant impact on how those you lead will experience you. Having one's identity anchored in performance, possession, or popularity is like building one's house on the sand. One's security or sense of self is going to be very much based on circumstances and this in turn enslaves one to a self-centered view of leadership. One cannot be free to serve others when so much is personally at stake in terms of identity in his or her leadership interactions. The Apostle Peter offer these words to the person tempted to find their security in fleeting and worldly sources: "Humble yourselves, therefore, under God's mighty hand that he may lift you up in due time." (1 Pet. 5:6)

Personal security for the ministry leader must be anchored in one's identity as established by their relationship with Christ. Through Christ, one experiences unconditional love and approval that is secure and eternal. Because the ministry leader is found in Christ, there is no need to seek out elsewhere what one already has (Gal. 5:1). In Christ, there is a freedom to lead without making things about one's own identity (Phil 2:3-4), because those core issues have been settled (John 8:38). Steinke summarizes this dynamic well writing, "The more you can feel safe as a child of God, the freer you will be to claim your mission in the world as a responsible human being."[15] The leader who is on the journey of internalizing one's identity in Christ in the context of community will be personally secure enough to lead towards the mission as an emotionally separate individual, but in the context of emotionally connected relationships. This is what Jesus modeled – that even on the cross in his moment of greatest rejection, he was still was moving towards his accusers by interceding to the Father for their forgiveness (Luke 23:34).

Differentiation and Communication

A common consequence of a leader who either emotionally fuses with their followers or who emotionally cuts off from their followers is the failure to open the channels for healthy, trust-building communication. One's partnering ability is going to be enhanced or hindered in large part due to their capacity for open and honest communication that can allow for greater levels of trust. Paul writes in his letter to the Ephesians that communication that is both truthful and loving is part of the process that leads to greater personal maturity (4:15) as well as greater community results (4:15-16). Paul warns the church in Ephesus to lay aside falsehood and engage in honest and open communication with his neighbor. Differentiated, emotionally mature leaders are able to put aside the falsehood that insecurity breeds and be beacons of truth and honesty in relationships, demonstrating a commitment to reality as well as the empowerment of the community.

Out of their fear and insecurity, the undifferentiated leader will have a hard time sustaining and cultivating this kind of open and honest communication. The failure to do so weakens the foundations of the team and distances team members from the leader. LaFasto and Larson write, "It's too hard for team members to contribute, much less explore the possibilities, when it is not safe for them to say what's on their minds."[16] In contrast, emotionally mature leaders "don't allow their insecurities to get in the way of the job at hand, and they don't labor to create their own persona."[17] Differentiated leaders are committed to environments of honesty where trust and safety can develop between leaders and followers. Maybe more importantly, differentiated leaders have the personal security to actually lead towards environments of trust and safety, while the emotionally insecure will have a hard time producing in a group what they do not possess in their inner person.

Emotionally immature leaders may exchange this open and honest communication for a kind of "controlled honesty." This controlled honesty gives the appearance of trust building communication, but it lacks some of the ingredients necessary for trust to be built between people, especially between leaders and followers. The lack of differentiation in leadership leads to a lack of safety in communication. Followers or those without the organizational power are going to determine the safety of the environment on the basis of how secure and differentiated their leaders are. If followers perceive their leaders to be overly anxious or personally insecure in their leadership, they will hold back greatly because this lack of differentiation hinders trust. Followers engage open and honest communication with their leaders when they trust that their leaders are secure enough to handle the communication and that there will not be backlash for truthful communication.

Leader Self-Differentiation and Culture

Emotionally immature or poorly differentiated leaders who "cutoff" from or "fuse" with their teams and followers set in motion "unspoken rules" that begin to shape the architecture of their working environment that tend to conform to the level of anxiety within the leader. "Because they are not said out loud, you don't find out that they're there until you break them."[18] Unspoken rules can effectively silence the community on important matters and function as a "fortress wall of protection," protecting the emotionally immature leader from any challenge or criticism. The implicit culture that is driven by the character, identity, and behavior of the leader or leaders is almost always more powerful that the explicitly communicated norms and values.

Emotionally mature leaders embrace the reality that, "The team leader has the greatest responsibility for making free expression safe."LaFasto and Larson add that, "It is the team leader's job to remove artificial barriers to communication and lower the real ones."[19] Healthy, honest, and adult communication protects against unspoken rules and silent agreements, and promotes clarity and responsibility in the working environment for everyone. Promoting healthy and honest communication requires a secure leader as well as a leader who, as McCloskey discusses, is committed to a humble and honest assessment of reality. Low differentiation of self in leadership will hinder and potentially even enslave team members through these unspoken rules while those with healthy differentiation of self are free to continually serve their people, helping to empower them towards making their greatest contribution to the Kingdom.

The unspoken rules and architecture of how people communicate and relate is really what many refer to as "culture." Culture can either work against the vision and direction of the community or serve as a powerful catalyst towards the community's desired results. Caruso and Salovey relay an example of how new Hewlett-Packard CEO Carly Fiorina challenged the culture of HP in her successful effort to lead change in their book *The Emotionally Intelligent Manager*.[20] She reflects, "When culture turns into groupthink, when culture turns into closed minds, when culture turns into 'act the same, be the same, look the same,' that is when culture starts to kill a company."[21] Even though Fiorina herself has a reputation as a fairly narcissistic leader, this piece of wisdom should not be neglected.

Undifferentiated leaders will tend to produce groupthink because differences and individuality are seen much more as a threat to their leadership success than a vital source of learning, sharpening, and creativity. Heifetz and Laurie state that, "A leader has to have the emotional capacity to tolerate uncertainty, frustration, and pain. He has to be able to raise tough questions without getting too anxious himself."[22] Emotionally mature leaders are able to keep one foot outside of the culture to be able to critically and humbly evaluate the honest reality, but are also able to stay connected with people and be a part of the culture so that they can continually build trust with their followers and empower them for service. Heifetz and Laurie call describe the big picture aspect of this balancing act as "going to the balcony," a needed discipline for a leader if he or she is going to avoid getting "swept up in the field of action."[23]

Self-Differentiation and Leadership Development (Next Steps for the Young Leader)

The concept of self-differentiation is fairly complex when one considers the numerous factors that all work together to shape our sense of identity and self. First, the leader needs to engage in honest and reflective self-work so that he or she can develop the self-awareness or capacity of emotional recognition. Second, the leader needs to learn how to regulate his or her emotional life in community. Peter Scazzero offers some very helpful thoughts on how a leader can grow in his or her emotional maturity in *The Emotionally Healthy Church*.[24] He explains what it means for the leader to "Break the Power of the Past" and "Embrace the Gift of Limits" among other things. This "self-work" that the leader must engage involves exploring family influences, life experiences, and personal limitations. All of this has as its aim continued sanctification through Christ and a humble and sober assessment of one's self and leadership (Rom. 12:3). Differentiation of self will not develop on its own. It requires the leader to work and exercise due diligence in developing an honest assessment of one's own character and worldview – and those powerful unseen forces that have helped shaped them. One cannot do this without honest and trusted input from other people.

Pastor Jan Hettinga of Northshore Baptist Church in Bothell, Washington reflects, "The safest, healthiest, most effective ministry leaders are those who tap into greater grace through lifestyle repentance and voluntary humility."[25] This reflects one of the ways that a leader can learn to lead from an emotionally mature foundation. McCloskey recommends that one of the best ways to move towards others, as a leader is to "lean into feedback."[26] So many of the problems created by a leader's lack of differentiation can be eliminated by a willingness to humbly and voluntarily go out of their way to get feedback about themselves or about the community at large. A leader who struggles with his or her level of self-differentiation may be able to better receive feedback or negative input if it is being offered at his or her own initiative. If a leader can proactively ask for help then they may be more able to hear and internalize where change is needed.

In addition to the work of developing self-awareness and proactively learning from community feedback is the work of developing one's own capacity for self-regulation. Over the years I've heard many express how odd it seems to them that self-control is listed by Paul as one of the fruits of the Holy Spirit (Gal 5:23). However, the above discussion of how undifferentiated leaders get derailed in their leadership by responding out of their own anxiety shows just how important it is for the leader to be able so exercise self-control over his or her emotions in leadership. Exercising self-control in the power of the Holy Spirit is not the same as being emotionally shut down. The fruit of self-control reflects what loving behavior looks like in those moments when there is ample temptation and opportunity to respond reactively as opposed to intentionally and lovingly. Ministry leaders who desire to become more secure in their identity and experience greater self-control in life and leadership can take some steps to grow, but they will not get very far without acknowledging the role of the Holy Spirit in their lives producing the life of Christ within them.

Self-differentiation is not a quest for the sake of self-actualization. The end game for the spiritual leader in becoming more differentiated is to be able to more completely and freely love others and give glory to God. Self-differentiation is the fruit of one's self-examined and Spirit-filled life as it plays out in community. The Holy Spirit and the constructive influence of the people of God are then necessary to one's personal growth and transformation. Self-control as a leader is not the exercise of sheer will or works of effort, which lead to self-focus on one's own performance. Ephesians 2:8-9 reinforces that sheer works or working harder does not achieve the transformation and righteousness that honors God. Self-control rather is the capacity through the Spirit to master one's impulses in a way that honors God and honors others.

Galatians 5:16-26 again provides us a picture of how the life of faith in the power of the Holy Spirit should produce the fruit of self-control (Gal 5:23). The Holy Spirit also produces the fruit of personally security as demonstrated in the fruits of peace and joy (Gal 5:22). And lastly the Holy Spirit produces the fruit of a loving presence in community as shown by the fruits of kindness, goodness, faithfulness, and gentleness (Gal 5:22-23). In fact, an argument can be made that Spirit-empowered self-control really can be loving action towards others even though it is primarily an internal work of the Spirit. It is love through restraint in relationships. It captures the kind of internal regulation and security that is needed to be able to move towards other people in maturity and grace. In this way, the fruit of self-control is connected to the concept of self-differentiation. Self-control flows from a posture of dependent obedience and submission to the power of the Holy Spirit and results in greater self-regulation as well as appropriate attentiveness to the needs of others. These are marks of a self-differentiated person and ultimately they lead to a greater capacity to respond appropriately to the relational demands of life.

Conclusion

At the core of the idea of transformational servant leadership lies the notion that genuine, authentic, and spiritually powerful authority in leadership is to be exercised towards the end of empowering followers in a way that results in a mutually beneficial relationship that yields greater results and satisfaction than what could be achieved if the leader–follower dynamic was merely a set of transactions. Ministry leaders that are concerned about multiplying laborers and leaders for the Kingdom cannot afford to lead through mere transactions, yet many continue to do so because of their lack of self-differentiation and emotional maturity. They simply aren't secure enough or emotionally mature enough to lead any other way. They tend to take the leadership short cuts found in reliance upon positions, hierarchies, and policies to get things done as opposed to doing the hard work of building the healthy team or working environments that can yield greater and more meaningful results.

Leighton Ford writes that servant leaders, "are those who are able to divest themselves of their power and invest it in their followers in such a way that others are empowered, while the leaders themselves end with the greatest power of all, the power of seeing themselves reproduced in others."[27] However, leaders can only give power away if they are secure enough in their person to do so. A lack of self-differentiation and emotional maturity in the leader will consistently hinder the leader's efforts to lead transformationally.

One's level of emotional maturity may not eliminate the anxiety of followers or team members in the short-run, but it can have a powerful impact on the long run. Differentiation of self in the leader frees both the leader and the follower for greater freedom, trust, and hope. While the undifferentiated leader grows anxious and gets lost emotionally amidst criticism, the emotionally healthy leader is able to inject a calm and steady presence into the community by continuing to lead as a responsible adult and by staying connected relationally. The secure and self-differentiated leader is free to serve and love well as a leader without having to abdicate the roles and responsibilities of leadership. The leader who can continue to do the work of leadership as well as stay in relationship with those they lead, even in anxious times, will more than likely find success for both themselves and the whole of the community.

---

[1]Peter L. Steinke, *Congregational Leadership in Anxious Times : Being Calm and Courageous no Matter What* (Herndon, Va.: Alban Institute, 2006), 121.

[2]Ronald A. Heifetz and Donald L. Laurie, "The Work of Leadership," *Harvard Business Review* 79, no. 11 (12 2001): 131-141. 65.

[3]Steinke, xi.

[4]Mark McCloskey, "The Components of Emotional Maturity," *ML736 Course Documents, Emotional Maturity and Spiritual Leadership,* Bethel Seminary, 2007, 1.

[5]Leroy T. Howe, "Self-Differentiation in Christian Perspective," *Pastoral Psychology* 46, no. 5 (05 1998): 347-362. 348.

[6]Parker J. Palmer, *The Courage to Teach: Exploring the Inner Landscape of a Teacher's Life*, 1std ed. (San Francisco, Calif.: Jossey-Bass, 1998), 72.

[7]McCloskey, Mark. "Emotional Maturity and Leadership Effectiveness," *ML736DE Emotional Maturity and Spiritual Leader Course Notes*, Bethel Seminary, 2007. 4-5.

[8]Steinke, 13.

[9]McCloskey, 3.

[10]Samuel D. Rima, *Leading from the Inside Out: The Art of Self-Leadership* (Grand Rapids, Mich.: Baker Books, 2000), 189.

[11]Steinke, 34.

[12]Peter Scazzero, *Emotionally Healthy Spirituality: Unleash a Revolution in Your Life in Christ* (Nashville, TN: Integrity Publishers, 2006), 75-77.

[13]Ibid, 82.

[14]Ronald A. Heifetz and Marty Linsky, "A Survival Guide for Leaders," *Harvard Business Review* 80, no. 6 (06 2002): 65-72. 73.

[15]Steinke, 158.

---

[16]Frank M. J. LaFasto and Carl E. Larson, *When Teams Work Best : 6,000 Team Members and Leaders Tell what it Takes to Succeed* (Thousand Oaks, Calif.: Sage Publications, 2001), 109.

[17]Ibid, 120.

[18]David Johnson and Jeffrey VanVonderen, *The Subtle Power of Spiritual Abuse: Recognizing and Escaping Spiritual Manipulation and False Spiritual Authority within the Church,* 2005) 67.

[19]LaFasto and Larson, 109.

[20]David Caruso and Peter Salovey, *The Emotionally Intelligent Manager: How to Develop and use the Four Key Emotional Skills of Leadership* (Hoboken: Books In Print, (c) 2007 R.R. Bowker LLC; Jossey-Bass [Imprint]; John Wiley & Sons, Incorporated Publisher Record, March 2004).

[21]Ibid, 207. From "Catching Up with Carly Fiorina." San Jose Mercury News, April 13, 2003. Available online: www.siliconvalley.com/mld/mercurynews/business/5624255.htm

[22]Heifetz and Laurie, 135.

[23]Heifetz and Laurie, 132.

[24]Peter Scazzero and Warren Bird, *The Emotionally Healthy Church : A Strategy for Discipleship that Actually Changes Lives* (Grand Rapids, Mich.: Zondervan, 2003), 223.

[25]Hettinga, Jan. "Protecting Our People From Ourselves." John R. Cionca, *Dear Pastor : Ministry Advice from Seasoned Pastors* (Loveland, Colo.: Group Pub., 2006), 91.

[26]McCloskey, 5.

[27]Leighton Ford, *Transforming Leadership : Jesus' Way of Creating Vision, Shaping Values & Empowering Change* (Downers Grove, Ill.: InterVarsity Press, 1991), 16.

❖

Appendix

An Interview with Lawrence Matthews on the LIM Experience

This interview captures the vision and history of the Leadership in Ministry Workshops from founder Larry Matthews. He served as faculty on Friedman's advanced seminary for clergy from 1991 till Friedman's death in 1996. Matthews served as coordinator of the workshops till 2010.

How did Leadership in Ministry workshops begin?

LM: First, a few words of background before fully answering this question. Rabbi Edwin "Ed" Friedman settled in the Washington, DC, area in the 1960's to serve a synagogue congregation and train to become a therapist. He received his training from psychiatrist, Dr. Murray Bowen, a pioneer in "family therapy." Bowen had named his attempt to construct a scientific basis for psychiatry the Bowen Family Systems Theory (BFST), or simply the Bowen Theory. Friedman's first book, *Generation To Generation: Family Process in Church and Synagogue*, was published in 1985.

This pioneering application of the Bowen Family Systems Theory to the emotional life of congregations and their leaders received an immediate positive response from leaders in the religious community which widened as Ed accepted invitations to speak before religious gatherings. A recurring question he heard from participants was, "How can we better understand and learn to apply these ideas to our ministry?"

For some time Ed had been leading small coaching groups for Washington, DC, area therapists and clergy. Then he began to offer a structured training program in Bethesda, Maryland, that he named "Post Graduate Ministers' Seminars in Family Emotional Process."

How did you start teaching with Edwin Friedman?

LM: I read Ed's book in 1986 and, like many others, decided that I needed help in understanding and applying these important concepts to my life and ministry. I joined one of his local coaching group's for ministers. We brought case studies from our ministries to our monthly sessions and Ed taught us how to view them through the BFST lens.

He recommended that we read Bowen's and Kerr's books and view the videos of Bowen's lectures available at the Bowen Center in nearby Georgetown. I also began to attend the monthly "Theory Days" he led for the clergy and therapists in his coaching groups.

Ed was my coach as I embarked on my family of origin work, a commitment that has become a life-long journey. In 1991 he added an advanced level to the Ministers' Seminars and invited me to join his faculty as a coach for one of the small groups focused upon participants' family of origin work.

During my first year as a faculty coach in the Ministers' Seminars, although I was impressed by the variety of congregational and denominational leaders attending, I observed that there were few participants from smaller congregations outside the immediate Washington, DC, area.

The basic tuition was not inexpensive and non-resident participants also had to provide for their travel costs, lodging and meals for the two three-day sessions. I began to ask myself: would it be possible to create a quality training program similar to the Seminars that would be more affordable?

How did the first workshops begin?

LIM: I knew colleagues who were either seminar faculty members or who had studied with Ed. So I made some inquiries and shared what was a still-in-the-rough-draft-stage idea with a few of them. The congregation I served in Vienna, VA, owned a retreat center in West Virginia. In spite of not receiving any encouragement when I shared my idea with Ed (I could always count on him for an honest response!), in the spring of 1991 I contacted all of the clergy I knew who might be interested in participating in a low cost ($125) Leadership In Ministry Conference at Lost River Retreat Center in Lost River, West Virginia, September 21-23. The invitation noted that "It would be a conference on ministering to the church as a family system — with special emphasis upon leadership as understood by Bowen Theory. The overall focus will be upon the practical integration of theory and practice." My minimum number for a "go" was twelve, although I noted that the group would be "limited to 25, or 30 at the max." I received five registrations plus four "interested" responses. So I wrote my "not this time" notes to the few who had responded.

The following spring I drafted a second invitation letter announcing a workshop for September 20-22, 1992. Fourteen male clergy and two female lay leaders registered and Leadership In Ministry Workshops was born. One of my colleagues from Ed's Seminar faculty, Myrna Carpenter, and a pastoral counselor friend, Mahan Siler, worked with me as the first faculty coaches. Two of those first registrants, Israel Galindo and James Lamkin, are still in the workshops and have served for years as faculty coaches.

For the most part the LIM workshop format has retained the general pattern of the Friedman seminars. One-third of the time is spent in large group presentations where faculty coaches, workshop participants and guest presenters focus on teaching Bowen Theory and its relevance for leadership. Guest presenters have included psychiatrist and former Bowen Center Director, Michael Kerr, M.D., psychiatrist Roberta Gilbert, M.D., and other Bowen trained professionals as well as Angelo Bolea, Ph.D, teacher of neurophysiology and neurofeedback.

A major change in the LIM format was the decision to assign a central role to small peer groups of no more than four persons, led by faculty coaches. Two-thirds of every workshop is spent in these groups where the focus is upon both the participants' case studies and their family of origin work. A second major change was the decision that all three-day LIM workshops would take place in residential retreat centers. This meant that the teaching/learning setting itself would offer individual and group relationship building opportunities as clergy and lay leaders from different places in the USA and other countries lived and learned together. Although the workshops began in the West Virginia retreat location, new sites were added in Atlanta, Georgia, the Boston area in Massachusetts, and Colorado Springs, Colorado.

What is the goal of the LIM workshops?

LM: The goal of LIM has remained the same from its beginning: teaching and practicing a different understanding of "leadership." Bowen wrote that in his early research he was "always looking for the family leader" and maintained that in "differentiating change" in the family emotional process, probably the most important principle was the movement of one family member towards more differentiation of self. He also observed the crucial importance of his own functioning as the "leader" in the groups of psychiatrists he was training in this new understanding of psychiatry.

Friedman coined the phrase, "leadership through self-differentiation," as his way of succinctly expressing this insight of Bowen. "Through" was the word he emphasized. In his writing and teaching, he focused upon this radical understanding of the importance of persons in the leadership (L) position. He emphasized that, for better or for worse, the functioning of those in the "L" position profoundly affects the emotional process of the systems they lead. He taught that leaders who are working on their own process of differentiation have four characteristics:

(1) Self-regulation — the awareness and management of one's own anxiety and reactivity. Ed initially used the term "non-anxious" to describe this characteristic; however, "self-regulation" became his preferred way of more clearly describing what he intended to communicate.

(2) Self-definition — the ability to express one's thinking and to take stands in ways that are neither reactive nor manipulative.

(3) Staying connected — the refusal to cut off emotionally from those being led.

(4) Dealing with the reactivity and sabotage resulting from the leader's more differentiated functioning.

He applied this understanding of leadership not only to religious institutions (see Chapter 9 in *Generation To Generation*), but also to all human institutions (see *A Failure of Nerve: Leadership in the Age of the Quick Fix*, a book he considered the summation of all his ideas). The LIM focus is upon this process of differentiating a self in one's own life first, then in relating this understanding of leadership to one's family and the larger communities and institutions in which one lives and works.

What kind of background and training do the faculty coaches have?

LM: Since the small peer groups of four persons occupy a central place in the format of the workshops, the need for a faculty coach for each group has always been a major challenge. The goal is to select persons who are not only committed to their own life-long process of differentiating a self, but also skilled in leading group learning experiences. During LIM's almost twenty years, the workshop faculty has included more than 22 small group coaches. Many have backgrounds in educational or pastoral ministry. Others are therapists or counselors and some are from other professional or business backgrounds.

All have the skills needed for coaching in small groups and many of them have been, or still are, participants in workshops where they are not coaching. Faculty coaches have written a number of the books on BFST and leadership.

Are the workshops about leadership in general or only clergy leadership?

LM: We think the unique understanding of leadership that is taught and experienced in the workshops is applicable to all of the systems in which we live and work. As Friedman was fond of saying, "This is for everyone, from parents to presidents." Non-clergy men and women have always participated in the LIM workshops. Beginning in 2006, this participation was further encouraged by the addition of a second registration for "Leadership in Organizations" (LIO), which clarifies the availability of this training for everyone.

Are the workshops for therapy?

LM: No, they are not. One of Ed Friedman's sayings about his training program was, "Although the seminars are not therapy, they are often therapeutic." This also has been the experience of workshop participants who use the workshops to continue work on their life-long process of differentiating a self.

Are the workshops open to persons from all religious backgrounds?

LM: Yes! The title "Leadership in Ministry" expresses the original intent to provide this training for clergy and lay religious leaders. However, the process of differentiating a self has significant dimensions for many people who are not religious leaders. As subjects regarding the interface between scientific theory, therapy, and spirituality surface in either the large group presentations or in the small groups, they are dealt with in a manner that respects differences in individual commitments and thinking. Just as the workshops are not about doing therapy, they are not about doing theology or religion. But neither are the religious dimensions of life avoided or dealt with in a manipulative or coercive way when they arise.

How many years of participation are required before one finishes the program or "graduates?"

LM: This understanding of leadership is an invitation to a life-long process of growing "self." Participants are welcome to return for as many years as they desire. Each year there are returning registrants who were in the earliest workshops, for whom this has become a major continuing education commitment.

Bibliography

Bowen, Murray. *Family Therapy in Clinical Practice.* Northvale, New Jersey: Jason Aronson, 1985.

Bregman, O. C. and White, C. M. *Bringing Systems Thinking to Life.* Routledge, 2010.

Broderick, C. B. *Understanding Family Process : Basics of Family Systems Theory.* Newbury Park, Calif., Sage Publications, 1993.

Brown, Jenny. *Growing Yourself Up.* Exisle Publishing, 2012.

Comella, Patricia et al., eds. *The Emotional Side of Organizations: Applications of Bowen Theory.* Washington, DC: Georgetown Family Center, 1996.

Cummings, T. G. *Systems Theory for Organization Development.* New York: John Wiley & Sons, 1980.

Friedman, Edwin H. *Generation to Generation: Family Process in Church and Synagogue.* New York: The Guilford Press, 1985.

_____. *A Failure of Nerve: Leadership in the Age of the Quick Fix.* Ed. E. Beal and M. Treadwell. Seabury Books, 2007.

Galindo, Israel. *101 Systems Theory Quotes.* Didache Press, 2017.

_____, Boomer, E. and Reagan, D. *A Family Genogram Workbook.* Educational Consultants, 2006.

_____ and Brock, Timothy, eds. Bowen Family Systems Theory in the Congregational Context. *Review & Expositor Journal.* Issue vol. 102 no. 3, (2005).

_____. "Ministry Years." *Congregations* (Winter 2004)

_____. "The Myth of Competence." *Congregations* (Winter 2003).

_____. *The Hidden Lives of Congregations.* Bethesda: The Alban Institute, 2004.

_____. *Perspectives on Congregational Leadership.* Educational Consultants, 2009.

Gilbert, Roberta. *Extraordinary Leadership: Thinking Systems, Making a Difference.* Leading Systems Press, 2006.

_____. *Extraordinary Relationships.* Minneapolis: Chronimed Publishing, 1992.

_____. *The Eight Concepts of Bowen Theory.* Falls Church, VA: Leading Systems Press, 2004.

Goleman, Daniel; Boyatzis, Richard, and McKee, Annie. *Primal Leadership: Realizing the Power of Emotional Intelligence.* Boston: Harvard Business School Press, 2002.

Marcuson, Margaret. *Leaders Who Last.* Seabury Books, 2009.

McGoldrick, Monica & Gerson, Randy. *Genograms in Family Assessment.* New York: W. W. Norton & Co., 1985.

Mikesell, R. H., D.-D. Lusterman, et al. *Integrating Family Therapy: Handbook of Family Psychology and Systems Theory.* Washington, DC, American Psychological Association, 1995.

Nyengele, M. F. *African Women's Theology, Gender Relations, and Family Systems Theory : Pastoral Theological Considerations and Guidelines for Care and Counseling.* New York, Peter Lang, 2004.

Oshry, B. *Seeing Systems: Unlocking the Mysteries of Organizational Life.* San Francisco: Berrett-Koehler Publishers, 1995.

Papero, Daniel V. *Bowen Family Systems Theory.* Boston: Allyn and Bacon, 1990.

Richardson, Ronald W. *Becoming A Healthier Pastor.* Minneapolis: Augsburg Fortress Press, 2005.

_____. *Family Ties That Bind: A Self-Help Guide to Change Through Family of Origin Therapy.* Bellingham, Washington: International Self-Counsel Press Ltd., 1984.

_____ and Richardson, Lois A. *Birth Order and You: How Your Sex and Position in the Family Affects Your Personality and Relationships.* Bellingham, Washington: International Self-Counsel Press Ltd., 1990.

_____. *Becoming Your Best Self.* Augsburg, 2008.

_____. *Creating a Healthier Church: Family Systems Theory, Leadership, and Congregational Life.* Minneapolis: Fortress Press, 1996.

Sagar, R. R., K. K. Wiseman, et al. *Understanding organizations: applications of Bowen family systems theory.* Washington, D.C., Georgetown University Family Center, 1982.

Schein, Edgar H. *Organizational Culture and Leadership.* San Francisco: Jossey-Bass Publishers, 1985.

Steinke, Peter L. *Congregational Leadership in Anxious Times: Being Calm and Courageous No Matter What.* The Alban Institute, 2006.

_____. *Healthy Congregations: A Systems Approach.* The Alban Institute, 2006.

Steinke, Peter L. *How Your Church Family Works: Understanding Congregations as Emotional Systems.* New York: The Alban Institute, Inc., 1993.

Stevens, R. Paul and Collins, Phil. *The Equipping Pastor: A Systems Approach to Congregational Leadership.* Bethesda, Md.: The Alban Institute, 1993.

Titelman, Peter. *Clinical applications of Bowen family systems theory.* New York, Haworth Press, 1998.

_____. *Differentiation of Self: Bowen Systems Theory in Perspectives.* Routledge, 2015.

_____. *Emotional Cutoff: Bowen Family Systems Theory Perspectives.* Haworth Press, 2003.

_____. *Triangles: Bowen Family Systems Theory Perspectives.* Haworth Press, 2007.

49874640R00163

Made in the USA
San Bernardino, CA
06 June 2017